ESSENTIALS
OF FINANCIAL
MANAGEMENT

Ernest W. Walker
Professor of Finance
University of Texas at Austin

ESSENTIALS
OF FINANCIAL
MANAGEMENT

Second Edition

Prentice-Hall, Inc., Englewood Cliffs, New Jersey

PRINTED IN THE UNITED STATES OF AMERICA

13-286104-6
Library of Congress Catalog Number 70-143029

Current printing (last digit)
10 9 8 7 6

Prentice-Hall International, Inc., *London*
Prentice-Hall of Australia Pty. Ltd., *Sydney*
Prentice-Hall of Canada, Ltd., *Toronto*
Prentice-Hall of India Private Limited, *New Delhi*
Prentice-Hall of Japan, Inc., *Tokyo*

To Margaret, Marshall, and Eledith

Preface

This edition of *Essentials of Financial Management* incorporates several changes. Rather than including cost of capital, capital structure, and planning fixed-assets expenditures in one chapter, I have presented each of these subjects in a separate chapter. The chapter on planning fixed-assets expenditures has been broadened to include the techniques presently used to evaluate investment proposals—e.g., payback, average rate of return on average investment, internal rate of return, net present value, and profitability index. A new section on methods to compensate for risk has been added.

The chapter on capital structure includes a discussion of the current thought on capital structure theory. Particular attention is given to the impact of the asset mix, as well as the capital mix, on a firm's cost of capital.

The material on working-capital management has been substantially changed. Not only is a theory of working capital presented but techniques used to ascertain the size of cash discounts, length of credit terms, and selection of credit risks are thoroughly discussed. The discussion of decisions covering cash and inventories has also been revised.

The revision has aided the book in achieving its primary goals of making available to students and practitioners of finance a concise treatment on decision making in the utilization and procurement of funds. This book, when used in conjunction with current readings on financial management and case problems, comprises a complete package for both undergraduate students and first year M.B.A. students.

The author is grateful to his many friends in the academic and business communities for their constructive criticisms of the first edition as well as this edition of the book. I wish to thank especially Professor Lee Tavis of the Graduate School of Business of The University of Texas at Austin for his advice on the material covering risk and working-capital theory. I wish also to thank Miss Nettie Webb and Mrs. Trudy Conlee for their efforts in the preparation of the several drafts of the manuscript.

ERNEST W. WALKER

The University of Texas at Austin

Contents

         Steps in Fixed-Assets Management.   Methods of
         Selecting from Among Proposals.   Adjusting for Risk.

7   Working-Capital Management   59

         Concepts of Working Capital.   Classification of Working
         Capital.   A Four-Part Theory of Working Capital.
         Summary.

8   Working-Capital Management (continued)   67

         Receivables Management.   Cash Management.
         Inventory Planning.   Control of Working Capital.

9   Equity versus Debt Financing   81

         Terminology.   Relative Importance of Equity and Debt
         Financing.   Choosing Between Debt and Equity Capital.

10   Capital Structure Determination   92

         Capital Structure.   Theories of Capital Structure.
         Other Approaches Used to Determine the Optimum
         Capital Structure.

11   Income Taxes and Financial Planning   101

         Influence of Taxes on Cost of Capital.   Effect of Legal
         Structure on Tax Liability.   Effect of Taxes on Financial
         Policy.   Further Ways to Minimize Tax Losses.

12   Dividend Policies   111

         Classification of Dividends.   Mechanics of Dividend
         Distribution.   Dividend Policy.

13   Short-Term Capital   119

         Importance of Short-Term Credit.   Factors Influencing
         the Use of Short-Term Debt.   Trade Credit.

14   Short-Term Credit, as Supplied by Financial
     Institutions   129

         Commercial Banks.   Commercial Paper Houses.   Business
         Finance Companies.   Factors.   Miscellaneous Sources.

1

Role of Financial

Management in

the Business Firm

The primary purpose of a business firm is to produce and distribute goods and services to the society in which it exists. Achieving this goal requires the performance of such business functions as production, distribution, and finance. If these functions are to be performed efficiently, it is necessary that the managerial functions of planning and control be effected. Financial management is the application of the planning and control functions to the finance function. An examination of this process reveals the significance of business finance and the role it plays in the production and distribution processes.

MANAGERIAL FUNCTIONS

Production and distribution require an investment of both fixed and working capital in order to produce a flow of funds. That is, cash is invested in raw materials that are processed by fixed assets into finished goods that, in turn, are sold and ultimately converted back into cash. It is this flow of funds that vitally concerns financial management, because if the flow is slowed down for any reason, the profit position of the firm will be affected. The processes involved in maintaining the flow may be broadly classified as financial planning, coordination, control, and replanning.

Financial planning is the act of deciding in advance the financial activities that are necessary if the firm is to achieve its primary goal. It involves three fundamental steps: first, determining both long-and short-term financial objectives; second, formulating and promulgating financial policies; and third, developing procedures that aid in the promulgation of the firm's policies.

If a firm is to reach its ultimate goal of optimizing the potential of all factors of production, it should establish objectives in each of its operational areas, one of which, of course, is finance. The primary or long-term objective of financial planning is to secure and employ capital resources in the amount and proportion necessary to increase the efficiency of the remaining factors of production. Under perfect conditions, this means that the finance manager would synchronize the flow of funds into the firm with the flow of funds out of the firm. In other words, the finance manager has as his goal full employment of funds at all times. In a dynamic economy, a perfect synchronization is not possible; therefore, he must at times establish short-term or temporary objectives that on the surface would appear to contradict the firm's long-run objective. For example, the finance officer may set up reserves in working capital in order to assure solvency. The amount of these reserves is predicated on the amount of risk that the firm can safely assume at a particular stage of the business cycle.

The second step in the planning process is the determination of policies that act as guides to the firm in achieving its primary objective. The following policies are required by most profit-oriented firms:

1. Policies that determine the amount of capital required for firms to achieve their financial objectives
2. Policies that determine the control by the parties who furnish the capital
3. Policies that act as a guide in the use of debt and equity capital
4. Policies that guide management in the selection of the sources of funds
5. Policies that govern the determination and distribution of income
6. Policies that govern the credit and collection activities of the enterprise
7. Policies that determine the amount of funds to be invested in fixed and working capital

It was mentioned above that the financial executive is responsible for the efficient use of capital resources. To fulfill this responsibility, he must see that the financial activities, in addition to being planned, are coordinated. Coordination requires that each function and subfunction be performed at the proper time; to achieve this requires that these functions be organized. Organizing the various activities necessitates two primary steps: (1) grouping all financial activities into departments or divisions, and (2) delegating adequate authority to individuals who have been assigned the responsibility for the performance of these functions.

The organization structure of the business enterprise is nothing more than the hierarchy of its functions. The size of the structure is dependent upon the size and nature of the various functions; that is, as a general rule, each function increases in size as it increases in complexity. In order to minimize waste and inefficiency, management subdivides each function into various subfunctions and assigns these functions to specialists, thereby creating a system.

In determining the kind of financial system that is needed, management must consider whether to centralize or decentralize the financial activities. Decentralization of the production and sales functions has characterized business establishments for some time, but this practice has not been followed to any great degree when firms act to organize the finance function. This may be explained by the fact that the growth and development of the business firm is directly related to the finance function; therefore, top management does not wish to delegate financial planning and control to lower echelons. A second important reason for not decentralizing financial authority is that top management is vitally concerned with the firm's solvency position. Solvency is directly related to the firm's flow of funds, and if decisions affecting the flow are delegated to various divisions, it may be more difficult to secure the degree of coordination necessary to assure solvency.

Financial control consists of two steps: developing standards of performance and comparing activities with these standards. The former, although difficult to determine, is especially significant, since these standards serve as a basis for the replanning process. In the past, standards were derived primarily from past experience, but with improved knowledge in the area of statistics and mathematics, it is becoming easier for finance managers to look into the future and develop standards that directly relate to future activities. Moreover, with the advent of computers, it is easier for management to maintain accurate and up-to-date records of activities. As a result, it is possible for the financial staff to compare today's activities with predetermined standards. This not only allows management to ascertain immediately discrepancies that occur, but it also enables it to take remedial action before deviations become too "wide." The control process will be discussed in connection with each of the policy areas as they are developed.

The replanning process is the last function performed by financial managers, and it, like each of the other functions, is vital to the ultimate success of the business firm. If the evaluation of performance reveals that the end results of the firm's activities will not meet predetermined standards, it may be assumed that either the firm's policies or personnel are not effective. If it is the former, management must first ascertain which of the policies are ineffective, and second, change the defective policies so that the firm can achieve its goals.

The student may ask when evaluation (control) and replanning should take place. Evaluation should be *continuous*, since the environment under which the firm is operating is constantly changing. Replanning, on the other hand, should be undertaken only when it has been proved that changes are needed. In other words, change for its own sake can be detrimental to the success of the firm. To avoid indiscriminate changes, management should be absolutely positive that the policy is at fault and not the personnel in charge of the policy.

Role of the Owner in the Finance Function

In noncorporate enterprises, the owners perform the majority of the financial functions, but in corporations the shareholders delegate much of their authority to the board of directors and to the officers of the corporations. Although they authorize the board to act for them in most cases, custom and law require that shareholders personally perform certain financial functions. First, by approving the articles of incorporation and bylaws, shareholders determine the following:

1. Amount and kind of capital stock as well as its par or stated value
2. Pre-emptive rights of shareholders
3. Rules governing the issue and transfer of stock
4. Provisions granting directors the right to declare dividends
5. Provisions allowing directors to choose a bank
6. Provisions authorizing directors to create reserves out of net profits for such purposes as contingencies and working capital

Second, shareholders are required to approve the following acts in annual or special meetings, if such plans are to be effected:

1. Sales of any substantial portion of the firm's assets, except during the ordinary course of business
2. Recapitalization or reorganization plans
3. Voluntary plans for liquidation
4. Plans for consolidation and mergers
5. Amendments to the charter and bylaws

The managerial activities of shareholders, as a general rule, would not be classified as either planning or control; rather, the action they take is to approve or disapprove of the planning and control activities of the board and officers of the corporation.

Role of the Board of Directors
in the Financial Organization

A corporation acts only through its board. This does not mean that the authority to perform the multiple functions required cannot be delegated to officers and employees of the firm; it means rather that the responsibility for management cannot be delegated. Although many financial functions are delegated to the various financial officers, boards retain several specific duties, the most important of which are to:

1. Translate the wishes and desires of stockholders into goals and objectives
2. Approve all financial policies
3. Compare actual with planned operations
4. Select senior officers such as president and vice-president for finance
5. Declare dividends
6. Set executive compensation

Relating these functions to those performed by shareholders, we can see that boards of directors actually perform many planning and control functions. It should be emphasized, however, that the detailed planning and control are delegated to the finance officer. Therefore, let us turn our attention to the duties of the financial vice-president, treasurer, or controller.

Role of the Chief Finance Officer

The size of the firm does not determine the number of functions performed by the finance officer, but it does determine their complexity. As a result of this complexity, the functions of larger firms are highly organized, whereas in small firms it is difficult to determine whether the functions actually exist. In the large firms the finance function is usually divided into treasurer and controller functions. Functions that may be assigned to the treasurer are as follows:[1]

1. Financial Planning
   a. Reporting financial results to the officers of the company
   b. Planning the company investment program
   c. Planning borrowing requirements
   d. Forecast of cash receipts and disbursement
   e. Advice on dividend payments
2. Cash Management
   a. Opening accounts and depositing funds in banks
   b. Management of petty cash and bank balances
   c. Payment of company obligations through proper disbursement procedures
   d. Maintaining records of cash transactions
3. Credit Management
   a. Determination of customers' credit risks
   b. Orderly handling of collections
   c. Handling cash discounts and terms of sale for prompt payment
   d. Collections
4. Security Flotations
   a. Recommendation of type of security most desirable for company borrowing requirements and correlation of these with company's long-term ability to pay
   b. Negotiation with investment bankers
   c. Provision for trustee; registration of transfer agent
   d. Compliance with governmental regulations
   e. Retirement of bonds and stocks
   f. Stockholder relations, disbursement of dividends, etc.

---

[1] Ernest Dale, *Planning and Developing the Company Organization Structure* (New York: American Management Association, 1955), p. 199.

5. Signing of checks, contracts, leases, notes, bond and stock certificates, mortgages, deeds, and other corporate documents, endorsement for deposits, collection of checks

6. Custody of funds and securities

Functions usually assigned to the controller are: [2]

1. Providing basic information for managerial control through formulation of accounting and costing policies, standards, and procedures; preparation of financial statements and maintenance of books of account; direction of internal auditing and cost controls

2. Budgeting and control of corporations and results

3. Specific control activities

   a. General accounts—primary and subsidiary accounts; devising checks on the company's finances and safeguarding its assets; checking invoices and accounts receivable and payable; controlling cash payments and receipts; payroll accounts, fringe benefits, plant and equipment records; cost accounting activities of the various management functions

   b. Preparation and interpretation of regular financial reports and statements

   c. Inventory control

   d. Statistics

   e. Taxes

4. Internal audits

5. Interpretation of control data

The reader should not assume that the treasurer's and controller's functions are separate and independent and are performed independently of each other. Although in some firms the treasurer's functions are delegated to one person and the controller's functions are assigned to another, these actions cannot be performed independently. Therefore, financial managers must not only be familiar with so-called financial principles and fundamentals, they must also be thoroughly grounded in accounting theory and fundamentals. In other words, there must be an amalgamation of financial and accounting knowledge at the financial manager's level of operation. *Duties and Problems of Chief Financial Executives*, a study recently conducted by Jeremy Bacon and Francis J. Walsh, Jr., for the National Industrial Conference Board, revealed that 157 financial executives included accounting as one of their primary responsibilities. The following were listed as the most important functions performed by this group:

1. Administration of funds

2. Planning and controlling business operations

3. Acquisition of funds

---

[2]*Ibid.*, p. 200.

4. Accounting
5. Protection of assets
6. Tax administration
7. Investor relations
8. Management of the company's financial organization
9. Consultation
10. Analysis of acquisitions
11. Government reporting
12. Appraisal of economic outlook[3]

ORGANIZATION AND STRUCTURE
OF THE FINANCE FUNCTION

Generally speaking, individuals in charge of the finance function of large companies are located on the same scalar level as the managers of production and distribution and report directly to the chief executive officer. This is borne out by a survey conducted by J. Fred Weston, which revealed that in most of the reporting firms, the finance officer reports to the president or to the president and the board of directors.[4] This points up the importance of the finance function to the welfare of the *total* operation of the firm. Its importance is further emphasized by the fact that half the companies reporting stated that the finance officer was a member of the board of directors. Furthermore, when the finance officer was not a member of the board, he usually attended the board meetings in order to advise and be consulted on financial affairs of the organization.

As a general rule, the size of the business firm determines the number and kinds of financial executives responsible for the finance function. This conclusion was reached by the American Management Association after conducting a study of the organization of the finance function of 278 companies. Included in Table 1-1 are the titles of the individuals in charge of the finance function of the firms included in the survey.

It should be noted that the larger companies have a vice-president of finance, whereas the middle-sized companies have both a treasurer and a controller but no financial vice-president. Smaller companies have only treasurers (78 companies with an average of 1,480 employees) but no controllers. Finally, in 22 of the smaller companies, the treasurer and controller are the same individual.[5]

Although there are no studies regarding titles of finance executives in small

---

[3] Jeremy Bacon and Francis J. Walsh, Jr., *Duties and Problems of Chief Financial Executives* (New York: National Industrial Conference Board, 1968), p. 4.

[4] J. Fred Weston, "The Finance Function," *Journal of Finance*, September 1954, p. 274.

[5] Edward T. Curtis, *Company Organization of the Finance Function*, Research Study 55 (New York: American Management Association, 1962), pp. 12-13.

TABLE 1-1

COMPANY OFFICIAL IN GENERAL
CHARGE OF FINANCIAL AFFAIRS IN THE
278 PARTICIPATING COMPANIES

	Number of Companies	Percent	Total Employees	Percent	Average Number of Employees in Company
Total	278	99[a]	1,719,445	100	6,185
Company has vice-president–finance or executive vice-president–finance who is not also treasurer or controller	32	12	601,306	35	18,790
Company has a director of finance or a vice-president–planning and control or a vice-president–administration as top financial man	4	1	44,100	2	11,025
Company has both treasurer and controller but none of the above	135	48	934,441	54	6,921
Company has a treasurer but no controller	78	28	115,488	7	1,480
Treasurer and controller are same man	22	8	19,655	1	893
Company has neither treasurer nor controller	1	--	190	--	190
No answer on some point of information, or unclear response	6	2	4,265	--	710

[a]Because of rounding, percentages do not total 100.

Source: Edward T. Curtis, *Company Organization of the Finance Function,* Research Study 55 (New York: American Management Association, 1962), p. 12.

companies, it may be assumed that an even wider variation exists among titles. This is primarily because the finance function in small firms is not as well defined nor as complex as in large firms; consequently, the function would more than likely be combined with other functions, such as sales or production.

Figure 1-1 shows the place of the finance officer in the management hierarchy, as well as the various subfunctions he is usually called upon to supervise. It may be noted that the finance committee reports directly to the board of directors. The primary reason for having a finance committee in most organizations is to facilitate coordination of financial policy, since committees are not very effective in performing the financial planning and control functions.

FINANCIAL MANAGERS OF THE FUTURE

In the past, the principal constraint on financial decisions has been the availability of capital resources. It is believed that although the scarcity of capi-

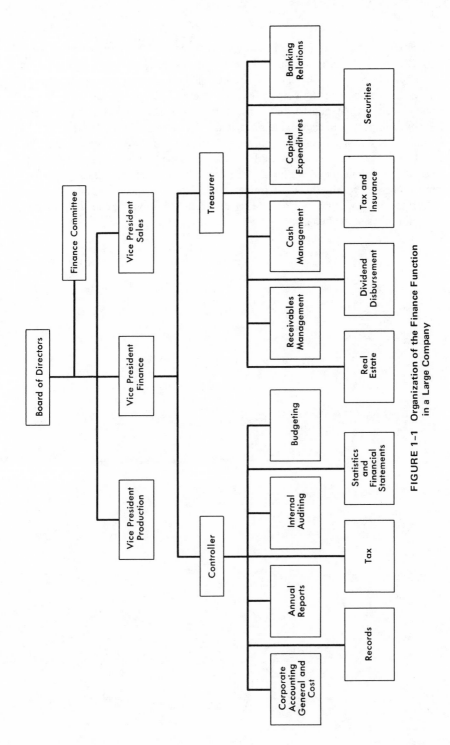

FIGURE 1-1 Organization of the Finance Function in a Large Company

9

tal resources will continue to influence investment decisions, there will be other constraints of equal importance. To illustrate, financial managers of the future must consider the impact that investments will have on society in general as well as on shareholders of the corporation. For example, it is possible that an investment decision may add to the "present value of the shareholders' wealth" and yet be completely unacceptable since it fails to increase the "present value" of the wealth of society. In addition, it may also fail to satisfy the legal constraints that have been imposed not only by statutory law but also by guidelines established by administrative agencies. Obviously, the financial manager of the future must operate within the total framework of society; therefore, he should be educated in the behavioral as well as the technical disciplines such as finance, accounting, and mathematics.

2

The Legal Forms
of Business
Organization

Proprietorships, partnerships, and corporations are by far the most important forms of legal organization in the United States today. Major emphasis in this chapter is on a discussion of the characteristics of proprietorships, partnerships, and corporations, and the effects of these characteristics upon the financial activities of the firm. The function of forming the organization belongs to management's legal advisors; however, the responsibility for the choice of the type of organization the business assumes is the sole responsibility of the firm's owners. In making this decision, management should select the type of legal organization with characteristics that aid rather than impede the firm in achieving its goals. Although many of the characteristics do not directly affect the finance function, there are many that do; therefore, it is mandatory for students of finance to know and understand thoroughly the characteristics of each organization as well as the impact of each on the firm's financial activities.

To accomplish this end, the following factors are used to describe the types of organizations mentioned above, since each plays an important role in management's decision: (1) ease of formation, (2) cost of formation, (3) liability of owners, (4) durability and stability of each firm, (5) directness of control and ease of direction, and (6) legal status and sphere of activity.

PROPRIETORSHIPS

Although relatively speaking, more business firms operate as proprietorships than as corporations and partnerships, the former are far less important from the standpoint of the dollar volume of business receipts. To illustrate, the number of proprietorships accounted for 79.2 percent of business firms in these three categories in 1966, but they accounted for only 13.0 percent of all business receipts (see Table 2-1). It is interesting to note also that although the relative number of proprietorships underwent little or no change between the years 1963 and 1966, their share of business receipts declined during this period; e.g., they accounted for 14.4 percent of the business receipts in 1963, but by 1966, their share had declined to 13.0 percent.

TABLE 2-1
PROPRIETORSHIPS, PARTNERSHIPS, AND
CORPORATIONS, NUMBER AND BUSINESS
RECEIPTS FOR SELECTED YEARS
(in millions)

Organization	1963	1964	1965	1966
Proprietorships				
Number	9,136	9,193	9,078	9,087
Percent	79.2	80.0	79.5	79.2
Business receipts	$181,551	$188,738	$199,385	$207,447
Percent	14.4	14.0	13.6	13.0
Partnerships				
Number	924	922	914	923
Percent	8.1	8.0	8.0	8.0
Business receipts	$ 73,274	$ 74,822	$75,259	$ 79,776
Percent	5.8	5.5	5.1	5.0
Corporations				
Number	1,323	1,374	1,424	1,469
Percent	11.6	12.0	12.5	12.8
Business receipts	$1,008,743	$1,086,739	$1,194,601	$1,306,313
Percent	79.8	80.5	81.3	82.0
Total Number	11,383	11,489	11,416	11,479
Total Business Receipts	$1,263,568	$1,350,299	$1,469,245	$1,593,536

Source: Statistical Abstract of the United States, 90th ann. ed. (Washington, D.C.: U.S. Department of Commerce, 1969), p. 472.

The proprietorship type of business was the earliest and by far the simplest of all legal forms of organization. The proprietorship is a common-law form of organization and requires no formally drawn documents. Moreover, the state does not require the owners to pay any organizational fees or taxes before the firm starts doing business. Since the proprietorship has no legal status, it ceases to exist at the will of the proprietor or upon his death. It is true that the assets of the firm can be bequeathed upon the death of the owner and the firm can continue to operate, but the resultant business is not the same as the original proprietorship.

The owners of individual proprietorships, unlike owners of corporate enterprises, are personally liable for the debts of the business firm. This characteristic has certain advantages from a capital-raising viewpoint, since creditors may look to the owner's personal assets as security. However, it may also serve as a deterrent, since it jeopardizes the personal assets the proprietor may have accumulated from other sources. It is for this reason that proprietors look to the corporate form of organization as quickly as is feasible.

The low cost and ease of forming the proprietorship is one of its chief advantages when compared to other forms of organization. Although the owner must pay certain license fees in order to do business, they are usually very nominal. From the viewpoint of creating the proprietorship, no agreements are necessary, since the proprietor is the sole owner of the assets; and as long as the business engages in lawful endeavors, no permission is required of state officials.

In most instances, the owner is also the manager and does not share control with anyone. Moreover, this form of business is relatively free from legal restrictions. As long as the owner adheres to the basic laws regarding contracts, negotiable instruments, deeds, and mortgages, he is free to move in any direction that he chooses.

The profits of the proprietorship are taxed at the owner's tax rate whether they are retained in the business, paid out in the form of salaries, or withdrawn as profits. Furthermore, they are taxed only one time, whereas in the corporate organization, income is taxed when made and then taxed again when distributed to the shareholders as cash dividends. Finally, a proprietorship may operate without incurring abnormal expenditures in any state the owner chooses.

PARTNERSHIPS

A general partnership is a voluntary organization of two or more individuals who combine their capital, skills, and effort in order to increase their profit. Although the partnership is a common-law organization, several states have passed statutes governing its formation and operation. In states where no statutes exist, the partnership agreement may be implied, oral, or written. In any event, agreements usually cover these points: names of the partners; name and nature of the business; amount and type of capital invested; duration of the partnership; agency powers of the various partners; and method of dividing profits and losses. (The last point is most important because in the absence of an agreement, the law holds that each partner will share profits and losses equally.)

The general partnership has many of the same characteristics as the proprietorship; for example, it is relatively easy to form, from the standpoint of both cost—organizational fees, taxes, and miscellaneous expenses—and effort required to bring it into existence.

As a general rule, it is better to have an attorney draw up the articles of copartnership since this action tends to reduce misunderstanding concerning the sharing of profits and losses and the powers of each partner. Even when an attorney is used, the charges are small compared to the attorney's fees for securing a charter for a corporation. The agreement does not need to be filed with any state official; once drawn, the partnership is in effect and ready to begin doing business. The only costs of formation are the attorney's fee and license fees when required.

Larger sums of equity capital can usually be raised by partnerships than by proprietorships, since several individuals may be called upon to supply equity capital. Moreover, it is also possible to obtain larger amounts of debt capital, since each partner has unlimited liability. Although this may be an advantage in some cases, it often serves to limit the amount of equity capital that can be acquired. That is, many individuals are hesitant to enter into a partnership, since they are liable for the firm's debts. Although each partner may limit his liability by agreement, he may still be sued by the creditors for the entire amount of the claim. It is true that he in turn can sue the other members of the partnership for their share; but if they do not have sufficient personal assets to satisfy their share, he will be liable for the entire sum. It is easy to see why a person with large personal assets would be hesitant about entering into an agreement with individuals whose personal assets are limited.

The partnership lacks stability; that is, the partnership ceases to exist when any one of the following occurs: (1) any partner dies, (2) any partner goes insane, (3) any partner withdraws from the partnership, or (4) any partner goes bankrupt. Although the remaining partners may reform and continue the business, the original business is dissolved and the assets must be divided according to the agreement, or equally in the event that no valid agreement exists.

Instability is one characteristic of the partnership that does create serious problems. Since the partnership is a voluntary association, it may have difficulty surviving. For example, no partner is required to remain in the business endeavor. A shareholder of a corporation may sever his relationship with the firm by selling his interest, but the firm will continue to function. This is not true with the partnership; if a partner wishes to sell his interest to another individual, the remaining partners can refuse to accept the newcomer. Even if they accept the new partner, another partnership must be created and all outstanding contracts must be renegotiated.

The general partnership is a common-law organization, but some states have created what might be referred to as a statutory partnership. The most common form is that of limited partnership. This organization differs from the general partnership in that it is formed under the limited partnership statutes and one or more of the partners may have limited liability; that is, their liability is limited to the amount that they have invested. In order for these special partners to enjoy limited liability, their names cannot appear in the name of the firm, nor can they actively engage in the management of the endeavor. If either of these two provisions is violated, the partner or partners lose their claim of limited liability. A serious disadvantage of the limited partnership is that states not having limited partnership statutes may refuse to recognize the firm as a limited partnership and may treat it as a general partnership.

CORPORATIONS

The corporation is by far the most important type of business organization in existence today from the standpoints of assets employed and sales made. The rapid rise in its importance supports the concept that without the corporation, the United States would not have achieved the economic position that it enjoys today. One authority had this to say about the corporation; "Its position in the Western world is the end result of men's effort to create a business unit that will maximize the production of economic goods, minimize capital risk and facilitate managerial control."[1]

It can also be said that the corporation is the outgrowth of need. That is, the corporation has, in most cases, corrected many of the weaknesses inherent in proprietorships and partnerships. In what way did the corporation correct these defects?

First, the corporation is organized under specific statutes. Like a citizen, it can sue, be sued, buy, sell, or own property, commit a crime, and be punished by sentences up to and including death. However, unlike a citizen, it must request and receive permission before doing business in its home state or in other states.

Second, individuals who invest equity funds in the corporation have limited liability; however, if shareholders pay less than par or stated value for stock, they are liable for the difference, should it become necessary to satisfy creditors' claims. (Some states provide that stockholders may be assessed an amount up to but not exceeding the par value of their stock for unpaid wages of labor.) This provision makes it possible for corporations to accumulate large sums of capital. Had it not been possible to assemble large sums of capital, it is highly probable that our economy would not have achieved its present importance. When viewed in this way, the corporation may be called the "father of modern industry."

The corporation makes it possible for individuals to transfer ownership without interrupting the business endeavor. This is one of the essential differences between the corporation and the general partnership or proprietorship. In the latter two forms, the owners own the assets of the business; but corporate shareholders own the stock and the corporation owns the assets. Since this is true, the shareholders may sell or dispose of the shares in whatever way they wish without affecting the status of the corporation.

The corporation's life is said to be permanent. In most states incorporators receive a permanent charter, although a few states set a maximum number of years for which a charter may be issued. It should be emphasized that the renewal of the charter in these states is a perfunctory act, and the corporation possesses permanency and stability. This is a very important characteristic, since investors do not have to worry about reinvesting their funds or renegotiating the

---

[1] W. Bayard Taylor, *Financial Policies of Business Enterprise*, 2nd ed. (New York: Appleton-Century-Crofts, Inc., 1956), p. 21.

terms of their agreement every time an "owner" dies, goes insane, or becomes bankrupt.

The corporation possesses certain characteristics that may be considered disadvantageous. These are: cost and difficulty of forming the corporation; taxation; inability to do business in states other than the one in which it is domiciled without paying additional fees; legal restrictions; and the lack of interest by many stockholders.

Each state has enacted legislation setting forth the requirements for the formation of the corporate organization. Chapter 3 emphasizes the cost, time, and effort involved in creating a corporate organization as compared with proprietorships or partnerships. This in no way implies that the formation of the corporation is prohibitive, but only that management should consider these factors when selecting the legal form of organization.

At one time, taxation was a major factor in determining whether to incorporate. However, now that corporations may elect to be taxed as unincorporated businesses, this factor is of considerably less importance.

It was stated earlier than a corporation is regarded as a "citizen" of the state in which it is incorporated. If the firm wishes to do business in any other state, it must qualify. To qualify simply means that the firm is required to pay the necessary fees and taxes and file such documents as articles of incorporation, bylaws, statements of financial condition, and statements revealing the amount of capital and assets to be employed in that state. It should be noted that if the firm performs only functions that are *interstate* in nature, it does not need to qualify; but if it performs functions that are considered to be *intrastate*, it must qualify. The following acts are considered doing intrastate business:

1. Sales of goods by salesmen who possess the power to make contracts
2. Storage of goods in a warehouse
3. Ownership of real property
4. Purchase and temporary storage of goods prior to shipment to home office
5. Sale of goods requiring installation by an agent

Business enterprises of all kinds are subject to governmental regulations provided that: (1) they are big, (2) they affect the public interest, or (3) they possess a corporate structure. The government does not look with favor upon any business that may be large enough to create either a monopoly of a monopsony; and to prevent these conditions, the government requires businesses to subject themselves to certain regulatory provisions. Businesses such as public utilities are subject to legal restrictions because their activities affect public interest. Government, both state and federal, requires corporations to file statements revealing their financial conditions. Although individual proprietorships and partnerships are subject to a degree of governmental control, the corporation is subject to even more; however, it should be emphasized that corporations do not consider themselves too highly regulated in comparison to other forms of organization. Whether management considers that it should be regulated by the government at all is another question, and a discussion of this matter is not within the scope of this book.

Some managers consider it to their advantage for shareholders to be uninterested in the affairs of the corporate organization, but even if this is the case, management has the problem of informing owners of past accomplishments and future plans. All except a very small number of corporations submit quarterly and annual reports to their shareholders. The finance executive is vitally interested in this requirement, since each report received by shareholders contains financial information; in fact, many reports contain little else. Since owners of proprietorships and partnerships are so close to the affairs of the business, their reports are less formal and require much less effort to prepare.

OTHER TYPES OF ORGANIZATIONS

In addition to proprietorships, partnerships, and corporations, several other types of organization may be utilized in the business process. The majority of these types were developed to offset one or more of the disadvantages of partnerships and proprietorships.

Limited Partnership Association

The limited partnership association is similar to the limited partnership in that the owners have limited liability. In addition, ownership is transferable, but the new owner is not allowed a vote unless this is approved by the majority of the old owners or shareholders. Unlike the partnership, the firm is managed by a board of directors elected by the shareholders. Only four states recognize this form of organization: Michigan, Ohio, New Jersey, and Pennsylvania. Although this type of organization enjoys the advantages of limited liability and the ability to transfer shares of stock with reasonable ease, the following disadvantages exist: first, it is treated as a general partnership outside the state in which it is domiciled; second, it is treated as a corporation for income tax purposes.

Joint Groupings

The *joint stock company* is characterized by (1) the transferability of its shares and (2) the permanence of life it enjoys compared to the partnership. It is taxed as a corporation and its owners are jointly and severally liable for the obligations of the firm. The *joint venture* is a temporary grouping together of individuals, partnerships, or corporations for the specific purpose of performing a particular project. Once the project is completed or after an agreed period of time, the venture is dissolved.

Business Trust

The business trust, often referred to as the Massachusetts Trust, closely resembles the corporation in that it possesses the following characteristics: (1) it

is formed by adopting a trust agreement; (2) shares of ownership, called certificates of beneficial interest, and bonds may be issued and sold; (3) shareholders
have limited liability; and (4) the trust is taxed as a corporation.

The above characteristics are similar to those of a corporation, but certain
characteristics are dissimilar. The more important are: (1) shareholders are not
permitted to vote for the members of the board of trustees, who manage the
business (if they do vote, they lose their right to limited liability); (2) the life of
the business trust is limited; and (3) only the trustees are empowered to fill
vacancies on the board. The trust claims two primary advantages: it may be used
in areas in which the corporation is not allowed to operate, and it is relatively
free from government supervision. The trust, like other legal forms of organization, also has certain disadvantages; for example, shareholders have unlimited
liability if they attempt to manage the affairs of the trust, and the trust may be
treated as a partnership in states other than its legal residence.

EFFECT OF THE CHARACTERISTICS
ON FINANCIAL MANAGEMENT

It was pointed out earlier than the actual formation of the legal organization
should be delegated to the firm's attorneys, but it was also emphasized that the
choice of organizational form is the responsibility of the owners of the business
enterprise. Although many factors influence this decision, one of the more important areas of consideration is that of finance. How then do financial considerations influence the decision of whether to create a proprietorship, partnership,
or corporation?

One of the more significant factors to be considered is the amount and kind
of capital the firm should have in order to achieve its purpose. In areas where
small amounts of capital are needed—service establishments and many retail
businesses—proprietorships or partnerships are capable of providing the necessary
equity and debt capital. If large sums of capital are involved, the proprietorship
and partnership forms of organization are at a distinct disadvantage, primarily
because of the unlimited liability of the owners and their inability to transfer
their equity readily. The corporation's owners are neither burdened with unlimited liability nor are they restricted in transferring shares of stock that represent ownership.

Another important feature serving to limit the partnership from raising large
amounts of capital is the possession by each general partner of agency powers.
This means that each partner is a manager of the firm and is responsible for the
decisions of the others. Since each partner's assets may be used to satisfy business debts, a wrong decision on the part of one partner could jeopardize the
assets of every member of the firm. In addition to this, it is difficult to obtain
harmony among large numbers of partners with equal authority. Moreover,
many investors do not want to participate in the day-to-day operations, yet they

feel obliged to take an active interest since they are jointly and severally liable to the firm's creditors.

The corporate form of organization allows management to plow a larger amount of its earnings back into the business than is the case with the unincorporated firm, because the profit of the unincorporated firm is considered income of its owners and is taxed at their individual rates regardless of its disposition. The earnings of the corporation are not considered the property of the owners until they have been declared in the form of cash dividends. Suppose a corporation earns $25,000 per year. The tax on these earnings amounts to $5,500, which means that the firm can retain $19,500 in the business process. If the same amount is earned by a proprietorship whose owner is in the 30-percent tax bracket, the amount that may be reinvested in the business will be $17,500, or $2,000 less.

Furthermore, the corporation owners may never be called upon to pay the tax on these earnings, since the directors may never pay them out in the form of cash dividends. In such a case, if corporate owners want cash, the firm can declare a stock dividend and the owners can sell the stock. It is true that they will have to pay a capital gains tax on the profit from the sale, but the corporation will not have to pay the tax. In other words, it can keep the extra $2,000 invested in assets. (This situation is true only in those firms where the owners' tax rate exceeds the corporate tax rate.)

The discussion above does not pertain to the subject of taxation per se; it is concerned only with the ability of the corporate form of organization to retain funds for operational purposes rather than distributing them to the owners. Under existing tax laws, taxation is not an important factor in choosing the legal form of organization, since certain corporations may elect to be taxed as unincorporated units. It is true that corporate earnings are subject to "double" taxation, whereas unincorporated firms are not. For example, a corporation pays an income tax as a business unit; that is, the corporate income is taxed at a corporate rate (22 percent on the first $25,000 and 48 percent on all income exceeding $25,000). If the net income after corporate taxes is paid out in the form of cash dividends, the shareholder is also required to pay a tax on these dividends. Whether it is better to be taxed as a corporation or as an unincorporated firm depends entirely on the tax rate of the owners. If the tax rate of the owners is less than the corporate rate, obviously, the advantage rests with the unincorporated firm. If the opposite is true, the advantage rests with the corporate firm.

Although their income may be taxed two times, corporations enjoy certain tax privileges not available to unincorporated firms. For example, salaries paid to owner-officers are deductible as expenses. Furthermore, owner-executives of corporations are considered employees and as such enjoy certain tax advantages with respect to stock options, pension and profit-sharing plans, group insurance, death benefits, medical and wage continuation plans, and expenses incurred for meals and lodging.

3

Formation and Control of the Business Corporation

Sound financial principles and fundamentals are not normally associated with any one particular type of institution. It is equally important for a proprietor and for the president of a multimillion-dollar corporation to know and understand financial principles and fundamentals, since the success or failure of each is based upon the formulation and promulgation of effective financial policies. However, since the corporate enterprise dominates the business scene insofar as assets and sales are concerned, it is essential that students of finance know and understand the techniques employed in the formation and control of the business corporation.

The modern business corporation is a result of the changing economic structure in which we live. Originally, simple business enterprises, such as proprietorships, could produce and distribute all required economic goods; however, as the environment changed, the institutions serving this environment also changed. From this evolution emerged the modern corporation.

According to the sovereignty theory, the corporation owes its legal existence to the state in which it obtains its charter. This is true, but in order for a state to act, an association of individuals must request the action; therefore, it is the opinion of the writer that the corporation owes its true existence to the group of individuals who recognized the need for the corporation at that particular time and in that particular environment.

FORMATION OF THE CORPORATION

Although statutes governing the formation of business corporations vary among states, the procedures for their formation tend to follow a common pattern. In forming a corporation, incorporators are called upon to make decisions concerning the following: (1) the name of the corporation, (2) the location of the principal office, (3) the period of corporate duration, (4) selection of the incorporators and first board of directors, (5) the state of incorporation, (6) the nature and scope of business activity, and (7) the plan of capitalization, including the method of distributing the securities.

Name of the Firm

Those selecting the name of the firm should be mindful that the name will help advertise and exploit the firm's products and services. Since most names do perform this function, state laws protect the names of firms by disallowing a name designed to deceive or cause confusion. Many states require that the name indicate its corporate character. Furthermore, the statutes generally prohibit the use of names in the title which improperly imply (1) that the business is performing a function prohibited by law, (2) that it is some form of public agency, or (3) that it is a part of some other organization when in fact it is not. When selecting a name, it is unwise to indicate a local or regional area. If the name of a state or section of the country is made a part of the corporate name, potential customers in other areas or states may become discouraged from using its products or services.

Location of the Principal Office

Since all incorporation laws require that the name of the principal office as well as the name of the registered agent be included in the articles of incorporation, these decisions should be made prior to the drafting of the articles of incorporation. In most cases the registered office need not be the same as the corporation's place of business. The registered agent may be an individual resident of the state, whose business office is identical with such registered offices; or a domestic corporation; or a foreign corporation authorized to do business in the state. The principal function of the registered agent is to receive any notice, process, or demand that is served.

Period of Duration of the Corporate Charter

Generally speaking incorporators want the life of the corporation to be permanent; therefore, in states that provide for perpetual existence, the charter will ordinarily stipulate this. If, however, the statutes limit the period of duration, the articles of incorporation show and set forth the maximum number of years permitted.

Identity of Incorporators and Directors

Although statutes vary concerning requirements with respect to the identity of incorporators and directors, most states require that the names and addresses of both incorporators and the board of directors be included in the articles of incorporation.

State of Incorporation

The selection of the state in which to incorporate is usually a very simple matter if the firm is small or if the product is distributed locally. On the other hand, for firms that are international, national, or regional in character, the selection of the state of incorporation is far from a simple process. In arriving at the decision of whether to incorporate in one state or another, the following factors must be considered: (1) citizenship requirement of incorporators; (2) statutes pertaining to directors; (3) requirements for capitalization; (4) requirements regarding liability of shareholders; (5) requirements regarding dividends; (6) stockholder rights regarding books and records of corporation, limitations with respect to prosecution of stockholders' suits, dissenters' rights, and pre-emptive rights; (7) costs, including taxes, required in the formation as well as the operation of the business endeavor; and (8) statutory provisions regarding sale of assets, amendment of charter, and merger.

A brief explanation of these factors will give the student an insight into the problem of selecting the "home" of the business. First, a few states require that at least one of the incorporators be a resident of the state in which it is incorporated. This in itself presents no problem since "dummies" may be used to satisfy the requirement; however, some states may require that the annual shareholder meeting be held in the state of incorporation. This could present a problem, particularly if management wants to hold regional stockholder meetings in order to improve stockholder participation.

Second, citizenship and residence requirements for members of the board of directors are very liberal. For example, the Texas Business Incorporation Act does not require directors to be residents of the state of Texas unless the articles of incorporation or bylaws so require. Most states require that directors be shareholders, but again this presents no problem, since ownership of one share generally satisfies the requirement. Furthermore, this requirement can be modified by the articles of incorporation and bylaws. Classification of the board is permitted in most states and therefore presents no problem. Also, statutory requirements concerning removal and changing the number of the board members are generally lenient.

Third, the statutory provisions concerning capitalization should be examined thoroughly before deciding on the state in which to incorporate. For example, statutes concerning classification of stock—par or no par, voting and nonvoting, and preferred, common, or classified—should be carefully examined, since these characteristics do influence the success or failure of the firm. Moreover, the statutes should be examined to determine whether there is a limitation with respect to the amount and character of debt. (Arizona, for example, limits debt to two-thirds of the capital stock.)

Fourth, a few states require that shareholders be liable beyond their investment for corporate debts resulting from unpaid wages.

Fifth, as a general rule, the corporation can pay dividends out of surplus or profits, but a few states require that dividends be paid out of current profits. This provision may seriously limit a corporation, since there is always the possibility that a firm will not operate at a profit. In this case, the payment of dividends must be curtailed for that period regardless of the state of the surplus and cash account.

Sixth, the operations of a corporation may be influenced by the statutes regarding (1) the rights of shareholders to inspect the books; (2) limitations regarding the prosecution of shareholders suits; (3) the right of the shareholder to dissent, particularly in the case of the sale of assets; and (4) the right of shareholders to purchase their proportionate share of any new stock that is issued. For example, in Texas the pre-emptive right is guaranteed unless specifically limited by the articles of incorporation and bylaws. Furthermore, this exclusion must also appear on the certificate of ownership. Only two states require pre-emptive rights; three-fourths of all states specify that the pre-emptive right is provided unless specifically denied; and five states deny this right unless provided by the charter.

Seventh, the cost of incorporation is probably the most important of the above factors. Careful analysis should be made of organization taxes and fees as well as annual taxes and fees.

Nature and Scope of Business

With certain exceptions,[1] a natural citizen of a state can enter into and carry on any specific business endeavor that is not otherwise prohibited by the laws of the state without securing prior approval of the state. This is not true with the corporation. In order to engage legally in business endeavors, the corporation, through approval of its petition to incorporate, is delegated by the state certain "powers" to act. If a corporation engages in transactions that are outside the purposes for which it was created, it may be enjoined by the state, since it is performing *ultra vires* acts.

There often exists in the minds of students of finance a confusion regarding "purpose" and "power" clauses. The "purpose" clauses are intended to set forth the nature of the business of the corporation, whereas the "power" clauses set forth the manner and means through which the firm can achieve its goals. Early incorporation acts required that a corporation list each "purpose" for which the

---

[1] In certain instances this is not true; for example, some states require that a person obtain permission to operate a liquor store. Furthermore, some endeavors require that a tax be paid before actual operations can be started—e.g., sale of tobacco, liquor, etc.

firm was incorporated. These specific purpose provisions have been replaced by a "general purpose" clause, which allows the corporation to state in more general terms the nature of the business enterprise.

The statutes of most states grant corporations the necessary general "powers" to carry out the firm's objectives. These powers are supplemented by "implied" powers that are "reasonably" necessary for the corporation to carry out its stated purposes. To illustrate, the Business Incorporation Act of Texas sets forth eighteen "expressed" powers that a corporation has, plus the following "implied" power: "Whether included in the foregoing or not, to have and exercise all powers necessary or appropriate to effect any or all of the purposes for which the corporation is organized." Requirements with respect to enumeration of powers in the articles of incorporation vary among states. Therefore, it is wise to follow local precedent, which, of course, conforms to the law of the state involved.

Capitalization

Incorporators, in conjunction with their accountants and attorneys, must determine and set forth in the articles of incorporation (1) type, kind, and number of shares of stock to be authorized; (2) the par or no-par status of the stock; (3) voting rights of each type and class of stock; and (4) pre-emptive status of the stock. Although amending the charter is relatively easy to accomplish insofar as the state is concerned, it may be difficult as well as expensive to get the shareholders to agree to changes after the firm is in operation.

Also included in the articles of incorporation is the amount of stock to be issued initially and the amount that is to be paid for the stock. Statutes require a minimum consideration to be received before the corporation can begin doing business. This usually amounts to $1,000 or 10 percent of the authorized stock, whichever is smaller.

Incorporation Procedure

After the articles of incorporation have been drawn up, the document is filed with the appropriate official, usually the Secretary of State. This official will issue a certificate of incorporation only after confirming that the articles of incorporation adhere to the business incorporation act and that the required fees have been paid. Upon issuance of the certificate, usually called the charter, the corporate existence begins. At this time, the incorporators normally call an organization meeting of the board of directors, to adopt the corporate bylaws, to elect officers, and to transact other business.

Corporate Bylaws

In addition to the authority granted by the statutes and articles of incorporation, the corporation is also governed by its bylaws. It has been said that the bylaws govern the internal affairs of the corporate firm. Although the statutes differ with respect to the content, most bylaws contain provisions for the regulation and management of the affairs of the corporation, and generally include the following:

1. Time and place of annual and special meetings of the shareholders
2. Voting rights
3. Board of directors (number, classification, election, term of office, and regular and special meetings)
4. Officers of the corporation
5. Committees of the board of directors
6. Bank accounts
7. Certificate seal
8. Books and records
9. Stock certificate (issuance, signature, and transfer procedures)
10. Dividends and reserves
11. Fiscal year and annual audits
12. Contracts
13. Amendment procedures

MANAGEMENT OF THE CORPORATION

The management of corporate organizations, unlike that of proprietorships, is vested in its shareholders, directors, and officers. The shareholders, by virtue of ownership, are the true managers of the enterprise. As a practical matter, except in small firms, shareholders cannot manage the operation; therefore, they elect and delegate the authority to manage to the board of directors. The board, in turn, delegates the details of management to the officers. It should be pointed out that officers have no authority to act unless that authority is properly delegated by the charter, bylaws, the board of directors, or a specified combination of these. Moreover, the authority to act in certain areas cannot be delegated to either the board or the officers; generally these areas include (1) the sale of assets, (2) merger and consolidation, and (3) amending the charter or bylaws.

Shareholders As Managers

Shareholders manage the affairs of the corporation by (1) adopting the charter and bylaws, (2) electing the board of directors, and (3) approving or disapproving the board's actions. Each of the acts is accomplished through the voting process. Under common law each stockholder is guaranteed one vote regardless of the number of shares owned. This method of voting has been replaced by statutes that control the incorporation procedures. The statutes provide that each shareholder has one vote per share, which means that a simple majority of stockholders can control every act. In order to give minority interests a voice in the affairs of the corporation, cumulative voting for directors has been either required or allowed in nearly all states. Under cumulative voting, each shareholder has a number of votes equal to the number of voting shares he owns multiplied by the number of directors to be elected; and he can accumulate his votes and cast them for any one or several directors. An example illustrates the process: Assume there are 1,000 shares outstanding and nine members on the board of directors. If all nine are to be elected at one time, a shareholder with 101 shares can elect one director. That is, by casting all 909 (101 × 9) votes for one candidate, the shareholder is assured of his man's election. If a majority is desired, 501 shares are required. Staggering the terms of directors tends to offset some of the advantages gained from the cumulative voting technique. For example, if only three directors are elected each year rather than all nine, 251 shares are required to elect one director. It should be noted, however, that the owners of 251 shares would have three members on the board at all times, but if all nine are being elected at one time, it requires 301 or 50 more shares, to elect three directors.[2]

Only shareholders of record are allowed to vote; that is, unless the shareholder's name appears in the corporate records, he is not permitted a vote. To avoid confusion, the bylaws provide for the closing of the stock transfer book for a reasonable period. After this date and until after the shareholders' meeting, the buyers of stock are not allowed to vote on issues presented at that particular meeting. In some states, the law allows the corporation to prepare a list of shareholders as of a particular date—anywhere from 10 to 30 days before the shareholders' meeting—and this list becomes the official authority for whether a shareholder is allowed to vote.

Unlike board members, a shareholder may authorize another person to vote his stock by giving him his power of attorney in writing; this is called a *proxy*. It is revocable, and the holder of the latest-dated proxy possesses the right to these votes. Moreover, even though a stockholder transfers his right to vote to another person or group of people, he may at the very last minute revoke the proxy and cast the vote in person. It has been stated by many authorities that management has been able to perpetuate itself by being able to obtain the proxies of uninterested shareholders. Obviously, since existing management has easy access to stockholder records and since the expense of soliciting proxies is assumed by the corporation, present management has a tremendous advantage over any dissenting group wishing to obtain control.

The shareholders exercise their managerial duties at regular and special meetings. The rules governing these meetings are set forth in the statutes, the charter, or the bylaws and cover such things as the time, place, nature, quorum, and order of business. For the regular annual meetings of shareholders, each share-

---

[2]The following formula gives a method of determining the smallest number of shares necessary to elect the desired number of directors:

$$\frac{\text{Total Number of Shares Outstanding} \times \text{Number of Directors Desired}}{\text{Number of Directors to Be Elected} + 1} + 1$$

holder must be given adequate notice; for example, not less than 10 nor more than 50 days before the date of the meeting. The failure to hold a regular meeting is not sufficient ground to revoke the firm's charter; however, statutes set forth in detail the procedure that any interested shareholder may use to force management to hold annual meetings.

As a general rule, special meetings of the shareholders may be called by the president, the board of directors, the holders of not less than one-tenth of all shares entitled to vote at the meeting in question, or any officer designated by the corporate bylaws. Also, the statutes usually require that the notice of any special meeting of the shareholders set forth the purpose or purposes for which the meeting is to be held.

Directors as Managers

It is the law that a corporation can act only through its legally elected board of directors except in instances where the corporation has conferred special authority upon one or more of its officers. However, in order to carry on the many and varied functions that must be performed, directors delegate to officers and employees the authority to act on certain matters. It should be emphasized that although authority to act is delegated, the responsibility for the actions cannot be delegated. The law requires that directors maintain the highest fidelity to the interest of the corporation and that they use reasonable care in the discharge of their duties. The statutes, charter, and bylaws will, in most instances, set forth in detail the number, qualifications, duties, method of election, term of office, and classification of directors, as well as resignation and removal procedures and the method of filling vacancies.

In general, boards of directors are expected to perform the following: (1) select the major officers of the firm, (2) delegate sufficient authority to the officers to operate the business unit, (3) approve the broad objectives of the business operations, and (4) serve as a control unit with respect to predetermined objectives. These powers may be limited or restricted by statutes, articles, and bylaws.

The law, as well as the shareholders, holds directors responsible for their acts. Directors may be punished under common law if they (1) make secret profits, (2) waste the firm's assets, (3) lose the firm's assets while committing acts of negligence, (4) allow the corporate entity to act outside its purposes, or (5) make fraudulent statements and acts.

Directors are also governed by statutes and are liable under the statutes for (1) doing business without proper authorization, (2) allowing the corporation to perform an unlawful purpose, (3) issuing improper stock certificates, (4) failing to maintain proper entries in the books of accounts, (5) authorizing illegal dividends, (6) misappropriating corporate funds, or (7) violating the law regarding political contributions. Although this is not a complete list, it is sufficiently comprehensive to show the nature of acts for which directors are responsible by law.

Shareholders also hold directors responsible for their acts. In many instances it is the shareholders who bring legal action against directors. In addition, shareholders may relieve directors of their duties if they have sufficient reason to believe that the directors are not acting in the shareholders' best interest.

Since board members are not permitted to act individually, the statutes, charter, or bylaws set forth the rules and regulations governing the regular and special meetings necessary for boards to act collectively. These rules and regulations cover such items as (1) regular and special meetings, (2) time and place, (3) notice, (4) quorum, (5) order of business, and (6) the presiding officer. Since various state laws differ, it is advisable for the student to study the statutes governing corporations in his state as well as the bylaws of a business firm in order to see the specific regulations covering these items.

It should be emphasized that minutes of both regular and special meetings of directors must be carefully drawn and maintained, since court rulings are often based on this record. Furthermore, any committee designated by the regular board is governed by the same rules used to guide the procedures of the board; therefore, the minutes of meetings held by these committees should also be recorded and maintained.

Officers of the Corporation

The statutes will as a general rule set forth the minimum number of officers of a corporation, their titles, a general statement of duties, and provisions for removal. The bylaws usually set forth the officers' qualifications, term of office, duties, and compensation; for a discussion of the function of the finance officer, see Chapter 1.

4

Internal Financial

Analysis

Financial analysis, as the name implies, means the determination of a company's financial condition at any particular point during its life cycle. In approaching this important subject, several questions should be discussed. First, what groups are interested in the financial condition of a firm, and why? Second, what techniques should be employed when making the financial analysis? Third, what basic weaknesses are inherent in any financial analysis?

Three groups are vitally concerned with a firm's financial condition; (1) the firm's creditors, (2) the firm's investors, and (3) financial management.

In the first category, there are two different types of creditors, short- and long-term creditors. Each examines the firm's financial record with different objectives in mind. The short-term creditor is concerned with the firm's ability to meet its obligation when due. That is to say, his attention is centered upon the status of the firm's *flow of funds* and whether this flow will provide sufficient cash to meet the obligation at the time of its maturity. The long-term creditor is interested in the condition of the firm's earnings over a long period of time, since earnings should provide sufficient funds either to liquidate the debt at the time of its maturity or to allow the firm to refund the debt. The chief concern of the long-term creditor is not cash but the total amount of working and fixed capital that a firm has, since continued success cannot be assured unless there is enough capital to sustain operations.

The second group that maintains an interest in the financial conditions of a firm is composed of its shareholders and potential shareholders. Like the firm's creditors, this group is interested in the debt-paying ability of the business, since if maturities are not satisfied when due, the firm faces bankruptcy. Such an event not only would jeopardize the shareholder's investment but would cause him to lose a source of his income. In addition to the firm's ability to meet its debt promptly, shareholders are concerned with the rate at which capital is utilized and with the firm's profit margin. An analysis depicting both the rate at which capital moves through the various processes and the profit margin indicates the efficiency of management in the use of capital resources. All other things remaining the same, the greater the turnover and profit margin, the larger will be the return on investment. In addition, shareholders are interested in an analysis showing the relation between the amounts of debt capital and equity capital employed in the business process. Generally speaking, there is a direct relation between the amount of debt employed and the amount of risk that a business firm assumes. In order to determine the amount of risk that a company has, holders of equity securities employ techniques showing the ratio between debt and equity capital.

Finally, the firm's management has the responsibility of planning and controlling the affairs of the business endeavor. Measurements most often employed to indicate success are financial in nature; therefore, financial officers must provide tools that enable management to determine efficiency of operations. The various techniques discussed below are primarily used to measure past performance; that is, they are used in the control process. However, when these methods are applied to projected financial data, they greatly aid the planning function by helping to measure the effectiveness of existing and newly proposed plans. One note of warning: These tools can never take the place of sound principles and fundamentals in financial planning. For example, the efficient use of working capital does not result from financial management's employment of such techniques as the current ratio, funds flow statements, and cash budgets; it is rather the result of applying sound principles and fundamentals to the management of such areas as cash, inventories, receivables, and short-term investments.

Although managers on every level in the management hierarchy employ these techniques, each uses them for a different purpose. For example, top management is interested in techniques that reveal the results of the total operation, whereas the finance officer may use them to show specific aspects of the business operation—for example, the firm's solvency position, profit margin, flow of funds, or rate of profit on net worth. Since these techniques are used by different groups for different purposes, it seems logical that they should be categorized as methods useful in measuring total performance, liquidity, profitability, the efficiency of capital, and leverage.

METHODS OF MEASURING
TOTAL PERFORMANCE

The rate of return on investment is one of the more commonly known methods of measuring the overall efficiency of the business firm. Its principal value lies in its ability to focus attention on the total operation, thus allowing management to evaluate the effects of existing policies on the firm's objective. If a firm is not operating as expected, this technique calls this fact to the attention of those in charge, thus allowing them to seek out the principal causes and to replan the firm's activities. An example serves to illustrate this point. Suppose the analysis reveals that return on capital is experiencing a steady decline. Management, after analyzing the situation, finds that total investment is not being employed at the desired rate. Further analysis reveals that fixed capital is being employed at 95 percent of capacity but that working capital turnover has declined severely. Moreover, it is noted that although cash and inventories are adequate, receivables have constantly increased. This simple analysis shows that the credit policies of the firm are ineffective and further studies should be made in order to determine what changes should be effected.

Another important characteristic of this technique is that it permits top management to evaluate the utilization of resources by the several departments or divisions of the firm. Such an analysis allows management to shift resources to the most productive areas, thus improving overall performance. Finally, not only does this method serve as a technique of control, but it may be used effectively as a planning tool, for example, by projecting sales and costs, management can ascertain with a reasonable degree of accuracy whether it should undertake a proposed project. If an acceptable rate of return cannot be expected from the proposed project, it will be rejected, and the funds can be directed to more profitable uses.

Although the return on investment technique has many advantages, it also has several disadvantages that limit its usefulness. The principal weakness arises out of the different methods used by companies to evaluate their assets. One firm may follow a liberal policy concerning depreciation, whereas another will depreciate assets over a much longer time. Since depreciation affects profits, the rate of return is also affected. The same can be stated concerning expensing rather than capitalizing and the methods used in handling research and development cost. Another weakness that should be taken into consideration when using this method is the problem of a changing price level. Two firms may experience different rates of return although they have the same kind and number of fixed assets, and both may employ the same depreciation methods, since one may have purchased the assets during periods of high prices while the other purchased the assets during periods of low prices.

The following example illustrates the usefulness of this method of analysis. Assume that the financial statements of firms A and B reveal the information shown on page 32.

The increased efficiency experienced by firm B is the direct result of increased efficiency of capital; while firm A turned its capital two times, firm B turned its capital four times. The same results could have been obtained if firm B had increased its profit margin. This example reveals the comprehensiveness of the technique, which allows management to see at a glance which of many factors caused the increased efficiency or, for that matter, which factors caused

	Firm A	Firm B
Sales	$10,000,000	$10,000,000
Total Investment	5,000,000	2,500,000
Working Capital Investment	2,000,000	1,500,000
Net Fixed Investment	3,000,000	1,000,000
Earnings (before tax)	500,000	500,000
Total Cost	9,500,000	9,500,000

$$\frac{\text{Sales}}{\text{T.I.}} \times \frac{\text{Earnings}}{\text{Sales}} = \text{Rate of Return}$$

$$\text{Firm } A: \quad \frac{\$\ 500,000}{\$5,000,000} = 10\%$$

$$\text{Firm } B: \quad \frac{\$\ 500,000}{\$2,500,000} = 20\%$$

inefficiency. It would appear that the management of firm A overexpanded its fixed capital and also was overly conservative in its working capital policies—that is, maintained an excessive amount of cash and inventory. As a result, the capital of firm A was inefficiently utilized, whereas the opposite was true in the case of firm B.

A second useful tool in evaluating overall performance is the funds flow statement. This statement, or versions of it, has been called by many different names—for example, cash budget, statement of sources and uses of funds, and the like. Like the previous technique, the funds flow statement method of analysis is developed from historical data; but whereas the rate of return on investment technique showed in part the causes for increases or decreases in the rate of return, this technique reveals the sources and uses of funds. In a general sense, firms receive funds by decreasing asset accounts and increasing liability and equity accounts and utilize funds to increase assets and decrease liability and equity accounts. An absolutely accurate statement requires adjustments to several of these accounts, since changes in each do not represent an increase or decrease in funds.[1] When such exactness is not required, it is necessary for the finance officer to note only the balance sheet changes that take place between periods—months, quarters, or years. Once changes have been noted, the finance officer is able to determine not only the sources from which operational funds have been obtained, but also where these funds have been employed. In other words, he is able to ascertain when and if the plans of the firm are properly executed; if they are not, he has a basis for replanning. This tool of analysis is

---

[1] Illustrations of adjustments that do not involve either increases or decreases of financial resources include charge-offs of prepaid assets; undepreciated balances of abandoned property; and amortization of leaseholds, bond discounts, goodwill, and organizational expenses.

exceptionally good when used in conjunction with the cash budget, since it reveals the amount of funds required, as well as when they will be needed.

METHODS OF MEASURING LIQUIDITY

The degree of liquidity that a firm has is determined by its ability to meet its maturing debts. Since cash is used to meet a firm's obligations, it is essential to measure not only the amount of cash that a firm has at a particular time, but also the firm's ability to secure cash at a time when it is needed; in other words, to measure the credit position of the firm.

The most comprehensive measurement of the firm's ability to have cash when needed is the cash receipts and disbursement statement (see Table 4-1). If prepared daily, weekly, and monthly, this document is one of the most valuable tools that management has at its disposal, since it reveals the following: (1) the rate at which assets (fixed and working) are converted into cash, (2) the times when cash is needed, (3) the availability of cash in relation to need, and (4) the amount of cash that should be raised if the firm is to avoid embarrassment.

Stated somewhat differently, it depicts the state of liquidity that results from the operations of the period. It should be pointed out that it does not

TABLE 4-1

CASH RECEIPTS
AND DISBURSEMENT STATEMENT
(in thousands)

Cash Balance		$ 5,000
Cash Receipts:		
Cash received from collection of receivables and cash sales	$5,000	
Short- and long-term borrowing	-0-	
Sale of stock	-0-	
Cash receipts derived from sale of assets	2,000	
Total Cash		$12,000
Cash Disbursements:		
Disbursements resulting from operations	$9,000	
Interest payments	1,000	
Debt retirement	-0-	
Tax payment	-0-	
Dividends	500	
Payments for fixed assets	-0-	
Total Disbursements		$10,500
Cash Balance		1,500
Minimum Requirement		$ 5,000
Underage (or Overage)		$(3,500)

reveal a firm's total liquidity position, since, as noted above, the credit status affects this position.

Another method that indicates a firm's ability to liquidate its maturing obligations is the relation between current assets and current liabilities. If this ratio shows that a firm's current assets exceed its current liabilities, its solvency is guaranteed at that particular time. This assumes, of course, that current assets can be converted into cash at the value shown on the balance sheet.

This ratio has many limitations; a few of the more important are: (1) it depicts liquidity at a particular point in time; (2) it does not measure the quality of assets; and (3) since the ratio measures the past, it cannot measure the future solvency of the firm.

Managers recognize that certain assets, although classified as current, are not easily converted into cash. To offset this weakness, they developed the so-called acid-test or quick ratio. This ratio generally includes only cash or "near" cash items and is considered adequate when the total of these items equals current liabilities.

Too often financial officers have been led to believe that when the firm's current ratio is 2:1 and its acid-test ratio is 1:1, financial solvency is assured. Nothing can be further from the truth. For example, there have been times when a firm has been completely insolvent, yet both ratios were above the magic 2:1 and 1:1. Solvency is assured when the firm has *adequate funds* on hand or can borrow them *at the time* its obligations mature.

Another fallacy of using ratios to measure solvency is that the going-concern concept is ignored. If all current assets were liquidated in order to meet the firm's obligations, the firm would have no working capital to carry on its operations and, for all practical purposes, would be insolvent.

The going-concern concept calls for measuring solvency in other ways. One such way is the measurement of the efficiency of the firm's working capital. Stated simply, if a firm employs its working capital in an efficient way, solvency is guaranteed. Since the major components of working capital are cash, inventories, and receivables, the problem of solvency normally rests with the efficient use of these assets. The amount of working capital for any given volume of sales is determined by the rate at which these assets move through the various processes. If the turnover is smooth and rapid, the amount of working capital required for any given volume of sales is less than when the turnover is slow or irregular. The method used to measure the effectiveness of total working capital is to divide sales by total working capital. Generally speaking, the larger the turnover, the more effective is management in the use of its resources.

A word of caution is in order at this juncture. If the turnover is too high, management may find that the firm does not have sufficient working capital for sales in the event that adverse conditions are encountered. A low turnover may also be serious in that the firm may not be enjoying the correct rate of return. A low turnover results from (1) obsolete inventory, (2) excess cash, (3) delinquent accounts receivable, (4) excessive inventory, and (5) excessive short-term investments.

As a general rule, an excessive turnover combined with a low working capital turnover is indicative of poor financial planning.

The effectiveness of working capital management cannot be determined by measuring total working capital alone, since its turnover is the composite of the turnover experience of each of the components of working capital. Therefore, it is essential for management to measure the effectiveness of cash, inventories, and receivables.

No standard ratios exist to measure cash and its equivalents. Many firms use the following techniques to measure cash: cash as a percentage of working capital; cash as a multiple of sales; and the cash receipts and disbursement statement discussed above. The last method is the only one recommended by the writer.

Inventory, the second major component of working capital, is measured as cost of goods sold divided by inventory at the end of the fiscal period.[2] The result indicates the number of times that inventory is turned over during the period under consideration. By comparing the turnover of one company with that of another management obtains a fairly accurate guide to measure its efficiency. There are times when a firm will want to reduce its turnover; for example, if a price increase is anticipated, a firm may want to increase inventory to reduce the effects of the rising prices on profits.

The last major component of working capital is receivables. Management should attempt to reduce the number of days that its receivables are outstanding in order to reduce the length of time during which it finances its customers' sales. We should recall here that credit terms directly affect the number of times that receivables are turned over during any given period. Stated differently, turnover should be used to determine the effectiveness of the firm's collection policies. To illustrate, 30-day credit means that receivables will turn over 12 times each year; if the turnover is only 9 times, it is evident that the collection practices of the firm are not consistent with predetermined policy. The average collection period is determined in the following way: accounts and notes receivable outstanding X 360 ÷ annual net credit sales = the average collection period.

The effectiveness of a firm's working capital is a direct measurement of ability to meet maturing obligation, since it measures the speed with which the firm moves through the various processes. Unless this is accomplished in an efficient manner, the firm's management will not have cash at the time obligations come due and payable. Not only is the firm's solvency measured by the ability of management to move working capital through the firm, but it is also dependent upon the firm's borrowing policies. For example, if accounts payable become due every 30 days but receivables are turned over every 60 days, a problem of financing will be encountered. If funds from outside sources are not

---

[2] *Inventory,* as used here, means the aggregate investment of items of tangible personal property that (1) are held for sale in the ordinary course of business, (2) are in the process of production for sale, or (3) are to be currently consumed in the production of goods or services to be available for sale.

available, a problem of insolvency occurs unless an adequate reserve is maintained in the cash account. In other words, payout should coincide with receipts insofar as possible, to reduce the total amount of working capital that a firm maintains.

METHODS OF MEASURING PROFITABILITY

Profitability is vitally important in more ways than just assuring that a firm "stays in business." For example, a firm's profit position determines the price it can expect from the sale of its stock, the degree of credit risk it assumes, and the extent to which it must depend on external sources for capital. Therefore, management must employ various methods that reveal past profits as well as future profit prospects. In order to tell whether the firm is doing well, management should establish a norm. To illustrate, a firm may have a profit margin of 15 percent and still not be successful, since it may have had the opportunity to invest its funds in endeavors that would have yielded 30 percent.

The most common ratio employed by management to measure its profit position is as follows:

$$\frac{\text{Net Profit on Operation}}{\text{Net Sales}} \times 100 = \text{Profit Margin}$$

The result is the percentage of each dollar of sales that is represented by profit. If a firm has a profit margin of 5 percent, then for each dollar of sales the company is realizing five cents in profit. The profit margin is good or bad only when compared with other firms in the industry.

The margin of profit is not the result of the dollar volume of sales that is produced; it is the difference between gross revenue and total expenses incurred in the operational process. That is, the profit margin can also be determined by dividing net sales into total operating costs and multiplying by 100. Assume that a firm incurs total costs of $9.5 million in the production of $10 million of sales. The operating ratio is 95 percent and the profit margin is 5 percent.

In addition to these techniques of measuring the firm's profit position, there are several more ratios that reveal specific information.

Net Profit to Net Worth

This ratio is expressed as a percentage and indicates the rate of return upon ownership capital. This information is calculated by dividing net worth into net profit. The rate is directly influenced by management's policy regarding trading on equity. For example, the higher the ratio of debt to equity, the greater will be the rate of return on equity capital. See Chapter 9 for a discussion of this concept.

Net Profit to Total Investment

This ratio is also expressed as a percentage and is obtained as follows: net profit (usually after income tax) divided by invested capital. The results indicate the earning capacity of all capital invested in the business endeavor. The ratio is useful in measuring the desirability of the endeavor as compared to other opportunities available to management.

METHODS OF MEASURING
THE EFFICIENCY OF CAPITAL

One approach that may be employed by management to assess the effectiveness of a firm's capital is to measure the length of time it takes capital to move through the various business processes. This is accomplished by relating total capital to sales. The ratio indicates the number of dollars that a firm has invested for each dollar of sales. All other things being equal, the higher the ratio, the greater the efficiency of capital. This ratio should always be used in relation to profit ratios, since it is useless to turn over capital at a rapid rate unless a sufficient margin of profit is realized on each dollar of sales.

Another method of evaluating the efficiency of each dollar invested is to compare the firm's return on capital to the cost that the firm had to pay for its capital. For example, if management is required to pay 10 percent for its funds but is capable of earning only 8 percent, it is obvious that capital is not being used effectively. Very rarely will firms raise funds from external sources to finance projects whose return is less than the firm's cost of capital. This may not be true, however, with funds obtained from retained earnings and depreciation. This use of capital occurs also in firms whose management is overly conservative; for example, when management wants to maintain a high degree of liquidity. As a result of this policy, idle funds may be invested in government securities, which yield far less than their cost.

METHODS OF MEASURING LEVERAGE

As mentioned elsewhere in this book, management is able to increase the per-share earnings by adding debt to its capital structure. Theoretically, the total amount of debt that should be used in the business process is determined by the amount of risk that can be assumed at any given time. There are now no precise criteria for determining the amount of risk that a firm can assume; however, creditors use certain rules of thumb to measure a firm's ability to assume risk. These rules generally refer to the number of times that a firm's prior charges are covered. For example, two such rules of thumb are: (1) the ratio of earnings to fixed charges and debt retirement charges, and (2) the ratio of "cash flow" to these charges.[3]

---

[3]Fixed charges, as used here, include interest, preferred dividends, rental payments, taxes on preferred dividends, and taxes on the excess, if any, of sinking fund requirements over depreciation. No effort is made to list all the various ratios that have been suggested by various writers in this field.

Some authorities argue that preferred dividends and taxes on these dividends should not be included, since preferred dividends are considered a liability. It is the opinion of the writer that they should be included, since most creditors and investors look with disfavor upon a firm that passes preferred dividends. I also believe that the amount of funds that management agrees to set aside each year to retire its debt should be included. Finally, rental payments should be included in order to permit comparisons between companies that rent fixed assets with those that own them. To determine this ratio it is only necessary to divide fixed charges into earnings.

Funds from depreciation are available for use in the liquidation of fixed charges, provided they have not been invested in nonliquid assets. Therefore, a proper evaluation of a firm's capacity to trade on its equity would be obtained by comparing the amount of fixed charges that a firm is obligated to pay with its cash flow. The ratio is calculated as follows:

$$\frac{\text{EBIT} + \text{Depreciation}}{\text{Fixed Charges} + \text{Debt Retirement Charges}}$$

This ratio indicates the firm's short-run ability to meet its obligations.[4] Obviously, the larger the ratio, the safer the operation is considered to be; but it should be remembered that excess safety also means the firm is not employing the proper amount of debt in its structure. This ratio should be related to the industry in which it operates as well as to whether it meets the approval of the investing public. If not, the firm can expect its cost of capital to be excessive when compared to other operations of similar nature.

In addition to these rules of thumb, there are several sophisticated criteria that may be used to ascertain the "ideal" level of debt—for example, cost of capital, cash adequacy, etc. For a thorough discussion of these and other techniques, see Chapter 10.

---

[4] EBIT refers to earnings before interest and taxes.

5

Cost

of Capital

Businessmen invest funds in assets with the idea of increasing the present value of the firm's equity capital. This objective is achieved only if the return on all invested funds exceeds the cost of all debt capital and the return expected by the shareholder. If the return is equal to these requirements, then more than likely there will be no change in the value of the firm; however, if it is above or below, a change in value may be expected. An example will show these relationships. Assume that the Conec Company has the following capital structure:

Assets		*Capital*	
Cash	$ 50	Trade Payables	$ 200
Receivables	100	Notes Payable[a]	100
Inventories	200	Long-Term Debt[b]	200
Other Current Assets	10	Common Stock[c]	500
Fixed Assets	640		
	$1000		$1000

[a] Average maturity, 90 days; 7.5 percent interest.
[b] Due in 1980; 8.75 percent interest; market price equal to par.
[c] Par $1.00; anticipated earnings, $1.50; average market price, $5.00.

The weighted average cost of capital before and after income taxes is determined as follows:

	Book Value	Capital Structure Proportion	Before-Tax Cost of Capital	Weighted Average "Cost" Before Taxes	Weighted Average "Cost" After Taxes
Trade Payable	$200.00	20%	0 %	0 %	0 %
Notes Payable	100.00	10	7.50	.75	.375
Long-Term Debt	200.00	20	8.75	1.75	.875
Common Stock	500.00	50	30.00	15.00	7.500
				17.50%	8.750%

In the example above, short-term creditors expect to receive $7.50 on their investment; long-term creditors expect $17.50; and common stockholders expect a return of 30 percent on their investment before taxes. To fulfill each group's expectation the firm must earn at least 17.50 percent on capital before interest and taxes; for simplicity, the firm's taxes are assumed to be 50 percent. The following illustrates this conclusion:

$1000.00	Investment
175.00	Earnings before interest and taxes (EBIT)
- 7.50	Interest on notes payable
-17.50	Interest on long-term debt
$150.00	Earnings before taxes (150.00 ÷ 500.00 = 30%)
-75.00	Taxes
$ 75.00	Earnings after taxes (75.00 ÷ 500.00 = 15%)

If the firm's EBIT had been 20 percent, earnings on equity would have been 17.50 percent; on the other hand, had EBIT equaled only 10 percent, earnings on equity would have been only 7.5 percent. If this had occurred, the market price of the stock would probably have dropped.

The expected return of both types of investors has been defined as the cost of capital of the firm. That is to say, cost of capital is the cost—expressed as a rate—of acquiring the total amount of all funds employed in the project or projects, regardless of their source. Van Horne, in defining cost of capital, said:

> The explicit cost of a source of financing may be defined as the discount rate that equates the present value of the funds received by the firm, net of underwriting and other costs, with the present value of expected outflows. These outflows may be interest payments, repayment of principle, or dividends. Thus, the explicit cost of a specific method of financing can be determined by solving the following equation for k:

$$I_0 = \frac{C_1}{(1 + k)} + \frac{C_2}{(1 + k)^2} + \cdots + \frac{C_n}{(1 + k)^n}$$

where I_0 is the net amount of funds received by the firm at time 0; and C_t is the outflow in period t.[1]

---

[1] James C. Van Horne, *Financial Management and Policy* (Englewood Cliffs, N.J.: Prentice Hall, Inc., 1968), p. 111.

To measure the total cost of all funds used by the firm, it is necessary to "cost" each source; that is, to ascertain the cost of funds received from long- and short-term debt and all types of equity capital.

COST OF EQUITY CAPITAL

The cost of equity is not the out-of-pocket cost of using these funds—cost of flotation and dividends; it is rather the "cost" of the estimated stream of net capital outlays derived from equity sources. Equity funds are obtained from external as well as internal sources, and the cost of each source is computed slightly differently. First, let us direct our attention to the computation involved in determining the cost of funds obtained by selling common stock to the public.

The cost of obtaining funds through the sale of common stock may be determined in one of three ways. The first method uses the expected earnings/ price ratio. To illustrate, if E_a is the expected average earnings per share, and P_0 is the dollar price of the share of stock if sold, the cost is ascertained simply by dividing E_a by P_0 ($k_e = E_a/P_0$). This method implicitly assumes that: (1) future earnings will grow at a constant rate and can be expressed as an average, and that (2) market price is influenced only by variations in earnings.

A second method of costing equity is to find a rate that will equate the present value of all future dividends per share to the current market price. If the growth of dividends is constant, the cost of equity is ascertained by solving the following equation:

$$V_0 = \sum_{t=1}^{N} \frac{D_0 (1+g)^{t-1}}{(1+k)^t}$$

By algebra this becomes

$$V_0 = \frac{D_0}{k - g}$$

To express this verbally, the present value of common stock (V_0) is equal to the beginning dividend divided by a market discount factor (k) appropriate for the risk associated with the particular company involved, minus the growth rate (g). Translated in cost of equity capital, the equation becomes

$$k_e = \frac{D_0}{P_0} + g$$

For example, assume the following: (1) the current dividend equals $5 per share, (2) market value equals $100, and (3) the growth rate of dividends is expected to remain constant at 10 percent. Given these facts, the firm's cost of common stock is calculated thus:

$$k_e = \frac{5}{100} + 10 = 15 \text{ percent}$$

It is obvious that the growth rate will not remain constant over time. To resolve the problem of varying growth rates requires a separate computation for each period that the growth rate changes.

A third way to calculate the cost of equity capital is to substitute earnings for dividends. It should be emphasized that the growth rate for earnings will not be the same as that for dividends. It is believed that from a manager's standpoint it is easier to employ earnings than dividends because the latter is the function of the directors' attitude, whereas earnings is the function of the projects involved. The following equation is recommended:

$$k_e = \frac{E}{P} + g$$

In summary, the earnings model is preferable primarily because the growth of dividends would be extremely difficult—if not impossible—to calculate, since this is a function of the board's attitude toward such items as taxes, stock value, general economic conditions, and earnings. As a consequence, dividends are likely to change even though earnings remain unchanged.

The principal reason for recommending the earnings model is that cost of capital's primary purpose is to serve as a minimum criterion for investment decisions; and since earnings is the goal, we should approach the problem directly; that is, use the earnings model.

COST OF PREFERRED STOCK

The cost per share of preferred stock (k_p) may be found simply by dividing the net proceeds received from its sale into the dividend paid to its owner:

$$k_p = \frac{D}{P_0}$$

If the Conec Company were able to realize a net of $48 per share for preferred stock that pays 7 percent on par value of $50, the cost would be 7.29 percent—$3.50 ÷ $48.00 = 7.29 percent. There is no adjustment for taxes, since preferred dividends are paid after taxes.

Various provisions complicate the computation; for example, a preferred stock that is participating will have a cost different from one that is not participating. Also, a noncallable preferred stock is considered to be perpetual, whereas if management intends to call a preferred stock after a definite time period at a specific price, the cost will be derived by calculating the following equation:

$$P_0 = \frac{D_1}{(1+k)} + \frac{D_2}{(1+k)^2} + \cdots + \frac{D_n}{(1+k)^n}$$

where P_0 is the net amount of the funds received at time period 0, and D_t is the dividends paid in period t.

INTERNALLY GENERATED FUNDS

Cost of Retained Earnings

A large number of companies use current earnings as a primary source of funds. These funds should be considered the investment of existing shareholders, and they have the same cost as if they had been raised through the sale of stock.

In the past, various authors have suggested that the cost of retained earnings be reduced by the amount of the shareholders' tax rate (TR). That is, cost is obtained by solving the following equation:

$$k_r = \frac{E_a \left(1 - \frac{TR}{2}\right)}{P}$$

where E_a = anticipated earnings
P = current market price
k_r = cost of retained earnings

One common criticism of this method is the difficulty of establishing the tax rate of the stockholders. Another criticism is that common shareholders take into consideration the retention policies of the firm and adjust their price accordingly; therefore, it is not necessary to adjust anticipated earnings. In the light of these criticisms, it is suggested that retained earnings be costed in exactly the same way as common stock capital—for example,

$$k_e = \frac{E}{P_0} + g$$

Funds derived from depreciation should be considered to be derived from "funds" previously invested in fixed assets. That is to say, depreciation is the return of capital invested in depreciable assets. Since these funds have already been individually costed and a weighted average cost derived, it is recommended that their "cost" be equal to the weighted average cost of future funds. Since such a cost would not affect the weighted cost of capital, it is omitted from such calculations.

Cost of Debt Capital

The cost of debt capital may be derived by solving a formula similar to the one used to ascertain the interest rate (IRR) that equates the present value of the expected future receipts to the cost of the project. The only difference is that present value of tax-adjusted interest costs plus principal repayments is equated to the amount received at the time the loan is consummated. The formula used is

$$CI_0 - \sum_{t=1}^{n} \frac{CO_t}{(1 + k)^t} = 0$$

where CI_0 is the net amount received from the lender and CO_t is the tax-adjusted sum of interest costs plus principal repayments made in subsequent periods. The following example illustrates this technique.

The Conec Company has negotiated a term loan under the following conditions: (1) the interest rate is 7 percent, and (2) the principal of $1,000 is repayable in five equal installments.

The problem is solved in two steps: first, the cash flow required to service the debt is calculated (see Table 5–1); and second, the rate required to equate the present value of the cash outflow to the net amount of the loan is determined by the trial-and-error process.

In the case above, the cost of the $1,000 equals 3.5 percent. The student

TABLE 5–1

ACTUAL AND PRESENT VALUES OF
DEBT SERVICE CASH FLOWS

				PRESENT VALUE AT		
Year	Repayment Principal	Tax-Adjusted Interest Charges	Total Cash Flows	2%	3.5%[a]	4%
1971	$200	$35	$ 235.00	$ 230.30	$ 227.05	$ 226.07
1972	200	28	228.00	219.11	212.84	210.90
1973	200	21	221.00	208.18	199.33	196.47
1974	200	14	214.00	197.74	186.49	182.97
1975	200	7	207.00	187.54	174.29	170.15
PV CO_t			$1,105.00	$1,042.87	$1,000.00	$ 986.56
CI_0			1,000.00	1,000.00	1,000.00	1,000.00
			$-$ $ 105.00	$-$ $ 42.87	$ 0	$+$ $ 13.44

[a]The precise rate may be determined through interpolation. For example: present value of 2% and 4% equal $1,042.87 and $986.56; $42.87 ÷ $56.31 × 2% = 1.5%; 2% plus 1.5% = 3.5%.

knows that the method of repayment will cause the cost to vary. For example, the cost will rise if larger amounts are paid in the earlier years, and vice versa.

In most cases, the cost of debt can be calculated in a much more simple and direct way. Where there are no premiums or discounts involved, the cost is simply the interest rate adjusted by the tax rate. Generally speaking, this method of cost calculation is associated with short-term notes payable and commercial paper.

The method of computing the cost of long-term debt varies only slightly from the technique used to cost short-term debt capital. The cost of long-term debt is the investor's yield to maturity adjusted by the firm's tax rate plus distribution cost. Yield to maturity is determined either by approximation or by the use of bond tables indicating the exact or accurate rate.

To determine the yield to maturity by approximation, it is necessary only to divide the average investment into the average annual gain. For example, assume that a $1,000, ten-year, 7 percent debenture was sold on July 1, 1968, at a price of $900. The current yield on this bond is 7.78 percent (70 ÷ 900), but yield to maturity is 8.42 percent. This rate is derived through the use of the following formula:

$$k_i = \frac{C + (P - M)/N}{(M + P)/2} \times (1 - TR)$$

where C = annual dollar interest
        P = par value
        N = number of years to maturity
        M = price for bond

By substitution, we are able to approximate the yield to maturity:

$$\frac{70 + (1,000 - 900)/10}{(1,000 + 900)/2} \times (1 - 0.50) = 4.21\%$$

Adjusting the yield to maturity rate by the firm's tax rate (50 percent), we find that the actual cost of the debt capital obtained from the sale of the bond is equal to 4.21 percent.

If a premium is paid for the bond, the firm's cost of capital will be less than the contract rate adjusted for taxes. To illustrate, suppose the firm had sold the bond for $1,060 rather than $900. In this case the yield to maturity is equal to 6.21 percent and the firm's cost would have been 3.105 percent.

The accurate method, which employs bond tables, reduces the yield to maturity to a discount rate, compounded semiannually, that will reduce all future interest and principal payments to a present value equal to the quoted price. Bond tables are available and simple to use; however, the approximation method is reasonably accurate when the bond price is between 90 and 110 and the maturity date is within ten years.

TRADE DEBT

The business firm is not required to pay for the use of funds obtained from trade creditors if the debt is paid within the discount period. However, if a firm fails to take advantage of the discount, the cost of trade credit can be very high. For example, if the cash discount terms are 3/10, net 30, and the bill is paid on the thirtieth day, the firm pays an effective annual interest rate of 54 percent. Funds derived from such sources as taxes payable and advances and prepayments by customers should be considered free.

COMPUTATION OF THE COST
OF CAPITAL

The calculation of the overall cost of capital depends upon which of the following three approaches is used: marginal, equity, or weighted average. Although arguments may be advanced for the adoption of any of these methods, the weighted-average method is probably the most acceptable technique today.[2]

The weighted-average method of computing a firm's cost of capital is found by weighting the cost of each component of the capital structure by the relative proportion of that source of funds to the total. The relative proportion of each source is ascertained by using either the book value or market value of each type of capital. The example in Table 5-2 explains both methods.

It is noted that the cost of capital using market value is higher than the one derived through the use of book-value figures. The higher cost obviously results from the greater emphasis given to equity capital. Several authorities suggest that the market-value method is superior to the book-value technique primarily because market value reflects current cost whereas book value reflects historical cost. It is the writer's opinion that the use of market value tends to cause a shift toward larger amounts of equity funds when additional financing is undertaken. When this happens, earnings on equity will decline, which could create difficulty. A second weakness results from the capriciousness of market values; therefore, if market values are employed, they should be normalized.

In general, it may be said that book values will cause a firm's average weighted cost of capital to be on the low side, whereas market value tends to have the opposite effect. The manager, by knowing the effects of each, will be in position to adjust the method used by his firm.

It should be remembered that the weighted cost of capital can be affected

---

[2]To understand thoroughly the marginal and equity methods, the student is referred to Robert Lindsay and Arnold W. Sametz, *Financial Management, An Analytical Approach*, rev. ed. (Homewood, Ill.: Richard D. Irwin, Inc., 1967); and Franco Modigliani and Merton H. Miller, "The Cost of Capital Corporation Finance and the Theory of Investment," *American Economic Review*, June 1958, pp. 261-97.

by a change in the cost of each component, a change in the relative importance of each component, or both; therefore, care should be taken in the computation of each.

TABLE 5-2

CALCULATION OF WEIGHTED COST
OF CAPITAL

TYPE OF SECURITY	BOOK VALUE		MARKET VALUE		AFTER-TAX COST	WEIGHTED-AVERAGE COST	
						Book Value	Market Value
	Dollar	Percent	Dollar	Percent			
Notes Payable[a]	$ 50,000	0.05	$ 50,000	1.1	4.00	0.20	0.04
Advances by U.S. Government	20,000	0.02	20,000	0.4	0.00	0	0
Trade Payable[b]	100,000	0.10	100,000	2.2	0.00	0	0
Federal Income Taxes Accrued	10,000	0.01	10,000	0.2	0.00	0	0
Debentures[c]	100,000	0.10	90,000	2.0	4.21	0.42	0.04
Term Loans[d]	100,000	0.10	100,000	2.2	3.50	0.35	0.08
Common Stock[e]	200,000	0.20	4,000,000	89.5	15.00	3.00	13.43
Preferred Stock[f]	100,000	0.10	100,000	2.2	7.29	73	.02
Retained Earnings	200,000	0.20			15.00	3.00	
Capital Surplus[g]	100,000	0.10			15.00	1.50	
	$1,000,000	100.00	$4,470,000	100.0		9.20	13.61

[a]Interest rate at 8 percent; average maturity 90 days.
[b]All discounts taken.
[c]Ten-year, 7 percent bond sold for $900.
[d]Loan repayable in five equal annual payments; 7 percent interest.
[e]Par $1; average market price $20; earnings $3.00 after taxes.
[f]Nonparticipating preferred stock; 7 percent dividend; sold for $48.
[g]Received at the time the common stock was sold to the public.

6

Planning Fixed-Assets Expenditures

Many writers consider fixed-asset management to be one of the most important tasks facing management today. The principal reason for this importance is the risk that is related to the fixed asset. For example, fixed assets are recovered over a longer period of time than current assets, and since change is inherent in a dynamic economy, the longer the life of the asset, the greater the risk management assumes when it commits itself for these assets. Another factor is the relatively high cost of the fixed asset as compared to the current asset, so that any errors resulting from acquisition will have a greater impact on the firm's profits.

Fixed-asset management includes not only additions to fixed assets but also replacements and betterments or improvements. Additions to fixed assets involve the acquisition of a new asset or assets that increase existing capacity. Replacement includes assets that are acquired to take the place of existing assets with comparable capacity. (In most cases any replacement is likely to increase capacity, since technology is constantly improving equipment.) Betterments and improvements refer to capital expenditures that bring about a physical change or alteration of an asset.

This chapter is concerned with a discussion of steps in fixed asset management and methods for the selection of investment proposals.

STEPS IN FIXED-ASSETS MANAGEMENT

There is every reason to believe that investment in fixed assets will increase during the next few decades. The most important reasons for this belief are: (1) management will seek ways and means of substituting machines for labor if labor costs continue to rise; (2) new and improved methods are constantly being developed; and (3) increasing competition will require that present costs be reduced, which can and will be accomplished by the use of more efficient machinery.

With the increased importance of fixed asset management in mind, the subject may now be approached, with the awareness that at least two steps should be recognized: namely, classification of proposals and selection of investment proposals.

As a general rule, the finance officer does not originate capital expenditure proposals. These normally originate in one or more of the other primary business functional areas—for example, production, distribution, or research. However, once recommendations for expenditures are made, the finance officer is called upon to evaluate the various proposals. We should also point out that the finance officer seldom makes the decision to accept or reject proposals, since this decision is reserved for top management; however, he is responsible for collecting and arranging the data that serve as a basis for the final decision.

In evaluating proposals it is most helpful if the various projects are classified in some logical manner. For example, projects may be classified with respect to reasons for the expenditure, such as the replacement of depreciated or obsolete equipment, expansion of existing equipment, or improving quality; or they may be classified with respect to priority, for example, projects that cannot be delayed without loss of profit or those that may be delayed without incurring a loss. There are other ways of classifying projects just as satisfactory as these two. The method itself is not important; what is important is that the finance officer must employ a method of classification that reflects something other than increased profits, since many expenditures are required that cannot be· determined by profits alone.

Once a system of classification has been adopted, the financial officers must ascertain which proposal to accept. There are two principal reasons for this step. First, as a general rule, the firm will have more projects than it has funds available. Second, the finance officer will want to recommend only projects that are essential to the welfare of the firm; or if this is not pertinent, he will want to recommend the project that yields the greatest financial advantage.

METHODS OF SELECTING FROM
AMONG PROPOSALS

There are several methods presently used by business firms to select the most advantageous investment proposal. Each method is designed with a particular purpose in mind—for example, to determine the degree of risk or rate of return that each project will yield. The most commonly used methods are payback, average rate of return, internal rate of return, and net present value.

Payback Method

Investment in fixed assets is usually large and generally takes several years to recover. As a rule, the degree of risk assumed by a firm when "buying" a fixed asset is directly related to the length of time required to recover the investment from the firm's cash flow. The payback method of evaluating investment proposals stresses the length of time that is necessary for a firm to recoup its investment from profits and depreciation charges.

Table 6-1 illustrates this method of evaluating investment proposals. Assume that a firm is contemplating an investment in two projects, each of which requires an investment of $1,500. Each project has an expected life of five years, and each will be depreciated on a straight-line basis. From the data in Table 6-1 we can see that Project A will "pay for itself" in 2.8 years, whereas it will take Project B 3.5 years to liquidate itself.

TABLE 6-1

CASH FLOWS: PROJECTS A AND B

Years	SAVINGS BEFORE DIRECT EXPENSE		DIRECT EXPENSES[a]		DEPRECIATION		CASH FLOW[b]	
	A	B	A	B	A	B	A	B
1	$1400	$980	$440	$420	$300	$300	$650	$450
2	1200	980	440	420	300	300	550	450
3	1000	980	440	420	300	300	450	450
4	740	980	440	420	300	300	320	450
5	740	980	440	420	300	300	320	450
					$1500	$1500	$2290	$2250

[a]Does not include depreciation; interest cost equals $40. If after-tax cost of capital is used as the discount rate, then only after-tax interest charges are added back; if before-tax cost of capital is used, then interest before taxes is added back.
[b]Cash Flow = $(1 - TR)$[Gross Savings – (Direct Expenses + Depreciation)] + Depreciation + Interest. (Taxes assumed to be 50%.) Cash Flow includes $20 interest payment.

The payback method has several advantages but ignores at least two primary considerations. First, it does not consider the manner in which income is received and therefore ignores the time value of funds; second, it ignores income beyond the payback period.

The advantages the payback method claims are: (1) It is easy to calculate, thus allowing finance officers to determine quickly the degree of risk the firm assumes in committing itself to "purchase" a particular fixed asset. (2) If a firm is experiencing a shortage of cash, the payback method may be used to select investments that yield a quick return of cash funds. (3) All factors remaining the same, the payback method permits a firm to determine the length of time required to recapture its original investment, thus determining the degree of risk of each investment.

As mentioned above, the time value of money and the amount of funds received after the asset has been "paid out" have been ignored. To illustrate, suppose a firm compares the investment worth of two $700 projects with cash flows as follows:

Years	Project 1	Project 2
1	$500	$200
2	100	200
3	100	300
4	200	200

Both projects have a payout of three years, but Project 1 is more desirable from an investment standpoint because of the time value of money; that is, a dollar is worth more today than it would be if received at some later date. For example, Project 1 will return its investment plus a rate of return of 14.2 percent, whereas Project 2 will produce its investment plus a return of 10.6 percent, over the four-year period.

A second criticism of the payback method is that it ignores income that is produced beyond the payback period. Suppose a firm is contemplating two projects. Project x has a payback period of two years and Project y is "paid out" in four years. If payback is the only criterion, the former would be accepted over the latter. However, suppose Project y produced a stream of income over ten years but the stream of Project x's income ceased after two years. Obviously, Project y is more desirable, since the firm realizes a higher average return on investment from it.

Average Rate of Return

The payout method of computation does not take into consideration the relative profitability of the project. The average rate of return is designed with this purpose in mind and is computed by adding the total of all earnings after depreciation and taxes and dividing this amount by the number of years the project will last. After the average "earnings" is determined, the average rate of return may be calculated by dividing average earnings by the average investment of the project.[1] Referring again to the example illustrated in Table 6-1,

---

[1] Average rate of return is calculated as follows:

$$\text{Project } A: \quad \frac{(\$330 + \$230 + 130 + 0 + 0)/5}{\$1500/2} = 18.4 \text{ percent}$$

$$\text{Project } B: \quad \frac{(\$130 + \$130 + \$130 + \$130 + \$130)/5}{\$1500/2} = 17.3 \text{ percent}$$

Note: Profits are derived as follows: cash flow less depreciation and interest; e.g., $650 − $300 − $20 = $330 in period 1.

one project yields 18.4 percent return whereas the other earns 17.3 percent on average investment. If the projects are mutually exclusive, Project A is the more desirable.

The average-return method of selecting alternative uses of funds takes into consideration "savings" over the entire life of the project; nevertheless, it has a primary weakness in that the time value of funds is ignored. Since income may be reinvested time and again at some profitable rate, it follows logically that current income is more valuable than income received at a later date. The method that takes this into consideration is commonly called the discounted cash-flow method.

Internal Rate of Return

In determining which investment to accept by comparing the discounted rate of each proposal, the finance officer should first estimate the cash flow for each investment during its economic life, and then ascertain a rate that equates the present value of the expected future cash flows to the cost of the investment. This can be accomplished by solving the following equation:

$$IRR = \sum_{t=1}^{n} \frac{C_t}{(1+r)^t}$$

The following example illustrates this method. Suppose the management of Conec Company is contemplating two investments, each requiring an investment of $1,500, one having a cash flow that varies and the other with one that remains constant over time (see Table 6-1).

As we mentioned above, our first duty is to determine the cash flow of each project after taxes but before depreciation and interest. This has been accomplished and is shown in Table 6-1. In the case of Project A, cash flow varied from a high of $650 to a low of $320. Project B, on the other hand, maintained a stable cash flow of $450 in each of the five years. The second step is to discount this flow at a rate that will yield a present value equal to the present value of the investment. By trial and error we are able to determine that the rate of discount lies somewhere between 18 and 20 percent for Project A and between 15 and 16 percent for Project B (Table 6-2).

By interpolation, the rate is estimated to be 18.84 percent for Project A and 15.24 percent for Project B. It should be noted that the cash flow of Project A is only $40 more than that of Project B, but Project A's cash flow is considerably higher in the first two years and smaller in the last two years than the cash flow of Project B. The higher rate results because income received currently is worth more than if received at a later date. Since the rate of return on income from Project A is higher than from Project B, it is the more desirable investment.

The significance of this method of choosing among alternatives is to reveal the rate of return that a firm would receive discounted over the period of

TABLE 6–2

VALUE OF ALTERNATIVE INVESTMENTS

YEARS	CASH FLOW OF PROJECTS		PRESENT VALUES OF PROJECTS			
	A	B	A		B	
			18%	20%	15%	16%
1	$650	$450	$551	$541	$392	$388
2	550	450	395	382	340	334
3	450	450	274	261	296	288
4	320	450	165	154	257	248
5	320	450	140	129	224	214
	$2,290	$2,250	$1,525	$1,466	$1,509	$1,472

years required for it to recover its original investment (Table 6–3). Assuming a cost of capital that is lower than 15.24 percent, Project *A* will be accepted if the two projects are mutually exclusive; however, both will be accepted if they are independent.

TABLE 6–3

DISTRIBUTION OF CASH FLOWS
BETWEEN INCOME AND RETURN
OF PRINCIPAL

PROJECT A				
Years	Investment	Income on Investment at 18.84%	Theoretical Return of Principal	Cash Flows
1	$1,500	$282	$368	$650
2	1,132	213	337	550
3	795	150	300	450
4	495	94	226	320
5	269	51	269	320
	0	$790	$1,500	$2,290

PROJECT B				
Years	Investment	Income on Investment at 15.24%	Theoretical Return of Principal	Cash Flows
1	$1,500	$229	$221	$450
2	1,279	195	255	450
3	1,024	156	294	450
4	730	111	339	450
5	391	59	391	450
	0	$750	$1,500	$2,250

Net Present Value

Another method that may be used to select from among alternative investments is to calculate the net present value of the expected net cash flows of each
project. This method is accomplished by discounting the net cash flows of each
project by a discount rate that equals the firm's cost of capital. We may do this
by solving the following equation:

$$NPV = \sum_{t=1}^{n} \frac{CI_t}{(1+k)^t} - \sum_{t=1}^{n} \frac{CO_t}{(1+k)^t}$$

where CI_t is the net cash flow in year t; k is the firm's cost of capital; CO_t is the
cost of the investment; and n is the proposal's life.

The net present values of Projects A and B are shown in Tables 6-4 and 6-5.

TABLE 6-4

NET PRESENT VALUE OF PROJECT A

YEAR	CASH FLOWS, PROJECT A		PRESENT VALUE FACTOR WHEN COST OF CAPITAL IS 10%	PRESENT VALUES OF CASH FLOWS	
	Cash Out	Cash In		Cash Out	Cash In
0	$1,500	$ 0	1.000	$1,500.00	$ 0
1		650	.909		590.85
2		550	.826		454.30
3		450	.751		337.95
4		320	.683		218.56
5		320	.621		198.72
				$1,500.00	$1,800.38

Net present value = $300.38 ($1,800.38 − $1,500.00)

TABLE 6-5

NET PRESENT VALUE OF PROJECT B

YEAR	CASH FLOWS, PROJECT B		PRESENT VALUE FACTOR WHEN COST OF CAPITAL IS 10%	PRESENT VALUES OF CASH FLOWS	
	Cash Out	Cash In		Cash Out	Cash In
0	$1,500	$ 0	1.000	$1,500.00	$ 0
1		450	.909		409.05
2		450	.826		371.70
3		450	.751		337.95
4		450	.683		307.35
5		450	.621		279.45
	$1,500	$2,250		$1,500.00	$1,705.50

Net present value = $205.50 ($1,705.50 − $1.500.00)

It may be observed that the net present value of Project A is \$94.88 greater than that of Project B. All other things remaining the same, management would accept Project A over B if the projects were mutually exclusive; however, both would be acceptable if they were independent, since there is a positive net present value.

It may also be useful to calculate the relationship that exists between the present values of the net cash inflows and the present values of the cash outflows (required investment outlay). This relationship is frequently called the profitability index (PI) and may be found by solving the following equation:

$$PI = \frac{\sum\limits_{t=1}^{n} \dfrac{CI_t}{(1+k)^t}}{\sum\limits_{t=1}^{n} \dfrac{CO_t}{(1+k)^t}}$$

In the case of the example above, Project A has a profitability index of 1.20, whereas Project B's ratio is only 1.14. This technique permits management to made exactly the same decision as would have been made had it used the payback, IRR, or net present value methods. The following data show the decisions that would be made under each method if the projects were mutually exclusive:

Method	Project A	Project B	Preferred Project
Payback	2.8 yrs.	3.6 yrs.	A
Average Rate of Return on Average Investment	18.4%	17.3%	A
Internal Rate of Return	18.8%	15.2%	A
Net Present Value	\$300.38	\$205.50	A
Profitability Index	1.20	1.14	A

ADJUSTING FOR RISK

The principal difficulty with the methods of evaluating an investment given above is that none of the techniques takes into consideration the business risk associated with the project. (Risk encompasses both the risk of possible insolvency and the variability in the earnings available to shareholders.) One method that may be used to adjust for risk is to substitute an expected cash flow for the modal cash flow. To accomplish this, management must ascertain a probability distribution of the annual cash flows of the various projects. That is to say, rather than assuming that Projects A and B will have the cash flows that were depicted in Table 6-1, management would calculate an expected cash flow by using a probability distribution that it believes will occur in each of the next five years (Table 6-6).

TABLE 6-6
EXPECTED CASH FLOWS DERIVED
FROM PROJECTED PROBABILITY
DISTRIBUTIONS

	PROJECT A					
Years		*Probability Distribution*				*Expected Cash Flow*
	0.20	*0.20*	*0.40*	*0.10*	*0.10*	
1	$300	$500	$650	$750	$800	575
2	300	400	550	700	800	510
3	300	400	450	500	600	430
4	100	200	320	400	500	278
5	100	200	320	400	500	278

	PROJECT B					
Years		*Probability Distribution*				*Expected Cash Flow*
	0.10	*0.20*	*0.40*	*0.20*	*0.10*	
1	300	350	450	550	600	450
2	300	350	450	550	600	450
3	300	350	450	550	600	450
4	300	350	450	550	600	450
5	300	350	450	550	600	450

It may be noted that the expected cash flows for Project A are different from the cash flows that have the greatest probability of occurring; e.g., the expected cash flow in year 1 equals $575, but the cash flow that has the greatest probability of occurring (0.40) is $650. In Project B this is not true; that is, the cash flows with the greatest probability of occurring and the expected cash flows are identical. Discounting the expected cash flows by the firm's cost of capital will give an answer different from the one obtained when using the cash flows with the greatest probability of occurring (Table 6-7).

By interpolation, the internal rates of return of Projects A and B are 13.86 and 15.24 percent, respectively. It is recalled that when the cash flows with the greatest probability were used, Project A was superior to B; but now the reverse is true.

Another method of adjusting for risk is to vary the discount rate; that is, to increase the discount rate when the risk associated with the project is high and reduce it when the risk is low. A quick evaluation of Project A would indicate that it is more risky than Project B since the distribution of the cash flows of the latter is normal whereas the distribution of cash flows of Project A is negatively skewed. (Further analysis indicates that the standard deviations of the cash flows in Project A are greater than those of Project B in four out of the five

TABLE 6-7

PRESENT VALUES OF EXPECTED CASH
FLOWS OF PROJECTS *A* AND *B*

YEARS	EXPECTED CASH FLOWS		PRESENT VALUE FOR DIFFERENT DISCOUNT RATES			
	Project A	Project B	A		B	
			12%	14%	15%	16%
1	$575	$450	$ 513	$ 504	$ 392	$ 388
2	510	450	406	392	340	334
3	430	450	306	290	296	288
4	278	450	177	169	257	248
5	278	450	158	140	224	214
			$1,570	$1,495	$1,509	$1,472

years.) In this case, management decided to use a discount rate of 15 percent
for Project *A* and 10 percent for Project *B*. Observe that Project *B* is now more
acceptable than Project *A* and would be accepted if the projects were mutually
exclusive. See Table 6-8 for the net present value calculations when varying
discount rates are used.

TABLE 6-8

NET PRESENT VALUE OF PROJECTS *A*
AND *B* WHEN DISCOUNT RATES VARY

YEAR	CASH FLOWS			PRESENT VALUE OF CASH FLOWS	
	Cash Out A and B	Cash In A	B	Project A (Discount Rate = 15%)	Project B (Discount Rate = 10%)
0	$1,500	$ 0	$ 0	$ -1,500.00	$ -1,500.00
1		650	450	565.50	409.05
2		550	450	415.80	371.70
3		450	450	296.10	337.95
4		320	450	183.04	307.35
5		320	450	159.04	279.45
	Net Present Value:			$ 119.48	$ 205.50

The major weakness of this technique is the difficulty in arriving at the
adjustment that should be made in the discount rate. That is to say, it is extremely difficult to ascertain how much more risky one project is than another.
It is true that the standard deviation and coefficient of variation techniques may
be used in determining which project is more risky, but neither technique indicates the amount that should be added to the discount rate. Nevertheless,
varying discount rates is a useful technique, applicable in many situations.

A third method that may be used to compensate for risk is to adjust the
firm's cash flow (numerator) rather than the discount rate (denominator). In
the process by which this method is applied, management evaluates the degree

of risk inherent in the cash flows. If the cash flow has a large degree of uncertainty, then the certainty-equivalent coefficient will be high, and vice versa. To arrive at this coefficient, management is asked to choose between a *certain* cash flow and an expected cash flow. For example, if management is indifferent about whether it would rather have the distribution of cash flow depicted in Table 6-7 with an *expected* cash flow of $450 or a *certain* cash flow of $337, then the certainty-equivalent coefficient is 0.75. Management establishes a coefficient for each cash flow under consideration. After these coefficients have been ascertained and applied to the expected cash flow, each is discounted by a risk-free rate. The use of a risk-free rate rather than the firm's cost of capital is logical, because in using the latter there would be an overadjustment for risk, since it is presumed that the cost of capital includes a premium for risk.

TABLE 6-9

ADJUSTED NET PRESENT VALUES,
PROJECTS *A* AND *B*

						ADJUSTED DATA	
Modal Cash Flow		*Certainty-Equivalent Coefficient*		*Adjusted Cash Flows*		*Present Value at 6% Rate*	
A	*B*	*A*	*B*	*A*	*B*	*A*	*B*
$650	$450	0.90	0.95	$585.00	$427.50	$ 551.65	$ 402.66
550	450	0.85	0.90	467.50	405.00	416.08	360.45
450	450	0.70	0.85	315.00	382.50	264.60	321.30
320	450	0.60	0.80	192.00	360.00	152.06	285.12
320	450	0.60	0.75	192.00	337.50	143.42	252.11
						$1,527.81	$1,621.64
						−1,500.00	−1,500.00
			Net Present Value:			$ 27.81	$ 121.64

NOTE: The following formula may be used in this method:

$$NPV = \sum_{t=0}^{n} \frac{\alpha_t A_t}{(1 + i)^t}$$

where α_t = certainty-equivalent coefficient for period t
         A_t = cash flows
         i = risk-free interest rate

The data of Table 6-9 depict how this technique is employed. It may be observed that Project *B* is superior to Project *A* and would be selected if the two were mutually exclusive.

7

Working-Capital
Management

A firm's profitability is determined in part by the way its working capital is managed. That is, when working capital is varied relative to sales without a corresponding change in production, the profit position is affected. Furthermore, if the flow of funds created by the movement of working capital through the various business processes is interrupted, the turnover of working capital is decreased, as is the rate of return on investment. It is important, therefore, for management to pay particular attention to the planning and control of working capital.

The primary purposes of this and the following chapter are threefold: first, to discuss the various concepts of working capital essential to effective planning; second, to discuss the principles that the author believes to be the basis of a "theory" of working capital; and third, to discuss techniques that may be employed in planning and controlling working capital.

CONCEPTS OF WORKING CAPITAL

There are two general working-capital concepts: net and gross. *Net working capital* is the difference between current assets and current liabilities. This concept is useful to groups interested in determining the amount and nature of assets that may be used to pay current liabilities. Moreover, the amount that is left after these debts are paid may be used to meet future operational needs.

Gross working capital refers to the amount of funds invested in current assets that are employed in the business process. This is a going-concern concept, since it is these assets that financial managers are concerned with if they are to bring about productivity from other assets. The gross concept is used here, since one of the principal functions of the finance officer is to provide the *correct amount* of working capital at the *right time* in order for the firm to realize the greatest return on its investment.

CLASSIFICATION OF WORKING CAPITAL

Working capital may be classified in two ways. The first classification is directly related to the gross concept of working capital; that is, working capital may be classified as capital invested in the various components of current assets, such as cash, inventories, receivables, and short-term unexpired costs. From the financial manager's viewpoint this classification is helpful, since it categorizes the various areas of financial responsibility. For example, funds invested in cash, inventories, and receivables require careful planning and control if the firm is to maximize its return on investment. (Since short-term unexpired costs account for such a small portion of capital invested in current assets, they are not considered.)

This classification is most important to financial management, but it is not completely adequate, since it makes no mention of *time*. And since time is vital in the formulation of procurement policies, a second classification alluding to time is necessary. Using time as a basis, working capital may be classified as either permanent or temporary.

Permanent working capital is that amount of funds required to produce the goods and services necessary to satisfy demand at its lowest point. Such capital possesses the following characteristics: First, unlike fixed assets, which retain their form over a long period of time, permanent working capital is constantly changing from one asset to another. Second, the fund of value representing permanent working capital never leaves the business process; therefore, suppliers should not expect its return until the business ceases to exist. Third, as long as a firm experiences growth, the size of the permanent working capital account will increase.

Temporary or variable working capital, like permanent working capital, changes its form from cash to inventory to receivables and back to cash, but it differs in that it is not always gainfully employed. Businesses that are seasonal and/or cyclical in nature require more temporary working capital than firms that are not so influenced. Therefore, managers should obtain the capital that is temporarily invested in current assets from sources that will allow its return when not in use. If this policy is followed, the turnover of investment will be more favorable, thus permitting a more efficient use of capital. It should be pointed out that although seasonal and cyclical working capital may be obtained from the same source, the contractual terms vary widely. For example, banks may be the principal suppliers of both types, but the charges may be different.

Moreover, contractual restrictions upon short-term loans will differ considerably from those placed upon term loans and long-term contracts.

A FOUR-PART THEORY OF WORKING CAPITAL[1]

A firm's fixed capital is determined by its scale of production; once committed, the capital remains invested regardless of production levels. Working capital, on the other hand, is employed only when actual production is undertaken, and the volume required is generally determined by the level of production. The precise level of investment in working capital is predicated on (1) management's attitude toward risk and (2) factors that influence the amount of cash, inventories, receivables, and other current assets required to support a given volume of output.

Risk as used here means the risk of not maintaining sufficient current assets to (1) meet all financial obligations as they mature, and (2) support the proper level of sales. It is the writer's opinion that four principles involving risk serve as the basis of a theory.

First Principle

The first principle is concerned with the relation between the levels of working capital and sales. Briefly, it may be stated as follows: *If working capital is varied relative to sales, the amount of risk that a firm assumes is also varied and the opportunity for gain or loss is increased.* This principle implies that a definite relation exists between the degree of risk that management assumes and the rate of return. That is, the more risk that a firm assumes, the greater is the opportunity for *gain* or *loss.* An examination of Figure 7-1 reveals that when the level of working capital relative to sales *decreases*, the opportunity for gain from investment *increases* but the opportunity for loss also *increases* and vice versa. (Here sales and output are considered equal.) It should be noted that while the gain resulting from each *decrease* in working capital is measurable, the losses that may occur cannot be measured. For example, return on investment increased from 7.6 percent to 16.6 percent when working capital fell from $120,000 to $50,000 (see Table 7-1). Gains that would be reflected in reduced costs are also measurable—for example, savings resulting from a reduction in warehouse space when inventory is reduced. Moreover, it is believed that while the potential gain resulting from each decrease in working capital is greater in the beginning than potential loss, the exact opposite occurs if management continues to decrease working capital; that is to say, potential losses are small at first for each decrease in working capital but increase sharply if it continues to be reduced.

---

[1] This theory is taken from Ernest W. Walker, "A Theory of Working Management," *Proceedings of the Southwestern Finance Association* (Bureau of Business Research, The University of Texas at Austin, 1966), and Ernest W. Walker, "Toward a Theory of Working Capital," *Engineering Economist*, Vol. IX, Nov. 2 (January-February 1964).

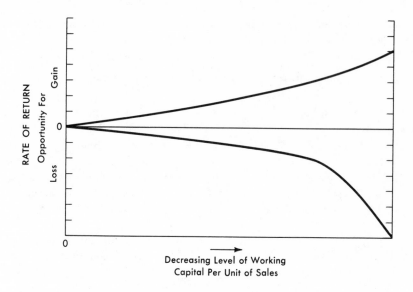

FIGURE 7-1 Working Capital Relative to Sales

Obviously, it should be the goal of management to select the level of working capital that optimizes the firm's rate of return. This level is defined as *that point at which the incremental loss associated with a decrease in working-capital investment becomes greater than the incremental gain associated with that investment.* It is emphasized that each company will have a unique set of curves, since the shape of each curve is determined by the risk associated with the firm, as well as by the size of the working-capital account relative to total assets.

It is presumed that by analyzing correctly the factors determining the amount of the various components of working capital as well as predicting the state of the economy, management can determine the ideal level of working capital that will equilibrate its rate of return with its ability to assume risk;

TABLE 7-1

XYZ MANUFACTURING COMPANY
FINANCIAL DATA

	Working Capital		
	$ 50,000	$ 90,000	$120,000
Fixed Capital	$ 10,000	$ 10,000	$ 10,000
Liabilities	30,000	30,000	30,000
Net Worth	30,000	70,000	100,000
Sales	100,000	100,000	100,000
Fixed Capital Turnover	10.0	10.0	10.0
Working Capital Turnover	2.0	1.1	0.833
Total Capital Turnover	1.66	1.0	0.761
Earnings (as Percent of Sales)	10.0	10.0	10.0
Rate of Return (Percent)	16.6	10.0	7.6

however, since most managers do not know what the future holds, they tend to maintain an investment in working capital that exceeds the ideal level. It is this excess that concerns us, since the size of the investment determines a firm's rate of return on investment.

As stated in the first principle, if the level of working capital is increased, the amount of risk is decreased and the opportunity for gain or loss is likewise decreased. On the other hand, if the level of working capital is decreased, the exact opposite is true; therefore, management's attitude toward risk definitely affects the level of working capital maintained for a given volume of sales. That is, a more conservative management employs more working capital for a given volume of sales than one which can and is willing to assume more risk.

Up to this point we have been talking about industries in general. Now let us turn our attention to specific situations. Financial managers of certain industries have more to gain or lose by following aggressive working capital policies than do managers in other industries. That is, the rates of return caused by changes in working capital in such industries as chemicals, retail trade, and drugs are much larger than those in the steel and paper industries. To illustrate, the management of an average chemical firm can increase the rate of return on investment 100 percent by decreasing working capital 50 percent and holding everything else constant. On the other hand, a 50 percent decrease in working capital in the average steel firm would increase the rate of return only 24 percent.[2]

The obvious conclusion is that managers should determine whether they operate in businesses that react favorably to changes in working capital levels; if not, the gains realized may not be adequate in comparison to the risk that must be assumed when working capital investment is decreased.

Second Principle

As we mentioned above, management is faced with the problem of determining the ideal "level" of working capital. It is not the purpose of this section to develop techniques that may be used by management in the solution of the correct level; rather, it presents a principle that will serve as a basis for its determination. In the writer's opinion, the concept that each dollar invested in fixed or working capital should contribute to the net worth of the firm should serve as a basis for such a principle. If this is true, the following principle qualifies and is applicable for investments made not only in various components of working capital but in fixed capital as well. Stated succinctly it is as follows: *Capital should be invested in each component of working capital as long as the equity position of the firm increases.*

Third Principle

Whereas the first principle dealt with the risk associated with the amount of working capital employed in relation to sales, the third principle is concerned

---

[2] Walker, "Toward a Theory of Working Capital," p. 29.

with the risk resulting from the type of capital used to finance current assets. This principle may be stated as follows: *The type of capital used to finance working capital directly affects the amount of risk that a firm assumes as well as the opportunity for gain or loss and cost of capital.*

There is no question but that different types of capital possess varying degrees of risk insofar as the business firm is concerned. Moreover, investors relate the price for which they are willing to sell their capital to this risk; that is, they charge less for debt than for equity capital, since debt capital possesses less risk. Since this is true, management is able to increase its opportunity for higher returns on its equity capital through the use of debt capital. A firm wishing to minimize risk will employ only equity capital; however, in so doing, it foregoes the opportunity for higher returns on equity capital. A word of caution is necessary at this juncture. It has been stated that return to equity capital increases directly with the amount of risk assumed by management. This is true, but only to a certain point. When excessive risk is assumed, a firm's opportunity for loss will eventually overshadow its opportunity for gain, and at this point return to equity is threatened. When this occurs, the firm stands to suffer severe losses. This concept is well known by students of finance and requires no further elaboration.

Unlike rate of return, cost of capital moves inversely with risk; that is, as additional risk capital is employed by management, cost of capital declines. This relationship prevails until the firm's optimum capital structure is achieved; thereafter, the cost of capital increases. This is because not only will creditors increase the amount of interest charged, but also suppliers of equity capital will decrease the price they are willing to pay for various types of equity securities. For a more detailed discussion of the impact that changing debt/equity ratios have on a firm's cost of capital, see Chapters 9 and 10.

Fourth Principle

As noted above, the use of debt is recommended, and the amount to be used is determined by the level of risk management wishes to assume. It should be noted that risk is not only associated with the amount of debt used relative to equity, it is also related to the nature of the contracts negotiated by the borrower. Some of the more important characteristics of debt contracts directly affecting a firm's operation are restrictive clauses of the contracts and dates of maturity. I believe that maturity dates are the more important of the two insofar as solvency is concerned; therefore, particular attention is directed to this area.

Lenders of short-term funds are particularly conscious of this problem, and in an effort to protect themselves by reducing the risk associated with improper maturity dates, they are requiring firms to produce documents depicting cash flows. These documents, when properly prepared, not only show the level of loans necessary to support sales but also indicate when the loans can be repaid. In other words, lenders realize that a firm's ability to repay short-term loans is directly related to cash flow and not to earnings, and therefore, a firm should make every effort to tie maturities to its flow of internally generated funds.

This concept serves as the basis for the final hypothesis of this presentation. Specifically, it may be stated as follows: *The greater the disparity between the maturities of a firm's short-term debt instruments and its flow of internally generated funds, the greater the risk, and vice versa.* Incidentally, management is not compensated for assuming the risk referred to in this concept; therefore, under no circumstances should it be assumed.

To illustrate this concept, assume the following about X Company, a small manufacturer of toys: (1) sales are highly seasonal, with 75 percent occurring between July 1 and August 30; (2) the firm relies on short-term bank loans and trade credit to finance seasonal inventory requirements; (3) credit terms are for 60 days; and (4) no cash discounts are given. Inventories and receivables were low relative to cash at the beginning of the year primarily because customers had liquidated last year's receivables and production had not begun for the year. In the first quarter, the firm, realizing that orders would start pouring in during July and August, began to manufacture for inventory. During this quarter, cash declined and inventories increased but receivables remained constant. In the second quarter a few sales were made, and as a result, accounts receivable increased slowly; however, cash outflow was greater than inflow, which meant that cash continued to decline. To offset this decline and to finance the continuing build-up in inventories, the finance manager negotiated a 60-day promissory note on May 15. As predicted, sales began to rise gradually in early July and increased rapidly during the latter part of the month and in August. The cash account began to increase due to the reversed flow of funds, but it did not reach its peak until the fourth quarter. The firm was therefore unable to meet its obligation with funds from internally generated sources.

This simple example shows how it is possible for a firm to face insolvency or embarrassment even though it might be making a profit. A word of caution is necessary at this point. It is extremely difficult to predict accurately a firm's cash flow in an economy such as ours. Therefore, a margin of safety should be included in every short-term debt contract; that is, adequate time should be allowed between the time the funds are generated and the date of maturity.

SUMMARY

The fundamental basis for a working capital theory is risk; that is, in most cases the opportunity for gain or loss varies directly with the amount of risk that management assumes. The theory briefly stated is that the policies governing the amount and type of working capital are determined by the *amount of risk* management is prepared to assume. To illustrate, by increasing the amount of risk it is willing to assume, management can reduce the amount of working capital required and thus increase the efficiency of capital, resulting in an increase in total profits. Further, by employing more risk capital, management can increase the rate earned on equity capital, also reducing its cost of capital; and finally, management can employ more debt capital, provided it can accurately determine the firm's ability to repay its obligations and can schedule its maturity dates accordingly.

8

Working-Capital Management (continued)

It may be remembered that cash, inventory, and receivables are the three primary components of working capital. In the preceding chapter there was a discussion of the various concepts of working capital essential to effective planning as well as the development of certain principles which, the writer believes, serve as a basis for a theory of working capital. This chapter contains a discussion of factors and techniques that should be considered when planning receivables, cash, and inventory.

RECEIVABLES MANAGEMENT

In the years 1967-1969, corporations used more funds to finance receivables than to finance any other asset except nonresidential fixed investments: $14.2 billion, or 17.3 percent of all funds, were invested in receivables. It should be noted that receivables have risen in importance from a dollar standpoint since 1967—$8.8 billion in 1967, $14.8 in 1968, and $17.3 billion in 1969 (see Table 9-1, p. 83). Also, the importance of receivables relative to other assets increased in each of these years. For these reasons it is imperative that management formulate effective policies if it intends to protect shareholders' net worth.

Factors Influencing Investment in Receivables

It was stated in Chapter 7 that no investment should be made in working capital unless each dollar invested contributes to the firm's net worth. Capital invested in receivables is exactly the same as that invested in other assets; that is, a cost is associated with the investment, and the value of each sales dollar sold on terms will be greater if it is received in the immediate future than it would be if it were received at some later date. As a result, both the cost and time values of funds must be given consideration when credit policy is being set.

Generally an increase in receivables investment results from several causes: an increase in sales, size of the cash discount, length of credit terms, and the volume of delinquent accounts. The first is not a part of the receivables policy and is not discussed here.

Cash discounts directly affect a firm's cost of capital in that they may cause it to increase or decrease. To illustrate, assume that a firm's cost of capital is 1 percent per month but its cash discount terms are 2 percent cash, net 30 days. If the discount is taken, the firm's cost of capital doubles—24 percent instead of 12 percent—and the net worth of the firm suffers. If the cash discount is taken, the present value of the sale will be less than it would have been if the account had been collected at the end of 30 days. A simple example illustrates this. Assume an article costing $0.80 sells for $1.00 with terms of 2 percent cash, net 30 days. If the cash discount is taken, the present value will equal $0.18:

Sale	$1.00
Cash discount 2%	0.02
Cash or present value	$0.98
Cost (present value)	0.80
Present value	$0.18

If the cash discount is not taken by the customer, the present value of the profit is equal to $0.19, a gain of $0.01; the computation is as follows:

Present value of sale 30 days hence, when cost of capital is 1%	$0.99
Cost (present value)	0.80
	$0.19

Since the cost of capital is 1 percent and the cash discount is 2 percent, the firm will have sustained a loss of 1 percent (reduction in net worth) if the discount is taken. If the two are equal, it makes no difference to the credit manager whether the discount is taken; however, if the discount is less than the cost of capital and it is taken, the net result will be to raise the present value of the firm's net worth.

In the establishment of credit terms, the same basic concepts are involved. To illustrate, assume the following:

1. Cost of capital, 1 percent per month
2. Terms, 90 days
3. No cash discounts
4. Sales of 10 units at $10 per unit
5. Fixed and variable costs, $9 per unit

The dollar value of the sale equals $100 but the present value of the firm's profit varies directly with the length of credit terms and the firm's cost of capital. These changes are depicted in Table 8-1.

TABLE 8-1

ILLUSTRATION OF THE
TIME-VALUE-OF-FUNDS CONCEPT

TERMS	SALES REVE- NUES	PRESENT VALUE FACTOR OF COST OF CAPITAL:		PRESENT VALUE AT COST OF CAPITAL:		PRESENT VALUE OF COST	GAIN OR LOSS IN NET WORTH WITH COST OF CAPITAL:	
		1%	*2%*	*1%*	*2%*		*1%*	*2%*
Cash	$100.00	1.000	1.000	$100.00	$100.00	$90.00	$10.00	$10.00
30 days	100.00	0.990	0.980	99.00	98.00	90.00	9.00	8.00
90 days	100.00	0.971	0.942	97.10	94.20	90.00	7.10	4.20
180 days	100.00	0.942	0.888	94.20	88.80	90.00	4.20	(1.20)
270 days	100.00	0.914	0.837	91.40	83.70	90.00	1.40	(6.30)
300 days	100.00	0.905	0.804	90.50	80.40	90.00	.50	(9.60)

The data in Table 8-1 illustrate how the cost of capital and the length of credit terms directly affect the firm's net worth. In the case where the cost of capital equaled 1 percent per month, the firm's net worth increased only as long as the credit terms did not exceed 330 days. On the other hand, if the firm's cost of capital were 2 percent per month it would realize an increase in net worth *only* if the credit terms were for five months or less. From a practical stand-point, management will want to maintain the shortest credit terms possible along with the lowest cost of capital.

Delinquent accounts have the same effect on net worth as an increase in (1) the cash discount, (2) the credit terms, or (3) the cost of capital. If a deterioration in net worth is to be avoided in the event of delinquent accounts, management should do one of three things: (1) eliminate the account by either collecting the account or eliminating the customer; (2) lower the firm's cost of capital; or (3) charge the customer an amount equal to the firm's cost of capital for the period of the delinquency.

The last major policy affecting receivables is the selection of credit risk (customers). Traditional theory stated that the selection of credit risk is determined by relating bad debt losses to the profit margin; that is, the greater the firm's profit margin, the more risk it can absorb. If the firm's objective is to optimize profits, it will sell to customers in the lowest risk category for which profits on sales exceed bad debt losses. For example, the credit manager in one firm divides the customers into four categories. Each group includes all customers with the same risk characteristics; that is, customers in group *A* always pay promptly; customers in group *B* are expected to have bad debt losses of 3 percent; group *C*'s expected bad debt losses will be 7 percent; and group *D*'s will equal 10 percent. If the firm's profits before bad debts equal 10 percent on sales, the theory says that the firm should sell to groups *A*, *B*, *C*, and *D* since no loss will result from sales. From a practical standpoint, management will probably not sell to group *D* since no profits will be realized (see Table 8-2).

This theory does not take into consideration the concepts of the cost of capital and the time value of funds. When both are considered, it is extremely doubtful that the firm would break even if it sold to customers in groups *C* or *D*.

TABLE 8-2

PROFIT POTENTIAL BY RISK CATEGORIES

Risk Category	Gross Sales	EXPECTED BAD DEBTS		Loss of Profit from Bad Debt	Loss of Profit from Operating Cost	Profit
		Percent	Dollar			
A	$20,000	0	$ 0	$ 0	$ 0	$2,000
B	30,000	3	900	90	810	2,100
C	40,000	7	2,800	280	2,500	1,200
D	60,000	10	6,000	600	5,400	0

To understand why this is true as well as to ascertain correctly the type of customers acceptable from a risk standpoint, the following should be considered.

First, the amount of time required to collect an account increases directly with risk; that is, it takes more time to collect the accounts in group D than C, C than B, B than A. Stated differently, the distribution of the collection experience will vary among groups. Second, the cost of collection increases as risk increases (in the example below, it is assumed that collection cost increases $1 per $100 of sales for each 15 days that an account is late). Third, the longer it takes to collect an account, the greater is the firm's investment in that account. Finally, the present value of the "return" on an account decreases in direct relation to the amount of time needed to collect the account. To incorporate these concepts into the theory that guides the firm in selecting credit risk, it is necessary to establish the collection characteristics of its customers.

In most cases it is possible to divide into groups those customers who have similar risk characteristics. Since each has different risk characteristics, the time to collect the accounts will vary. Table 8-3 depicts one method of determining the "expected" number of days required to collect the average account in each category.

A brief explanation of the preceding will be helpful to the analysis that follows. As previously mentioned, the amount of time required to collect an account increases directly with risk. To determine the expected amount of time that will be needed to collect the average account in each risk category, a probability distribution is established.

For example, there is a 100 percent probability that all customers in group A will pay within 30 days; therefore, the expected amount of time each account is outstanding is 30 days. The customers in group B will take more time to pay; i.e., 40 percent will pay in 30 days, 32 percent will pay in 45 days, 25 percent will pay in 75 days, and 3 percent will never pay. As a consequence, the management can expect to use an average of 45 days to collect from customers in this category. Employing the same technique for each group, we find that it will take an average of 60 days to collect from the customers in group C and 75 days to collect from the customers in group D. Moreover, it will cost an additional $1

TABLE 8-3

MEASURING THE EXPECTED DATE OF COLLECTION

Groups	Probability	Days to Collect	Expected Number of Days to Collect	Increase in Cost of Collection
A	1.00	30	30	0
	0.40	30	12.00	
	0.32	45	14.40	
B	0.25	75	18.75	
	0.03	0	0	
	1.00		45.15	$1
	0.23	30	6.90	
	0.30	45	13.50	
C	0.40	100	40.00	
	0.07	0	0	
	1.00		60.40	$2
	0.05	30	1.50	
	0.10	60	6.00	
	0.25	75	18.75	
D	0.30	90	27.00	
	0.20	105	21.00	
	0.10	0	0	
	1.00		74.25	$3

for each $100 of sales to collect from group B, $2 per $100 from C, and $3 per $100 from group D.

Let us now apply the cost of capital and the time value of funds concepts to these collection data and see which of the risks can be accepted. You will recall that there is a cost associated with each dollar invested in receivables and that each sales dollar sold on terms will have a greater value if received in the immediate future than if received at a later date. Applying these concepts to the above data, we can ascertain the present value of the sales in each category (Table 8-4).

TABLE 8-4

PRESENT VALUE OF THE SALES OF A FIRM
(by groups)

Group	Sales	Present Value of Sales	Present Value of Cost[a]	Expected Present Value of Sales
A	$20,000	$19,800	$18,000	$1,800
B	30,000	29,550	28,200	1,350
C	40,000	39,224	39,600	− 376
D	60,000	58,530	61,800	− 2,270

NOTE: It is assumed that the firm's cost of capital is 1%.

[a]Includes losses from bad debt, cost of collection, and operating cost.

The data in column 5 of Table 8-4 indicate that the present value of the sales that will be collected in 30 days exceeds the firm's direct cost and cost of capital by $1,800; the present value of the sales of group B will return direct cost and cost of capital plus $1,350. The present value of sales of groups C and D will be $2,646 *less* than direct cost and cost of capital, thus causing the present value of the firm's net worth to decline.

The following conclusions are obvious from Table 8-4: (1) If all sales were accepted ($150,000), the net present value of the firm's net worth would decline $504. (2) If sales were made to groups A, B, and C, the net present value of the firm's net worth would increase by $2,774. (3) If sales were made to groups A and B, net present value would increase $3,150.

Traditional theory directed that sales should be made to customers in groups A, B, C, and D; but according to the theory that no investment should be made unless a firm's cost of capital is at least recovered, sales should not be made to groups C and D.

Adjusting for Risk

Risk associated with receivables can be accounted for by adjusting either (1) the discount rate used to ascertain the present value of receivables—cost of capital, or (2) the cash flow resulting from receivables. To illustrate, rather than using 1 percent for each group of sales, management can increase the discount rate for those groups that it believes to be more risky. For example, 3 percent may be used to discount the sales in group D, 2 percent for group C, and 1 percent for B and A. The student remembers that the standard deviation and coefficient of variation are tools that may be used to determine the degree of risk associated with each group.

In adjusting the cash flow resulting from receivables, the first step is for management to derive a certainty-equivalent coefficient for the cash flows resulting from the sales from each group (risk category). It will be recalled that the coefficient has a value between 0.00 and 1.00 and it varies directly with

TABLE 8-5

PRESENT VALUE OF SALES
WHEN RISK IS ADJUSTED
BY THE CERTAINTY-EQUIVALENT TECHNIQUE

Groups	Sales	Certainty-Equivalent Coefficient	Adjusted Sales	Present Value of Sales[a]	Present Value of Costs	Increase (Decrease) in Expected Present Value of Net Worth
A	$20,000	1.00	$20,000	$19,900	$18,000	$1,900
B	30,000	0.95	28,500	28,286	28,200	86
C	40,000	0.90	36,000	35,640	39,600	(3,960)
D	60,000	0.90	54,000	53,325	61,800	(8,475)

[a]A 6 percent rate is considered risk-free in this example.

risk—the higher the risk the lower the coefficient. Suppose management computes the following certainty-equivalent coefficients for each group: 1.00 for group A, 0.95 for B, 0.80 for C, and 0.70 for D. The next step is to adjust the cash flows of each group by multiplying the certainty-equivalent coefficient by the cash flows. Finally, the adjusted cash flows are discounted by a risk-free rate. Observe that when this technique of analysis is used, the present value of the sales of each group changes considerably, thus causing management to reevaluate its decision to accept or reject sales to the various groups (Table 8-5).

CASH MANAGEMENT

All firms, regardless of size, type, or location, have the same motives for holding cash: transaction, precautionary, and speculative. Briefly, the cash held for transaction purposes is used to meet the *normal* cash needs of the business. Although the majority of a firm's cash flows—inflows as well as outflows—are nonrandom and predictable, some are random and difficult to predict. These flows, along with abnormal cash needs, are provided for by precautionary cash balances and lines of credit. The size of the precautionary cash balance is directly related to the firm's ability to assume risk. If management is averse to risk, the precautionary balance will be larger than it would be if management were willing to assume risk. To offset a complete loss of return on these balances, management will normally invest a large part of them in short-term securities. The final reason for holding cash—for speculative considerations—allows management to take advantage of profitable opportunities. For example, management may maintain large cash balances in order to be able to take advantage of an anticipated price increase. The ultimate in speculation occurs when productive assets are exchanged for cash in anticipation of a major break in the economy. In general, a business should not speculate with cash balances; this being true, no further attention will be given to this particular reason for holding cash.

Factors Influencing Cash Balances

The amount of cash for transaction requirements is predictable and depends upon a variety of factors, the more important of which are the credit position of the firm, status of the firm's receivables and inventory accounts, the nature of the business enterprise, and management's attitude toward risk.

The credit position influences the amount of cash required in two distinct ways. First, if a firm's credit position is sound, it is not necessary to carry a large cash reserve for emergencies. Second, if a firm finances its inventory requirements with trade credit, its cash requirements are considerably smaller, since the firm can synchronize the credit terms it gives to its customers with the terms it receives.

The amount of time required for a firm to convert its receivables into cash also affects the amount of cash needed and, of course, reduces total working capital employed. In other words, the longer the credit terms, the slower the turnover. When outflow is not synchronized with turnover, a firm must carry amounts of cash relatively larger than would otherwise be required.

The status of a firm's inventory account also affects the amount of cash tied up at any one time. For example, if one business firm carries two months' inventory on hand and another firm carries only one month's supply, the former has twice as much investment in inventory and will normally be called upon to maintain a larger investment in cash in order to finance its acquisition.

The nature of a firm's demand definitely affects the volume of cash required. To illustrate, a firm whose demand is volatile needs a relatively larger cash reserve than one whose demand is stable. Public utility firms exhibit stable demand whereas firms that deal with high-fashion merchandise or goods that tend to be "faddish" are subject to high degrees of volatility.

Another characteristic affecting the level of cash is the amount of sales in relation to assets. Firms with large sales relative to fixed assets are required to carry larger cash reserves. This is the result of having large sums invested in inventories (particularly finished goods) and receivables. It should be remembered, however, that cash requirements do not increase in the same proportion as sales. The rule is that as sales increase, cash also increases but at a decreasing rate. It is impossible to determine to what extent each characteristic affects the total volume of cash, but these examples indicate that different types of businesses have different cash requirements.

Finally, a more conservative management will hold a larger cash reserve than one that is less conservative. The former usually demands more liquidity than the latter and consequently does not experience the same degree of efficiency. A generalization is made that the firm that effectively plans its working capital policies is less conservative than one that does little or no planning. The obvious conclusion is that planning allows the firm to predict its requirements more accurately, thereby eliminating uncertainty, which is the basis for large cash reserves.

The Cash Budget as a Planning Device

The use of a cash budget as a means of determining the size of the cash account is superior to judging by past experience and to using pro forma balance sheets. A cash budget is a comparison of estimated cash inflows and outflows for a particular period, such as a day, week, month, quarter, or year.

The budgeting process begins with the beginning balance, to which is added *expected* receipts. This amount is reached by multiplying modal cash receipts by the probability distribution that management believes will prevail during the budgetary period. If outlays exceed the beginning balance plus anticipated receipts, the difference must be financed from external sources. If an excess exists, management must make a decision regarding its disposal—investing in short-term securities, repaying existing debts, or returning the funds to the equity owners.

The budget, in addition to revealing a cash deficiency, depicts the most opportune time to undertake the financing process. Two advantages result from this. First, funds will be available when needed and idle funds will not be on hand. Second, management will have sufficient time to raise the funds from the most advantageous sources.

In regard to the first advantage, management knows that inadequate liquidity may cause output to be reduced, which, of course, causes a decline in return. A second danger is that if funds are not available as needed, the firm will be unable to meet its commitments and will soon lose its credit standing.

The cash budget indicates when there will be excess cash and how much there will be at any given time. With this knowledge, management is able to ward off the disadvantages of excessive liquidity. One of the more important disadvantages is the decline in return on investment, which in turn adversely affects the cost of capital. The knowledge of excess liquidity allows management to instigate a short-term investment program, permitting an increase in the firm's overall return.

Information depicted by the budget also reflects the amount of time for which funds are needed, thus allowing management to relate the maturity of the loan to need. When funds are secured for a shorter period than needed, several problems are created. Immediately it is seen that the loan must be renewed or an entirely new loan must be negotiated. In any event, the negotiations are on a much shorter basis and the terms will probably be less favorable than they would have been if adequate planning time had been available.

Also, knowledge of the amount of time funds will be used in the business process is essential in determining the "best" source of funds. If funds are to be used for an indefinite period, management will more than likely resort to long-term sources. On the other hand, if the funds are for short periods, management will want to utilize short-term funds—see Chapter 14 for a more complete discussion of the correct sources of funds.

Finally, the cash budget establishes a sound basis for controlling the cash position. For this purpose it is necessary to prepare a budget report, which is nothing more than a comparison of actual income and expenditures with *expected* income and expenditures. If deviations occur, revisions to the cash budget for the succeeding period should be made. It is emphasized that if effective budgeting is to be achieved, management must make a thorough analysis of the deviation before corrective action is taken. If the analysis reveals that the variation is the result of an ineffective policy instead of an error in the budgetary process, action should be taken to correct the policy. However, if the error is the result of an ineffective budgeting technique, the technique should be improved or the individual employing the technique should be given whatever guidance is necessary to prevent a recurrence of the variation.

The student should keep in mind that control of cash calls for a complete replanning process. For example, objectives are reviewed, existing policies are examined, and changes made only if necessary, and finally, management corrects its procedures to assure that the correct policy is properly executed. When this process has been accomplished, a revised cash budget is prepared as a part of the planning process; and as each period is terminated, a cash report is made to determine whether the cash plan is effective.

Management of Cash Balances

The time value of funds concept tells us that a dollar received in the immediate future has more value than one received at some later time; all other things remaining equal, management should make every effort to speed up cash flowing into the firm and delay cash flowing out of the firm. It should be emphasized that management should not fail to meet its obligations when developing policies that delay the outflowing of funds. Many techniques may be used in reducing the span between the time a customer renders payment and the time the funds are available for use by the firm; some of the more important are: (1) the lock box system, (2) concentration banking, and (3) special handling of payments.

It is possible for management to reduce the time that funds are in transit (float) by creating postal boxes in post offices located near the customers. Customers send their payments to these boxes rather than to the company offices, thus saving several days. At regular times—daily or even more often—the firm has a bank pick up the checks and deposit them in a special checking account; after the checks are cleared locally, the bank remits by wire to the firm's bank of deposit. Such a system reduces float by several days, permitting the firm to use its cash more effectively.

A similar technique, referred to as concentration banking, also shortens the time that funds are in transit. To illustrate the process, a firm establishes one or more collection centers in areas close to a large number of customers. The centers bill the customers and collect the accounts. As soon as the payments are received, they are deposited in a local bank. At regular intervals, the funds in excess of compensating balances and local requirements are transferred by wire to a concentration bank or banks. The wire transfer technique is most frequently used, since it is much faster than a transfer of deposits by checks, which must be collected through the usual channels.

In some instances, firms expedite the movement of funds from the customer through the use of personal messengers or air mail. These techniques are generally employed only when there is a small number of accounts or when large payments are involved.

Obviously, firms can reduce their cash accounts by the number of banks that are used, reducing the total amount required for compensating balances. In some instances the level of cash may be reduced by paying banks for services rather than maintaining compensating balances.

Finally, financial managers can reduce cash requirements by developing techniques that effectively control the disbursement of funds. Although the techniques used to accomplish this vary with each situation, the idea is to time the payments to coincide with the due dates. Any technique that delays payment beyond the due date is generally bad and should not be utilized.

Models for Controlling Cash

It is not the purpose of a book of this nature to describe in detail each model that has been developed to optimize a firm's cash position. However, the reader should remember that the primary purpose of each model is to permit management to maintain an optimum level of cash at all times. Some of the more sophisticated models have been developed by Baumol, Miller and Orr, Tobin, and Archer.[1] The first three models are variations of inventory models and have certain limitations. Moreover, most firms would find it difficult to utilize them in day-to-day operations; nevertheless, they provide an insight into the problems of cash management and serve as a foundation to effective management. Archer, on the other hand, employs statistical techniques to measure both transaction and precautionary balances. His model is much more practical, and it or some variation of it is recommended for most firms.

INVENTORY PLANNING

Inventory is the largest current asset of most companies. For example, in the first quarter of 1970, inventories accounted for 23.3 percent of *all assets* in all manufacturing corporations except newspapers.[2] For this reason, inventory planning and control are of utmost importance. This section will deal with factors influencing the size of the inventory account and the level of inventories.

Several factors affect the amount of funds that a firm has invested in inventories at any one time. First, the amount of time needed for inventories to travel through the various processes directly affects the amount of investment. All other factors disregarded, the amount of capital invested for a given volume of sales is less when the turnover rate is high, and vice versa. In addition to the advantage gained by reducing the level of investment, high turnover rates reduce the risk associated with declining prices, obsolescence, and spoilage. Of the several disadvantages associated with high turnover rates, the most important involves the risk of not having sufficient inventories to continue production when external factors bring about a curtailment in the supply.

Second, there are certain costs associated with a large investment in inventories. Likewise, firms incur certain costs when investment is held to a minimum. Some of these costs are easy to measure, whereas others are almost impossible to

---

[1] See the following articles for a complete description of each model:

W. J. Baumol, "The Transactions' Demand for Cash: An Inventory Theoretic Approach," *Quarterly Journal of Economics*, November 1952, pp. 545-56.

M. H. Miller and D. Orr, "A Model of the Demand for Money by Banks," *Quarterly Journal of Economics*, August 1966, pp. 414-35.

James Tobin, "The Interest-Elasticity of Transactions' Demand for Cash," *The Review of Economics and Statistics*, August 1956, pp. 241-47.

S. H. Archer, "A Model for the Determination of Firm Cash Balances," *Journal of Financial and Quantitative Analysis*, Vol. 1, No. 1 (March 1966), 1-10.

[2] *Quarterly Financial Report for Manufacturing Corporations*, First Quarter, 1970 (Washington, D.C.: U.S. Government Printing Office, 1970), p. 12.

determine. Examples of the costs that are easy to calculate include storage costs, set-up and change-over costs resulting from short production runs, costs associated with increased ordering activity, and costs resulting from spoilage and obsolescence. Costs that are difficult to measure include opportunity costs of not being able to invest funds in more profitable ventures, costs resulting from changes in price levels, and costs resulting from loss of sales by not having adequate inventories to satisfy demand. The firm should have as its objective the minimization of costs; therefore, the level of inventory is determined by management's desire and ability to maximize the economies of holding large inventories with those of holding small inventories.

Third, the level of inventories is influenced by management's ability to predict the forces that may cause a disruption in the flow of inventories—for example, strikes and major shifts in demand. That is to say, a management that is able to predict these disruptions with a reasonable degree of accuracy will have less fear about the future and will maintain lower levels of inventories. The opposite is true when management is unsure of the future.

Finally, a firm's accounting procedures tend to influence the size of inventory investment. To illustrate, during periods of rising prices, a policy of costing on a last-in-first-out basis will cause the size of the investment in inventory to be smaller than it would have been if first-in-first-out had been used. The opposite is true when prices are declining.

No effort has been made here to list all the factors that influence the amount of investment in inventories; rather, it has been shown that management should consider a number of factors in determining the level of investment in inventories. Moreover, our purpose is also to show that too little investment can be as expensive as too much; therefore, considerable effort should be expended in deciding the amount of inventory that should be maintained.

Inventory Models

It is probably safe to say that models were used in inventory planning and control before they were used in cash or receivables management. Since there are numerous articles and books available on the subject of inventory decision models, there is no need to deal with them here. The student should be aware, however, that the primary purpose of each model is to ascertain the optimum size of the inventory investment, which has been defined as that level where the cost of holding additional inventory exceeds the total cost of *not* holding it.[3]

---

[3]The reader is directed to the following sources for a complete discussion of this important subject:

J. F. Magee, "Guides to Inventory Policy," I, II, and III, *Harvard Business Review*, January-February, 1956, pp. 34, 49-60; March-April, 1956, pp. 49-60; and May-June, 1956, pp. 57-70, 103-16.

Seymour Friedland, *The Economics of Corporate Finance* (Englewood Cliffs, N.J.: Prentice-Hall, Inc., 1966), Chap. 3.

Joseph Buchan and Ernest Koenisgberg, *Scientific Inventory Management* (Englewood Cliffs, N.J.: Prentice-Hall, Inc. 1963).

CONTROL OF WORKING CAPITAL

We can assume from the foregoing that a firm that adequately plans its cash, inventory, and receivables will have fewer problems of control than one that operates without effective policies in these areas. Therefore, the direct approach to working capital control is to develop effective policies for each of the components of working capital. Since deviations occur in actual operations, indirect control techniques are needed in order for management to reduce its working capital requirements.

The first step in the control process is to establish acceptable norms for each of the working capital components. In the case of cash, financial management should develop a cash budget at the beginning of each planning period.[4] Actual operations should be periodically compared with budgeted operations; if variations occur, the causes should be determined and corrected. When this has been done, management can replan its cash requirements if necessary.

Receivables and inventory control are somewhat more complicated, since the turnover of these accounts influences the total funds invested in each. Methods used to measure inventory and receivables turnover were discussed in Chapter 4 and need not be discussed further. We should emphasize, however, that these techniques *measure* turnover; they do not control the amount of investment needed for efficient operation. The determination of the amount of funds invested in inventory and receivables is a function of the firm's policies. If turnover, as measured, exceeds or falls below what is desirable, it is proof that the policies that were adopted are not being followed or are ineffective. To offset any serious repercussions that might result from an excessive or below-normal turnover, financial management should start an investigation into the causes for the deviation and, once these are ascertained, make the necessary correction.

In addition to the turnover technique, other methods available to management may be used effectively in the control of inventories. Management can employ the same budgets used in the planning process to control the amount of investment in inventories, since each budget limits the amount of investment that the firm has in each type of inventory at all times. That is to say, not only can actual operations be checked against planned performance, but production, finished goods, and material budgets may be used to indicate the original amount of inventories required to produce the quantity of goods necessary to satisfy demand (projected in the sales budget). Since production is continuous, inventories are constantly being depleted, and management must periodically replace its inventory. To assure that adequate, but not excessive, inventories are on hand at all times, minimum and maximum levels are established. That is, when inventories decline to a certain level, orders are immediately initiated that will bring the inventory back to the desired level. Some firms employ elaborate

---

[4]For a complete and thorough discussion of cash budgeting, see Glenn A. Welsch, *Budgeting: Profit Planning and Control*, 3rd ed. (Englewood Cliffs, N.J.: Prentice-Hall, Inc., 1971).

mathematical models to establish levels that will achieve a balance between the economies of holding large inventories and those of holding small inventories.

In the area of receivables, management has available to it several reports that, if used properly, will assist greatly in control of receivables. These reports include (1) percentage of collection reports, (2) report of aging accounts, (3) report of bad debts, and (4) report of delinquent accounts.

The student should remember that the use of reports is important, since they indicate when something is wrong; however, in order to correct the situation, one must determine the cause and initiate corrective action.

9

Equity versus Debt Financing

It is common knowledge that all funds employed by business firms are secured from either debt or equity sources. What is not common knowledge is the proportion of debt and equity that each firm should use or the sources from which the funds are obtained. The ratio of debt to equity and the sources of funds are determined by financial policies. Needless to say, these policies vary among industries as well as among companies within each industry.

TERMINOLOGY

In a discussion of the factors that influence management in the determination of its sources of funds, the first term of major importance is *capital structure*. Many business finance writers define the term to include only long-term debt and total stockholders' investment. Others define capital structure to include all items on the credit side of the balance sheet; that is, both short-term and long-term funds are included. Although both definitions have merit, the latter is used here.

The second term requiring consideration is *capital*. Capital has several meanings; for example, if used in the accounting sense, it generally means net worth or stockholders' equity. It should be pointed out that accountants have now come to recognize that capital means a variety of things. Businessmen use the term to mean the total of all assets or stockholders' equity. Economists define the term as wealth employed in the production of further wealth—that is, producer goods. When the term appears in legal documents, it usually means the stated or par value of the firm's capital stock. Since there are so many valid uses of the term, every effort will be made to use specific terms, such as stockholders' equity, capital stock, net worth, par value, and stated value, rather than the general term *capital.*

Finally, *capitalization* needs clarification, since, like capital, the term has many meanings. It may mean the sum of the par value of the stocks and bonds outstanding, the sum of the par value of the stocks outstanding, or the total value of all securities permitted by the charter. Capitalization of income refers to the process of estimating the present investment value of property by discounting to present worth the anticipated stream of future income. Accountants have used the term to explain the process involved when dividends are paid in stock. Since there is no single acceptable meaning of *capitalization*, the term will be used sparingly and its meaning will be made clear each time it is used.

RELATIVE IMPORTANCE
OF EQUITY AND DEBT FINANCING

The data contained in Table 9-1 indicate the importance of the various sources from which corporate organizations obtain their operational funds. An analysis of these data for the years 1967-1969 reveals several well-defined characteristics. First, corporations obtained a larger percentage of funds from internal sources than external sources; funds from internal sources accounted for 53 to 65 percent of all funds employed in this period. Second, the amount of long-term funds obtained from equity sources exceeded the total obtained from debt; this is not surprising, since the ratio of equity to debt capital is larger in most corporations. Third, corporations look to retained earnings as the primary source of equity funds; for example, in 1969, funds secured from retained earnings were five times greater than those obtained from the sale of stocks, but in 1967 and 1968, retained earnings were even more important. Fourth, long-term funds secured from the sale of bonds were more important in each of the years than the funds raised from "other" debt sources.

Turning our attention now to the sources from which corporations obtain short-term funds, it is noted that year-in and year-out trade credit is a major source of short-term debt capital. Two reasons may account for this: First, most suppliers make trade credit available as a matter of course to all purchasers who qualify; second, comparatively speaking, trade credit is cheaper. Short-term loans from commercial banks constitute the second most important source of short-term credit. It should also be pointed out that according to the data, the volume of short-term debt obtained from trade credit is much more usable than that secured from bank credit.

The data in Table 9-1 also indicate the stability characteristics of the various sources of funds. The following traits are discernible from these data: (1) the

TABLE 9-1

SOURCES AND USES OF FUNDS,
NONFARM NONFINANCIAL CORPORATE BUSINESS,
1967-1969
(in billions)

	1967		1968		1969	
	Amount	*Percent*	*Amount*	*Percent*	*Amount*	*Percent*
Total Sources	$ 94.2	100.0	$110.4	100.0	$118.8	100.0
Internal Sources	61.2	65.0	63.1	57.1	62.7	52.8
Undistributed profits	21.2	22.5	22.0	19.9	20.9	17.6
Corporate inventory valuation adjustment	− 1.1	− 1.2	− 3.2	− 2.9	− 5.6	− 4.7
Capital consumption allowances	41.2	43.7	44.3	40.1	47.4	39.9
External Sources	33.0	35.0	47.3	42.8	56.1	47.2
Stocks	2.3	2.4	− .8	− 0.7	4.3	3.6
Bonds	14.7	15.6	12.9	11.7	12.1	10.2
Mortgages	4.5	4.8	5.8	5.3	4.4	3.7
Bank loans, n.e.c.	6.4	6.8	9.6	8.7	10.9	9.2
Other loans	1.4	1.5	3.6	3.3	6.2	5.2
Trade debts	2.6	2.8	5.7	5.2	10.9	9.2
Profits tax liability	− 4.1	− 4.8	3.7	3.3	.8	.7
Other liabilities	5.2	5.5	6.9	6.2	6.5	5.5
Total Uses	86.0	100.0	103.5	100.0	111.7	100.0
Purchase of Physical Assets	72.5	84.3	76.9	74.3	87.5	7.8
Nonresidential fixed investment	63.8	74.2	68.0	65.7	77.2	69.1
Residential structures	2.2	2.6	2.3	2.2	2.9	2.6
Change in business inventories	6.4	7.4	6.5	6.3	7.4	6.6
Increase in Financial Assets	13.5	15.7	26.6	25.7	24.2	2.2
Liquid assets	.0	0	10.1	9.7	2.3	2.1
Demand deposits and currency	− 2.2	− 2.6	1.3	1.2	.5	.4
Time deposits	4.1	4.8	2.2	2.1	− 7.8	− 7.0
U.S. government securities	− 3.1	− 3.6	1.8	1.7	− 1.4	− 1.3
Open-market paper	1.5	1.7	4.5	4.3	8.7	7.8
State and local obligations	− .4	− 0.5	.4	.3	2.3	2.0
Consumer credit	.9	0.1	1.7	1.6	1.3	1.2
Trade credit	8.8	10.2	14.8	14.2	17.3	15.5
Other financial assets	3.8	4.4	.1	.1	3.4	3.0
Discrepancy (uses less sources)	− 8.2	− 9.1	− 6.9	− 6.6	− 7.0	− 6.3

Source: Survey of Current Business (Washington, D.C.: U.S. Department of Commerce, Office of Business Economics, May 1970), p. 18.

total volume of short-term funds fluctuates more widely than that of long-term funds. For example, the volume of long-term funds ranged from a low of $87.9 billion in 1968 to a high of $94.2 billion in 1967, a 7.2 percent variance. During the same period, the volume of short-term funds ranged from a low of $11.5 billion to a high of $28.8 billion, a variance of 151 percent. (2) When the sources of both long-term and short-term capital funds are considered, it is interesting to note that more funds were obtained from debt sources than from equity sources—depreciation and federal income tax liabilities were not included. This would not be true if short-term sources were excluded. (3) Finally, the majority of funds was used to finance plant and equipment rather than current assets.

CHOOSING BETWEEN DEBT AND
EQUITY CAPITAL

A firm may decide to use a financial mix consisting of both debt and equity capital for several reasons. The more important reasons are: (1) the use of debt capital increases the earnings on equity capital; (2) debt capital is cheaper than equity capital, which lowers a firm's cost of capital; (3) debt capital does not disturb the voting position of existing shareholders; and (4) debt capital provides a degree of flexibility that may bring about an improvement in the firm's rate of return on investment.

Trading on Equity

The use of debt capital in the financing process is one way that management may improve its return on equity capital without increasing the return on total investment. This is important because occasionally management finds itself in a situation where it is impossible to increase the overall return, and yet it is imperative to increase the return on equity investment. The process of using debt capital to increase the rate of return on equity is called financial leverage, or trading on equity. This means that the capital secured from debt securities is used in projects that produce a rate of return higher than its cost, thus allowing the difference to be distributed to the holders of equity securities.

The following illustration depicts how this principle works. Let us assume the following facts: (1) $10,000 is invested in assets; (2) the rate of return on invested capital is 10 percent; (3) all earnings (after taxes) are paid out in the form of cash dividends; (4) assets may be increased up to 100 percent without a decrease in the return on capital; (5) to keep the example simple, all flotation costs are ignored. The financial data illustrate the firm's present position:

Total Capital Employed	Equity Capital Invested	Debt Capital Invested	Rate of Return	Interest Payment	Dividend Payment	Return on Equity
$10,000	$10,000	None	10%	None	$1,000	10%

Assume that management decides to double its invested capital by raising $10,000 through the sale of common stock. The net effect of this transaction is indicated in the following financial data:

Total Capital Employed	Equity Capital Invested	Debt Capital Invested	Rate of Return	Interest Payment	Dividend Payment	Return on Equity
$20,000	$20,000	None	10%	None	$2,000	10%

It should be observed that there was no change in the rate of return on total investment, nor did the return to equity increase.

Now assume that management increases its assets with borrowed capital; in other words, it trades on its equity. After exploring the various sources of debt capital, management found that it could borrow at a cost of 5 percent. The effect of this transaction is as follows:

Total Capital Employed	Equity Capital Invested	Debt Capital Invested	Rate of Return	Interest Payment	Dividend Payment	Return on Equity
$20,000	$10,000	$10,000	10%	$500	$1,500	15%

It can be seen from these data that management is able to increase the rate of return on equity capital from 10 to 15 percent by using debt capital at a cost of 5 percent before taxes. The primary reason for this is the difference between the cost of debt capital and the amount that it earns; e.g., it costs 5 percent and earns 10 percent, allowing shareholders to increase their return by 5 percent without investing additional funds.

TABLE 9–2

ALL MANUFACTURING CORPORATIONS
EXCEPT NEWSPAPERS—DEBT/EQUITY
RATIOS, RETURN ON SALES, AND
RETURN ON EQUITY (AFTER TAXES)
(fourth quarter, 1969)

Asset Size	Debt to Equity	Return on Sales	Return on Equity
ALL	45/55	4.6	11.3
Under $1 Million	51/49	1.4	7.4
$1–5 Million	45/55	2.4	9.2
$5–10 Million	44/56	2.8	8.9
$10–25 Million	44/56	3.2	9.5
$25–50 Million	44/56	3.7	9.8
$50–100 Million	47/53	4.0	10.7
$100–250 Million	46/54	4.6	11.6
$250 Million–$1 Billion	47/53	4.9	12.3
$1 Billion and over	44/56	6.3	11.9

Source: Federal Trade Commission–Securities and Exchange Commission, *Quarterly Financial Report for Manufacturing Corporations*, 4th Quarter, 1969 (Washington, D.C., 1970), pp. 9, 11, 28–33.

The data in Table 9-2 depict the importance of trading on the equity. Note that in every case the return to equity is considerably higher than the return on sales. Also note the relationship between the size of the differential and the size of the debt-equity ratio; i.e., the larger the ratio of debt to equity, the greater the return to equity. Incidentally, companies with less than $1 million in assets have by far the lowest return on sales, but by employing a greater percent of debt than the larger companies, they are able to earn nearly as much for their shareholders. It should be emphasized, however, that in following this policy they are assuming more risk. These concepts will be more fully discussed later.

TABLE 9-3

RETURN TO EQUITY AND EARNINGS
PER SHARE WHEN VARYING LEVELS
OF DEBT ARE USED
($200,000 capital invested)

	FINANCIAL PLANS			
	A^a	B^b	C^c	D^d
Earnings Before Interest and Taxes	$20,000	$20,000	$20,000	$20,000
Interest on Debt	0	2,500	5,000	7,500
Profit Before Taxes	20,000	17,500	15,000	12,500
Profit After Taxes	10,000	8,750	7,500	6,250
Profit to Shareholder	10,000	8,750	7,500	6,250
Percent Earned on Equity	5.0	5.8	7.5	12.5
Earnings Per Share	$0.50	$0.58	$0.75	$1.25

[a] Plan A—equity capital invested, $200,000; common stock outstanding, 20,000 shares.
[b] Plan B—equity capital invested, $150,000; common stock outstanding, 15,000 shares.
[c] Plan C—equity capital invested, $100,000; common stock outstanding, 10,000 shares.
[d] Plan D—equity capital invested, $50,000; common stock outstanding, 5,000 shares.

It was mentioned above that return on equity and earnings per share are affected by the amount of debt employed. The data contained in Table 9-3 depict this relationship. In the case of financial plan B, the return to equity amounted to 5.8 percent and earnings per share equaled $0.58, a gain of 16 percent over the plan in which no debt capital was employed (plan A). Observe that when larger amounts of debt are used (plans C and D), the gains are even more impressive.

In addition to changing debt levels, changing levels of earnings before interest and taxes (EBIT) also affect return to equity and earnings per share. Figure 9-1 shows what occurs when EBIT is varied. The student should note carefully the changes that take place, for they are very significant and serve as the basis for several financial principles. First, as long as EBIT equals $10,000, it does not matter to management which financial plan (capital mix) is adopted, since return on equity and earnings per share are the same for each of the four plans[1]. However, management would certainly have a preference if EBIT ex-

---

[1] The indifference point is always at the EBIT level at which earnings per share or return to equity are the same regardless of the debt–equity combination. If either the total volume of funds employed or the interest rate on debt capital is changed, the indifference point is also changed. The point of indifference can be found by solving the following formula:

$$\frac{X - B}{S_1} = \frac{X}{S_2}$$

where X = indifference point
         S_1 = number of common shares outstanding when both debt and equity are used
         S_2 = number of common shares outstanding when only equity capital is used
         B = bond interest, in dollars

ceeded or fell below $10,000. That is to say, if management were assured that EBIT would be permanently above $10,000 it would always choose plan D, since it produces the greatest gains to equity and earnings per share. To illustrate, while EBIT increased four times from $10,000 to $40,000, return to equity and earnings per share rose 13 times. In the case of plans B and C, earnings per share and return to equity increased only four and seven times, respectively. It should also be noted that although the opportunity for gain is greatest under financial plan D when EBIT is rising, the opportunity for loss is greatest when EBIT is declining. For example, when EBIT fell to zero, shareholders under plan D lost $0.75 per share, but losses would have amounted to only $0.125 and $0.25 had plans B or C, respectively, been used. Herein lies the disadvantage of trading on the equity. That is to say, trading on the equity increases the degree to which earnings on equity fluctuate. When EBIT rises, the rate of return on equity increases at a rate faster than the growth in EBIT, but the opposite occurs when EBIT is falling. When no debt is used, return to equity moves proportionately to changes in EBIT (see Figure 9-1).

It should be emphasized that only firms with particular characteristics should employ debt to any degree. As a general rule, only those firms whose earnings are reasonably stable can afford the luxury of financial leverage. At one time in our economic development, it was safe to assume that all firms in certain industries could successfully "trade on their equity." For example, all firms that were classified as utilities could follow the practice without fear of financial embarrassment. On the other hand, firms that were classified as industrials were not supposed to employ debt in large volume, since it was presumed that earnings in these companies were highly volatile. Although the author will not argue with this generalization, it should be pointed out that financial managers who use this basis to determine whether to trade on their equity will not be practicing sound financial management. To determine accurately whether such a policy can be followed successfully requires an examination of the characteristics that cause earnings to fluctuate. If these characteristics are present, then care

---

Solving the problem above in which different levels of debt are used, we have:

$$X \times 10,000 = X \times 20,000 - \$5,000 \times \$20,000$$

$$10,000 = 20,000 - \frac{\$5,000 \times \$20,000}{X}$$

$$20,000 - 10,000 = \frac{\$5,000 \times \$20,000}{X}$$

$$X = \frac{\$5,000 \times \$20,000}{20,000 - 10,000}$$

$$X = \frac{\$100,000}{10,000}$$

$$X = \$10,000$$

earnings per share = $0.25

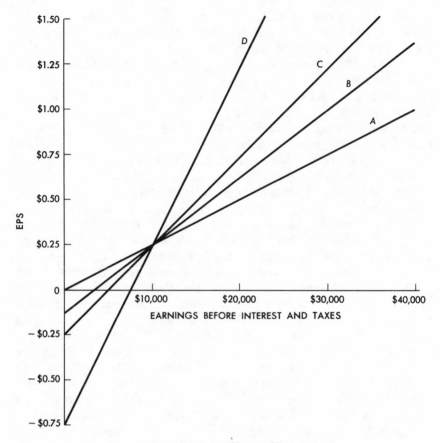

FIGURE 9-1 Indifference Chart

should be followed in determining the volume of debt that will be employed in the capital structure.

Cost of Debt Capital

The cost of capital is a very important aspect of financial management, since many financial managers use it as the basis for accepting or rejecting investment projects. Since the various costs of capital were discussed in Chapter 5, it is unnecessary to examine them here. Nevertheless, it should be remembered that debt is cheaper than equity capital not only because of the relative absence of risk from the viewpoint of the investor when compared to equity capital, but also because interest charges are a tax-deductible expense. Under the present income law, corporations pay a 22 percent tax on the first $25,000 of income and 48 percent on all income in excess of this figure. Since interest expense is deductible, the effective cost of debt capital is reduced by the amount of the firm's tax rate. To illustrate, if a firm's income is $25,000 or less, the cost of debt is reduced by 22 percent; debt capital with an interest rate of 6 percent actually costs the firm 4.68 percent. (For purposes of simplicity, all other "costs" are ignored and the tax rate is assumed to be 50 percent.)

TABLE 9-4

EFFECT OF USING DEBT CAPITAL

	Amount	Cost (percent)	After-Tax Cost (percent)	Ratio (percent)	Average Weighted Cost (percent)
			SITUATION A		
Debt Capital	$25,000	6	3	50	1.5
Equity Capital	$25,000	6	6	50	3.0
Weighted Average Cost					4.5
			SITUATION B		
Equity Capital	$50,000	6	6	100	6
Weighted Average Cost					6

The net effect of a lower cost of debt capital is to reduce the average cost of capital, thus allowing the firm to accept projects with lower "rates of return" or raise the per share earnings (see Table 9-4). The total amount of invested capital in both situations is $50,000, yet the weighted average cost of capital in situation A is 4.5 percent and the weighted average cost in situation B is 6 percent.

Nonfinancial Reasons for Debt

Several nonfinancial reasons explain the use of debt rather than equity capital; the chief of these are: (1) debt may be the only source available regardless of cost; (2) debt does not disturb the voting position of existing shareholders; and (3) debt instruments provide flexibility that may not be possible when equity securities are employed.

There are times during the life cycle of many firms when additional equity funds are not available at reasonable costs; but the same firms may have assets that would serve as security for either long- or short-term credit. In such cases, it is advantageous for the firm to accept the more "risky" funds, since these funds would be considerably less expensive, thus allowing the firm to accept projects with lower "returns."

It should also be remembered that many financial institutions are severely limited or completely prohibited from providing equity funds. Firms wishing to use these institutions as a source of funds must use debt in their capital structure. Finally, institutions that have been created or sponsored by the government to aid small businesses make available, at least in the beginning, only debt capital. For example, the Small Business Administration provides only debt capital. Although Small Business Investment Corporations ultimately take an ownership position, they rarely do so in the beginning. That is, they loan funds through the use of convertible debentures; if the firm succeeds, these securities are converted into common or preferred stock.

Many small and middle-sized firms employ debt capital in order to preserve control. If equity capital is secured through the sale of stock, existing shareholders are required to increase their stockholdings proportionally if they wish to preserve their position. The problem of dilution does not occur if debt securities are issued, since they do not enjoy the same voting privilege as equity securities.

It should be emphasized that the problem of control is of little consequence to "managers" of firms whose stock is widely distributed; however, for the small firm where the stock is concentrated, control is of major consequence, for in many cases the right to be an officer rests with the amount of stock held. Since control cannot be sacrificed, many smaller firms resort to the use of debt rather than equity securities.

Every firm operates in a constantly changing economy; therefore, financial managers must constantly plan for financial flexibility. Flexibility is secured when management is able to contract or expand the amount of capital that is invested in current or fixed assets as the need arises. As the result of the firm's flow of capital, all funds invested in either current or fixed assets will ultimately be converted into cash. A problem arises when cash cannot be reinvested in profitable projects; that is, if these funds are to remain idle, the rate of return on invested capital will decline. If the firm is able to return the "excess" capital to original investors, the rate of return is unaffected. If a certain portion of debt is used in the firm's financial mix, management can reduce the excess by repaying the debt obligations.

Debt instruments also provide flexibility by allowing management to take advantage of changing "costs" of capital. For example, suppose the market for equity securities is weak; in this case, management can use short- or intermediate-term debt to finance the firm's assets requirements and replace the debt either with retained earnings or from the proceeds of stock sold when the market rights itself.

Disadvantages of Debt

There is definitely more risk associated with debt than equity capital. This is primarily because interest and principal payments are fixed charges. Of course risk is greatest in businesses whose earnings tend to fluctuate widely; nevertheless, there is a certain degree of risk even in industries whose earnings are relatively stable, since no firm enjoys a demand that is completely inelastic.

Lenders of debt funds usually prescribe more severe restrictions than suppliers of equity capital because of the fixed nature of the debt. Given the dynamic nature of our economy, future conditions may be such that contract provisions at one time considered quite flexible may become so restrictive that the firm's future is threatened. Moreover, there is no certainty that the funds used to repay the debt obligation will have the same characteristics. For example, "dear" money may be required to repay a debt that produced "cheap" funds.

In summary, it is the writer's opinion that the use of debt funds necessarily depends upon the stability of the individual firm's earnings, level of earnings, and the attitude of management toward risk.

Finally, it is also my opinion that under no circumstances should the amount of debt used correspond to some magical debt-equity ratio that has been computed for an industry or suggested by some "authority"; rather, the amount of debt employed should be directly related to risk.

10

Capital Structure

Determination

In a recent study conducted by the National Industrial Conference Board, it was concluded that "the factor mentioned more often than any other as having a significant effect on corporate financial policy is the need to maintain a proper balance between borrowed funds and shareholder equity as components of a company's capitalization."[1] The maintenance of a proper debt-equity ratio is of major concern today, as indeed it has been since the very beginning. For example, Gerstenberg discussed this problem at great lengths in his 1924 edition of *Financial Organization and Management.* Almost every writer on finance has paid particular attention to this subject. Since it continues to be important, we too will focus considerable attention on the matter.

CAPITAL STRUCTURE

To avoid confusion, capital structure is defined here as including not only long-term obligations and equity capital but also short-term obligations. As I will explain in greater detail later, one of the primary reasons for using debt is to increase the earnings on equity capital. Although the use of debt in most cases increases the rate of return on equity capital, it also increases the financial risk of the firm. That is to say, the use of debt (leverage) increases the possibility of

---

[1] Jeremy Bacon and Francis J. Walsh, Jr., *Duties and Problems of Chief Financial Executives*, National Industrial Conference Board, 1968, p. 20.

insolvency as well as the variability in the earnings available to equity. A large majority of business firms are perfectly capable of assuming a certain amount of risk, and they are interested in employing a level of debt commensurate with their ability to assume risk. If this level is exceeded, it is generally believed that investors will reduce the price they are willing to pay for both debt and equity securities. Should this occur, not only is the firm's total valuation adversely affected but its cost of capital is similarly influenced. Briefly stated, then, an optimum capital structure is one that maximizes the market valuation of the firm's securities in order to minimize the cost of its capital.

THEORIES OF CAPITAL STRUCTURE

There have been several major contributors to a theory of capital structure. Among the more important are Durand, Modigliani and Miller, Donaldson, Solomon, and Schwartz. The following is a brief description of the two opposing concepts. The so-called traditional theory states that, up to a certain point, debt added to the capital structure will cause the market value of the firm to rise and the cost of capital to decline; however, after the optimum point has been reached, any additional debt will cause the market value to decrease and the cost of capital to increase. The second approach states that the cost of capital is unaffected by the amount of debt employed. One of the foremost advocates of the former concept is Ezra Solomon; the latter is defended by Modigliani and Miller.

Traditional Theory

Considerable differences exist among the followers of the traditional school, but all are in substantial agreement that the judicious use of debt will increase the value of the firm and reduce the cost of capital. The optimum structure is the point at which the value of the firm is highest and the cost of capital is at its lowest.

Solomon in his interpretation[2] of the traditional view concludes that there is a definite impact on a firm's total market value as leverage is increased; moreover, this impact can be divided into three distinct stages as leverage is increased from zero.

1. In the first phase the following are discernible: (a) the market value increases as leverage increases; (b) cost of equity (K_e) rises as debt is added but does not rise fast enough to offset the increase in the net earnings rate achieved through the increased use of lower cost debt capital; and (c) cost of debt (K_i) remains constant or rises only slightly. Each of these factors contributes to a condition that permits the market value of the firm to increase and the average weighted cost of capital (K_o) to decline.

---

[2] Ezra Solomon, *The Theory of Financial Management* (New York: Columbia University Press, 1963), pp. 93-98.

2. In the second phase, the addition of debt after a certain degree of leverage has been reached will produce only a moderate increase in market value. As a consequence, K_o remains relatively constant.

3. Finally, the addition of debt to a firm's capital structure after a critical point will cause a decrease in the market value as well as an increase in the K_o; that is to say, both K_i and K_e will rise at an abnormal rate.

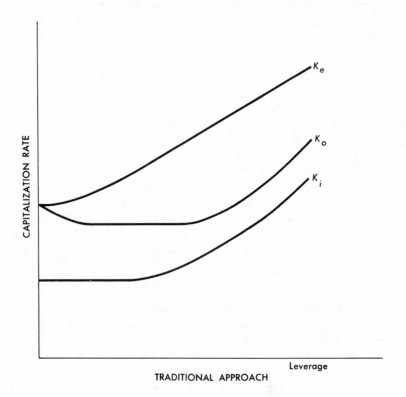

TRADITIONAL APPROACH

FIGURE 10-1 Traditional Approach

These concepts are depicted in Figure 10-1. It may be noted that the cost-of-capital curve K_o is saucer-shaped rather than U-shaped as traditional theory would dictate. In the case of the saucer-shaped curve there is an optimum range extending over the greater range of leverage. This is not true in the case of the U-shaped curve, since there is a precise point at which the market value will decline and K_o will increase. Solomon defines this point as that "precise point where the rising marginal cost of borrowing is equal to the average overall cost of capital."[3]

---

[3]*Ibid.*, p. 97.

Variations on the Traditional Theory

In the main, there is little or no disagreement with the general concept underlying the traditional theory as described by Solomon; however, there is disagreement about the shape of the K_e curve, which, of course, affects the shape of the K_o curve.

The traditional theory suggests that the shape of the K_o curve is primarily if not solely the function of leverage. The author is in substantial disagreement with this concept.[4] The major point of difference is that the slope of the K_e curve, rather than being the function of leverage, is dependent upon: (1) the asset mix combination as reflected in earnings before interest and taxes (EBIT), (2) the relation between K_i and K, and (3) the amount of debt employed in the structure.

There is no doubt in my mind that K is a function of a firm's asset mix, which in turn is an important variable in the determination of capital cost. In other words, K_e as well as K_o is not affected by only the amount of debt that a firm employs; both are also affected by the asset mix.

Let us direct our attention to the impact that the relation between K and K_i has upon cost of capital. It may be concluded that the expected return on equity capital is greatly increased when a firm's cost of debt equity (K_i) is small relative to the return on total capital (K) (see Table 10-1).

TABLE 10-1

GAIN DERIVED FROM THE USE OF
DEBT WHEN K AND K_i DIFFER

Firm	Total Capital	Source of Funds		K	K_i	Percent Return on Equity	Percentage Gain
		Debt	Equity				
A	$200	$100	$100	12%	6%	18	50
B	200	100	100	8	6	10	25
C	200	100	100	6	6	6	0

NOTE: For simplification, debt is not categorized and it is assumed that it has an average cost as shown.

In the example, the return to equity in firm A is much greater than for either B or C, yet all three firms use the same amount of leverage; therefore, the higher return of firm A is the direct result of the differential between K_i and K. It is difficult to believe that an investor would not pay more for an investment in A than in B or C; therefore, it is believed that the K_e curve of firm A will be lower

---

[4] The following ideas are incorporated in Richard H. Pettway and Ernest W. Walker, "Asset Mix, Cost of Capital, and Capital Structure," *The Southern Journal of Business*, April 1968.

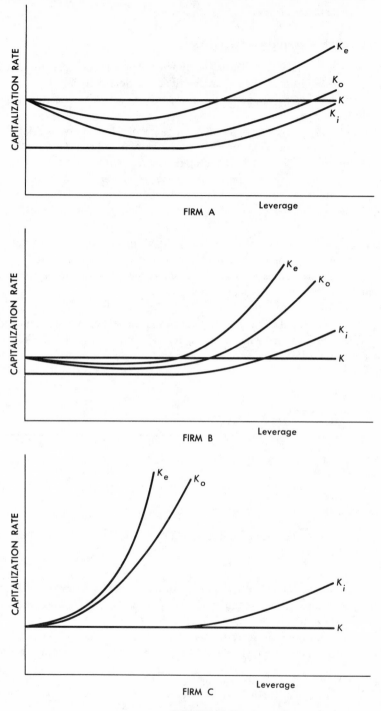

FIRM A

FIRM B

FIRM C

FIGURE 10-2

than the curve for either firm B or firm C. Also, the K_o curve of firm A will be lower than in either firm B or C (see Figure 10-2).

It is both interesting and important to note that at each level of debt the return to equity capital is greater in firm A than in either of the other two, (see Table 10-2). For example, firm A's return to equity was 2.22 percent higher than that of B and 6.67 percent greater than that of C when debt amounted to only 10 percent of total capital. Note that there was a gain of 5.33 percent in return to firm A when debt was increased from 10 percent to 50 percent; but there was a gain of only 3.55 percent in B when debt was increased to 50 percent, and there was no gain for C. The significance of this is that shareholders in companies with the greatest differential between K and the cost of debt (K_i) can expect to gain more for each additional unit of debt that is added than can shareholders in companies whose differential is smaller. Here we assume that K is larger because of a more effective asset mix.

TABLE 10-2

RELATION OF DEBT–EQUITY AND
SPREAD BETWEEN K AND K_i TO
RETURN ON EQUITY[a]

TOTAL CAPITAL	DEBT–EQUITY RATIO	EBIT			PERCENT RETURN ON EQUITY		
		A	B	C	A	B	C
$200	10/90	$24	$20	$12	12.67	10.45	6.00
200	20/80	24	20	12	13.50	11.00	6.00
200	30/70	24	20	12	14.57	11.72	6.00
200	40/60	24	20	12	16.00	12.67	6.00
200	50/50	24	20	12	18.00	14.00	6.00

[a]Taxes are not considered.

It is also important to note that should the differential $(K - K_i)$ decrease as a result of a decline in K, the resultant loss would be less in firm A than in firms B or C (see Table 10-3). In other words, from a standpoint of potential loss, there is less risk in a firm with a large differential between K and K_i than in one with a small differential. Since stockholders in a company with a large differential can expect to gain more from each additional unit of debt employed in the financing process as well as to assume less risk in the event that K declines, they are willing to pay a relatively larger price for the stock. This being true, the weighted cost of capital will decline more than it would in a firm with a smaller differential between K and K_i as debt is added to the structure.

Another important aspect is that, according to the foregoing logic, both K_e and K_o will rise after the optimum has been reached, but the rate of increase will be smaller for the company with the greatest differential between K and K_i and more rapid for a company with a smaller differential (see Tables 10-2 and 10-3 and Figure 10-1).

TABLE 10-3

EFFECT ON RETURN ON EQUITY
WHEN K DECLINES

DEBT–EQUITY RATIO	PERCENT RETURN ON EQUITY			PERCENT RETURN ON EQUITY			PERCENT LOSS		
	$A, K =$ 12%	$B, K =$ 10%	$C, K =$ 6%	$A, K =$ 10%	$B, K =$ 8%	$C, K =$ 4%	$A, \%$	$B, \%$	$C, \%$
10/90	12.67	10.45	6.00	10.45	8.22	3.78	17.5	21.3	37.0
20/80	13.50	11.00	6.00	11.00	8.50	3.50	18.5	22.7	41.7
30/70	14.57	11.72	6.00	11.72	8.86	3.14	19.6	24.4	47.7
40/60	16.00	12.67	6.00	12.67	9.33	3.00	20.8	26.4	50.0
50/50	18.00	14.00	6.00	14.00	10.00	2.00	22.2	28.6	66.7

The conclusion is that a change in K has as great an impact on both K_e and K_o as a change in leverage. Therefore, the maximum advantage is achieved when management is able to increase K through an improved asset mix or by assuming more business risk and using the correct amount of leverage.

Modigliani-Miller Position

Modigliani and Miller represent by far the most sophisticated support for the thesis that the total market value of the firm and the cost of capital are independent (exclusive of tax considerations) of the capital structure. If their thesis is accepted, it would seem that no capital structure is inherently more desirable than any other.[5] Their approach begins with the suppositions that (1) all firms are composed of equity capital; (2) they are divided into "equivalent return classes" with every firm in each class susceptible to the same degree of business risk; (3) the return on the shares outstanding of firms in a class is proportional to the return on the shares issued by any other firm in the class, so that the securities of each firm in the "equivalent return classes" are perfectly substitutable in the market; and (4) information about the market place is perfect and all investors are presumed to act rationally, thus creating a perfect market.

Under the assumption held by Modigliani and Miller, firms are not perfect substitutes when debt is introduced in the capital structure. Moreover, they contend that return to owners can be increased through the use of debt, but the increased returns are subject to more risk since there is an increased dispersion of the income. As a consequence, firms with different debt-equity ratios are no longer perfect substitutes.

---

[5] The description given here was taken principally from the following:

F. Modigliani and M. A. Miller, "The Cost of Capital, Corporation Finance, and the Theory of Investment," *American Economic Review*, Vol. 48 (June 1958), 261-97.

A. Barges, *The Effect of Capital Structure on the Cost of Capital* (Englewood Cliffs, N.J.: Prentice-Hall, Inc., 1963), pp. 7-18, 77-90, 100-113.

J. Fred Weston, "A Test of Cost of Capital Propositions," *The Southern Economic Journal*, Vol. 30 (October 1963), 105-12.

The following propositions outline the Modigliani-Miller argument about the relation of capital structure to the cost of capital and the market value of the firm.

1. The cost of capital and the market value of a firm are independent of its capital structure. The cost of capital is equal to the capitalization rate of a pure equity stream of income for its class, and the market value is ascertained by capitalizing its expected return at the appropriate discount rate for its class.

2. The second proposition, little more than a restatement of the first, maintains that the expected yield on a share of stock (K_e) is equal to the appropriate capitalization rate for a pure equity stream for that class, plus a premium, related to financial risk, which equals the debt-equity ratio times the spread between the capitalization rate (K_e) and yield on debt (K_i). Stated differently, the impact that a smaller K_e would have on cost of capital (K_o) is offset by an increase in K_e.

3. The cut-off point for investment in the firm is always the capitalization rate, which is unaffected by the types of securities used to finance the investment.

The theoretical validity of these propositions is difficult, if not impossible, to counter; however, they have been attacked by numerous authorities. Some of the criticisms are much more sophisticated and comprehensive than others, but all seem to attack the perfect market assumption and the arbitrage argument.

Modigliani and Miller argue that, through personal arbitrage, investors would quickly eliminate any inequalities between the value of levered firms and the value of unlevered firms in the same risk class. The basic argument here is that individuals (arbitragers), through the use of personal leverage, can alter corporate leverage. This argument cannot be supported in a practical world, for it is extremely doubtful that personal investors would substitute personal leverage for corporate leverage, since they do not have the same risk characteristics. The writer believes that the criticisms lodged against Modigliani and Miller's thesis are valid, thus limiting its use in an actual situation. Nevertheless, the propositions as well as their criticisms should be carefully studied, since they will serve as an aid in understanding capital structure theory.

OTHER APPROACHES USED TO DETERMINE THE OPTIMUM CAPITAL STRUCTURE

In addition to the two extreme viewpoints regarding the effect of leverage on cost of capital and market value of the firm, two additional concepts are useful in the formulation of an optimum capital structure. The first of these deals with a firm's ability to maintain adequate cash to meet future fixed charges such as interest payments, lease charges, repayment of principal on debt, and preferred stock dividends. To evaluate this ability, management must relate the future distribution of the firm's cash flows to future fixed charges. Obviously, management must ascertain future distribution of its cash flows in order to establish this relationship, since the information will serve as a guide to the amount of debt that may be employed.

Gordon Donaldson is the foremost advocate of this concept.[6] He establishes a refinement of the concept by suggesting that cash flows should be examined under the most adverse conditions. To determine debt capacity, management would compare these flows with the cash required to meet the firm's fixed charges at each level of debt. If there is no probability of being out of cash, the firm is said to have unused debt capacity. If, however, there is a probability that future cash flows will not meet the fixed charges during adverse periods (according to Donaldson, a recession), management must decide whether it wants to accept the risk involved; if not, debt must be reduced.

Another method used in determining the proper capital structure is suggested by John F. Childs.[7] He states that the following six determinants should serve as a guide in determining the level of debt that a firm can afford: borrowing reserve, financial insurance, cost of capital, leverage, tax savings, and pools of capital. Although each determinant must be considered, Childs thinks the first three are the most important; that is, debt should not be used in an amount that will (1) destroy the firm's reserve to borrow, (2) eliminate financial insurance, or (3) cause cost of capital to increase. Incidentally, Childs is in favor of a conservative debt policy so that the rating agencies will rate a firm's debt AAA or AA. Like all other financial authorities, Childs believes that the nature of the business and its inherent risks affect the firm's ability to carry debt; as a consequence, management must measure the risk associated with the firm and relate it to the amount of debt that will be employed. Otherwise, the credit rating of the firm will be affected.

Childs's approach in determining the optimum capital structure differs from that of the traditionalists, but both locate the optimum point where the cost of capital is at its minimum and the value of the firm's securities is at its highest.

---

[6]Gordon Donaldson, "New Framework for Corporate Debt Policy," *Harvard Business Review*, March-April 1962, pp. 117-31.

[7]John F. Childs, *Long Term Financing* (Englewood Cliffs, N.J.: Prentice-Hall, Inc., 1961), pp. 7-37.

11

Income Taxes
and Financial Planning

Economists have classified the costs of doing business as wages, interest, rent, and profits, but businessmen view costs from a much narrower viewpoint. For example, they do not regard profits as a cost, and in some cases they look upon income taxes as a true cost of doing business. Taxes do not have the same characteristics as other costs; for example, they are not paid unless the firm realizes a net income. Nevertheless, when an income is realized, the business is called upon to pay a tax before the owners receive a return on their investment. Since taxes are paid on all reported profits, management should take them into consideration in much the same way as it does other costs, seeking ways and means of reducing them in order to increase the profits available to the owners of the business.

. This discussion does not in any way attempt to criticize the income tax, nor is it concerned with the justification of income taxes. The primary purpose is to discuss ways and means of minimizing the tax bill and to relate such savings to the concept of tax planning. Tax planning is essential if management is to realize its greatest potential, because taxes influence asset procurement policies, capital procurement policies, payout policies, type of legal organization, and cost of capital.

INFLUENCE OF TAXES ON COST
OF CAPITAL

Recent literature on cost of capital indicates that this is one of the most important aspects of financial planning, primarily because of its influence on decisions to invest in fixed assets. For example, investments in fixed assets are not recommended unless the return exceeds the firm's cost of capital. Therefore, any forces that influence this cost should be of major concern to management.

Interest charges are considered expenses by the Internal Revenue Service and are deducted from income before taxes are computed. As a consequence, a firm using debt capital in its capital structure has a lower weighted average cost of capital than a firm employing little or no debt capital. The data of two operations shown in Table 11-1 point out this conclusion.

TABLE 11-1

FINANCIAL DATA

COMPANY *A*

Balance Sheet Data		Profit and Loss Data	
Current Assets	$ 525,000	Income	$6,000,000
Fixed Assets	475,000	Total Expenses	5,400,000
Total	$1,000,000	Interest	24,000
		Profit Before Taxes	576,000
Current Liabilities	$ 200,000	Taxes	269,980
Long-Term Debt	200,000	Profit After Taxes	306,020
Capital Stock	600,000		
Total	$1,000,000		

Number of Shares Outstanding ($10 par)	60,000
Market Value Per Share	$51.00
Present Cost of Equity Capital	10%
Earnings Per Share	$5.10
Weighted Average Cost of Capital	7.70%
Tax Rate	46.9
Interest (short- and long-term rate)	8%

COMPANY *B*

Balance Sheet Data		Profit and Loss Data	
Current Assets	$ 525,000	Income	$6,000,000
Fixed Assets	475,000	Total Expenses	5,400,000
Total	$1,000,000	Interest	0
		Profit Before Taxes	600,000
Current Liabilities	$ 200,000	Taxes	281,500
Long-Term Debt	0	Profit After Taxes	318,500
Capital Stock	800,000		
Total	$1,000,000		

Number of Shares Outstanding ($10 par)	80,000
Earnings Per Share	$3.98
Market Value Per Share	$39.75
Present Cost of Equity Capital	10%
Weighted Average Cost of Capital	8.85
Tax Rate	46.9
Interest (short- and long-term rate)	8%

We may observe that the weighted average cost of capital of company A is 7.70 percent, whereas in company B it is 8.85 percent. This lower cost is the direct result of using debt capital; for example, since interest is deductible, the cost of debt capital in company A is reduced by 3.75 percent (46.9 percent of 8 percent) to an effective rate of 4.25 percent, rather than the original 8 percent. This differential is in direct relation to the firm's tax rate; that is to say, the higher the tax rate, the lower the cost of debt capital. To develop this point more thoroughly, let us examine the current tax rate structure.

The corporate tax rates for 1963, the year before the rates were changed, for 1970, and the effective tax rates at various levels of income are shown in Table 11-2. An examination of these data reveals several very interesting facts regarding the effect of taxes on the cost of debt capital. First, the corporation reporting an income of $25,000 or less pays substantially lower taxes than the firm with a higher reported income; for example, in 1970 the firm reporting $25,000 pays a tax of 22 percent per $1 of taxable income, and the firm with an income of $50,000 pays 35 percent on each $1 of income.

TABLE 11-2

EFFECTIVE TAX RATES

	Prior to 1964 (percent)	1964 (percent)	1970 (percent)
Normal Tax[a]	30	22	22
Surtax	22	28	26
	52	50	48

Firm	Reported Income	1963 Rate (percent)	1970 Rate (percent)
A	$ 25,000	30.00	22.00
B	50,000	41.00	35.00
C	100,000	46.50	41.50
D	200,000	49.25	44.75
E	400,000	50.50	46.37

[a]Generally, a $25,000 exemption is allowed for surtax; therefore, the total tax applies to income in excess of $25,000.

Second, small corporations received a greater tax reduction in 1964 than large corporations. To illustrate, a firm reporting an income of $25,000 or less received a percentage reduction of 8 percent (30 percent to 22 percent), whereas a firm whose income is $400,000 received a reduction of only 2.25 percent.

Third, as pointed out above, since interest is deductible as an expense, the effective cost of debt capital is reduced by the amount of the tax rate. This means that when corporations received a tax reduction the actual cost of capital increased. This is borne out by the data included in Tables 11-3 and 11-4. Note

TABLE 11-3

EFFECT OF TAX ON
COST OF DEBT CAPITAL

Firm	Interest Rate (percent)	EFFECTIVE TAX RATE 1963 (percent)	1970 (percent)	NET COST AFTER TAX 1963 (percent)	1970 (percent
A	8.0	30.00	22.00	5.60	6.24
B	8.0	41.00	35.00	4.72	5.20
C	8.0	46.50	41.50	4.28	4.68
D	8.0	49.25	44.75	4.06	4.42
E	8.0	50.50	46.37	3.96	4.29

in Table 11-3 that firm A paid a higher effective rate for debt capital in 1970 than in 1963. For example, debt capital with an interest rate of 8 percent cost the firm 6.24 percent in 1970 as compared to 5.60 percent in 1963. The increase in the cost of debt capital also causes the weighted average cost of capital to increase (see Table 11-4.)

TABLE 11-4

EFFECT OF INCREASED TAX RATE
ON AVERAGE WEIGHTED COST OF CAPITAL

Firm	Debt-Equity Ratio	COST OF CAPITAL, 1963 Equity[a]	Debt (percent)	Weighted (percent)	COST OF CAPITAL, 1970 Equity[a]	Debt (percent)	Weighted (percent)
A	30/70	7.0	1.68	8.68	7.0	1.87	8.87
B	30/70	7.0	1.42	8.42	7.0	1.56	8.56
C	30/70	7.0	1.28	8.28	7.0	1.40	8.40
D	30/70	7.0	1.22	8.22	7.0	1.33	8.33
E	30/70	7.0	1.19	8.19	7.0	1.29	8.29

[a]Equity cost presumed to be 10 percent.
    Effective cost of debt capital computed from effective tax rates when income for the several companies amounted to $25,000, $50,000, $100,000, $200,000, and $400,000.

An increase in the cost of capital has three important effects on a firm's operation. First, the higher cost of capital reduces the profitability of each investment by the amount of the increase—compare costs of capital in 1963 with those in 1970. Second, smaller companies experienced the greatest loss in profitability because they realized the greatest tax reduction. This assumes that the capital structure is identical in both the large and small companies. Finally, the firm employing the largest amount of debt, relatively, experiences the greatest impact from the reduced tax rate; that is, its cost of capital experiences the greatest increase. The effect that the higher cost of capital will have in the future is difficult to determine, particularly since many firms do not base their investment decision entirely on the cost of capital.

EFFECT OF LEGAL STRUCTURE
ON TAX LIABILITY

The present tax laws allow incorporated businesses to be taxed as unincorporated organizations, provided, of course, they can qualify. Why should one type of organization want to be taxed as another? The obvious answer is to save tax dollars or to gain additional advantages for the taxes they are already paying. The following are conditions that the corporation must satisfy in order to qualify for the optional tax treatment.

1. The corporation must be a domestic corporation.
2. It may not be a member of an affiliated group, i.e., cannot own 80 percent or more of both voting and nonvoting stock of any domestic corporation.
3. There must be no more than ten shareholders.
4. Shareholders must be individuals or estates, not trusts or partnerships.
5. Shareholders must be U.S. citizens or resident aliens.
6. Stock must be of one class.
7. No more than 80 percent of gross receipts can be derived from sources outside the United States.
8. No more than 20 percent of gross receipts can be derived from royalties, rents, dividends, interest, annuities, or sale and exchange of stock and securities.

In making the election, the corporation must file a statement of election and a statement of consent by the firm's shareholders. In the latter case, all shareholders must agree. The election is terminated if one of the following occurs:

1. A new shareholder fails to consent.
2. The corporation and shareholders voluntarily consent to revoke the election.
3. The corporation ceases to be a small business corporation.
4. More than 20 percent of income is "passive investment income."

The effect of Subchapter S is to change the tax-paying status of the corporation; that is, it pays no corporate income tax but passes it on to the shareholders. The corporation's taxable income is computed in the same manner as regular corporation income except that the following are not allowed: (1) dividends-received deductions, (2) deductions for partially tax-exempt interest, (3) deductions for net operating loss carrybacks and carryovers, and (4) deductions for dividends received on certain preferred stock.

The amount of income or loss to be included each year is generally each shareholder's pro rata share of taxable income or net operating loss. Net operating losses, unlike income, are prorated among stockholders based upon the number of days each individual held stock in the company during the taxable year.

There are certain disadvantages associated with a Subchapter S corporation. Generally, the following are considered the most important:

1. There may be unintended disqualification.
2. Distributions in property other than cash result in shareholders' being taxed on the amount in excess of taxable income for the year.
3. Earnings and profits in excess of taxable income result in shareholders' being charged with a dividend on distribution of the excess amount.
4. Different taxable years of the corporation and of shareholders may cause a problem regarding the amount of loss or gain.

As a result of these disadvantages, a relatively small number of eligible corporations have elected to be taxed as partnerships.

It may be wise for a corporation to organize under Section 1244 of the Revenue Code if the endeavor is risky, since original investors are allowed to treat a loss on disposition or on total worthlessness of stock as an ordinary loss. To qualify, the following requirements must be met:

1. The corporation adopted a plan after June 30, 1958, to offer such stock for a period (ending not later than two years after the date such plan was adopted) specified in the plan.
2. The corporation was a small business corporation at the time the plan was adopted.
3. No part of a prior offering of stock was outstanding at the time the plan was adopted.
4. Consideration paid by shareholders is money or property other than stock or securities.
5. No new offering to issue stock is permitted until all original stock is issued under the plan.
6. The corporation at the time of loss must have derived more than 50 percent of its aggregate gross receipts from sources other than royalties, rents, dividends, interest, annuities, and sales or exchanges of stock or securities.

Although the loss in any taxable year is limited to $25,000 on a single return or $50,000 on a joint return, the 1244 corporation has many advantages and very few disadvantages.

EFFECT OF TAXES ON
FINANCIAL POLICY

Taxes affect the formulation of payout policies of all corporations, but they have a greater impact on the dividend policies of smaller corporate organizations. This is because the income of a corporation is taxed at the time it is reported by the corporation and again when it is paid out as cash dividends. Generally, when total income is paid out currently, the tax paid by a corporate organization is higher than that paid by an unincorporated business.

To reduce the tax bill, a corporate organization can retain the funds in the business rather than paying out cash, or, if the firm feels that some form of dividends is necessary, it can pay stock. In either case, the total tax bill is reduced. This is true when stock is issued in lieu of cash, provided the shareholder retains the stock for at least six months.[1]

A word of caution here to the student. If the retained funds are not "needed" by the firm, the firm is subject to a tax on the amount that is not needed but retained. For example, the tax amounts to 27.5 percent on the first $100,000 of unreasonably retained earnings and 38.5 percent on all above $100,000. As a general rule, if the accumulation does not exceed $100,000, the government does not impose a tax on the retained earnings.

Corporations can reduce the taxes of certain shareholders by following a stable dividend policy. The net effect of such a policy is to transfer income from high to lower brackets, thus reducing the amount of total taxes over the long run. Following such a policy also allows the firm to finance its requirements from internal sources rather than depending on the external markets.

Evaluation policies definitely affect the size of the tax bill. First, let us turn our attention to the method of evaluating inventories. If the firm is in a period of rising prices, it is advisable to employ the LIFO (last-in, first-out) method of costing inventory; however, if the firm is entering a period of declining prices, it is advantageous to value the inventory on a FIFO (first-in, first-out) basis. Data contained in Table 11-5 illustrate this concept.

Various methods of evaluating fixed assets also produce varying effects on the amount of taxes that must be paid. Depreciation, although not an out-of-pocket expense, is deductible from current income; therefore, any accelerated method of taking depreciation has the effect of reducing income, thereby lowering taxes during the early years of the asset's life. If all things remain constant, the total tax bill will equate itself, because expenses will decline during the latter part of the asset's life, causing the tax bill to be higher during this period.

The firm that uses an accelerated method of charging off depreciation enjoys a definite advantage over the firm employing the straight-line method. This advantage results because funds received several years from now are not as valuable as those received in the near future. Therefore, the firm should seriously consider the use of such methods as the declining-balance and sum-of-the-years'-digits methods (see Table 11-6). Certain advantages, however, may accrue to the firm that uses the straight-line method rather than an accelerated method. For example, a firm may be in a low tax bracket during the period when income is low (depreciation charges are high) and a high bracket during the years when income is high (depreciation charges are low). In this case the firm would lose the difference between the two rates by using the accelerated method. In taxable years beginning after June, 1972, corporations can use only the straight-line

---

[1] The maximum capital gains tax of corporations has been raised from 25 to 28.7 percent for the taxable year beginning in 1970 and to 30 percent for taxable years beginning in 1971 and thereafter.

TABLE 11-5

FIFO AND LIFO METHODS OF
EVALUATING INVENTORY

		PERIOD OF RISING PRICES		
		FIFO		*LIFO*
Sales (10,000 at $5.00)		$50,000		$50,000
Cost of Sales:				
Opening inventory				
(5,000 at $2.50)	$12,500		$12,500	
Purchases				
(10,000 at $3.50)	+ 35,000		+ 35,000	
	$47,500		$47,500	
Less: Closing Inventory				
FIFO (5,000 at $3.50)	17,500	−30,000		
LIFO (5,000 at $2.50)			12,500	− 35,000
Gross Profit on Sales		$20,000		$15,000
Tax		$ 4,400		$ 3,300

		PERIOD OF DECLINING PRICES		
		FIFO		*LIFO*
Sales (10,000 at $5.00)		$50,000		$50,000
Cost of Sales:				
Opening inventory				
(5,000 at $2.50)	$12,500		$12,500	
Purchases				
(10,000 at $1.50)	+ 15,000		+ 15,000	
	$27,500		$27,500	
Less: Closing Inventory				
FIFO (5,000 at $1.50)	7,500	− 20,000		
LIFO (5,000 at $2.50)			12,500	− 15,000
Gross Profit on Sales		$30,000		$35,000
Tax		$ 8,000		$10,500

TABLE 11-6

PRESENT VALUE OF FUNDS FLOW
RESULTING FROM DIFFERENT
DEPRECIATION METHODS[a]

	DEPRECIATION METHODS		PRESENT VALUE AT 6 PERCENT	
Year	*Sum-of-the-Years'-Digits*	*Straight-Line*	*Sum-of-the-Years'-Digits*	*Straight-Line*
1	$ 5,000	$ 3,000	$ 4,715	$2,829
2	4,000	3,000	3,560	2,670
3	3,000	3,000	2,520	2,520
4	2,000	3,000	1,584	2,376
5	1,000	3,000	747	2,241
			$13,126	$12,636

[a]Asset's original cost, less salvage value, equals $15,000.

method (or other method of ratable deduction over useful life) in figuring earnings and profits. The new rule does not prevent deduction in figuring taxable income of any available accelerated method.

FURTHER WAYS
TO MINIMIZE TAX LOSSES

Under the tax law prior to the Tax Reform Act of 1969, if a corporation transferred property, except money, to a new or formerly inactive 80-percent-owned subsidiary, the transferee's $25,000 surtax exemption could have been disallowed unless it was shown that tax savings was not the major purpose for the firm's creation. Under certain circumstances, multiple corporations could be created and one surtax divided among them, or, if they chose to retain their exemption, each then elected to pay an additional 6 percent on the first $25,000 of its taxable income.

Under the Reform Act of 1969, the election to retain multiple exemptions will be gradually phased out. Beginning in 1975, the group will be limited to one such exemption to be divided equally among the members or shared as they elect under regulations. In the interim, the multiple-surtax election continues, but each exemption above one will be reduced one-sixth each successive year. Thus the extra exemptions will be $20,833 for 1970, $16,667 for 1971, and so on. The group may choose which member is to receive the full $25,000 and which are to be limited to the reduced exemptions, which may not be allocated. If multiple exemptions are elected, the extra 6 percent tax is imposed, but only on income equal to the corporation's exemption.

A corporation may deduct 85 percent of dividends from another corporation. But the deduction is 100 percent in the case of dividends from one member of the affiliated group to another if the group so elected and did not elect multiple surtax exemptions. Under the Tax Reform Act of 1969, an increased dividends-received deduction may be elected even though multiple surtax exemptions are elected; in other words, that restriction has been removed. The increase is phased in over a specified time.

In addition to reducing multiple surtax exemptions, the act also gradually limits related corporations to one $100,000 exemption from accumulated earnings tax.

Prior to the Tax Reform Act of 1969, tax savings could accrue to a company that bought and sold its own stock, since no gain or loss was recognized when a corporation received property or funds in exchange for its stock. This has been changed somewhat in that the corporation will realize gain when it distributes appreciated property in redemption of its own stock. The rule does not apply to dividend distribution without surrender of stock or to distributions in partial or complete liquidation of the corporation. Nor does the rule apply to complete termination of the interest of an at-least-10-percent shareholder, distribution of stock of a 50-percent-or-more subsidiary, distributions under antitrust decree, redemption to pay death taxes, and certain redemptions from private foundations.

Taxes may also be minimized by retiring outstanding bonds. If outstanding bonds are retired with new bonds, the unamortized cost of the old issue plus the cost of retirement is added to the cost of the new bonds amortized over the life of the new bonds. If the outstanding bonds are retired with cash and new bonds are sold, the unamortized cost of the old issue plus the costs of calling in the old bonds are deductible in the year in which the bonds are called.

Reorganization, in the majority of cases, involves the transfer of property, and in most cases any differences in fair market value are taxed; however, gains or losses resulting from exchanges made in connection with reorganization are deferrable provided certain conditions are met by both parties. In order to qualify as a tax-free reorganization, the following conditions must be met:

1. The reorganization must be in accordance with the plan adopted in advance by all parties.
2. The reorganization must be for legitimate business purposes.
3. The parties to the reorganization must retain a continuity of interest in the business after a transfer of the property has taken place.
4. There must be a continuity of the business enterprise.

In addition to meeting these requisites, the reorganization must be classified as one of the following: (1) statutory merger or consolidation, (2) acquisition of another corporation's stock, (3) acquisition of another corporation's property, (4) transfer of assets to another corporation, (5) changes in capitalization, or (6) changes in corporate form.

Besides the six different types of reorganization just mentioned, in which gains and losses are not recognized at the time the reorganization takes place, there are also three divisive types of reorganization in which gains and losses are not recognized at the time of reorganization. These are split-up, split-off, and spin-off. The split-up refers to a situation where a corporation divides itself into two or more separate corporations, whereas the split-off refers to a corporation that exchanges its property for the stock of a new corporation. The spin-off type of reorganization is similar to the split-off except that the shareholders are not required to surrender any of their stock in the original corporation.

The above areas suggest only a few of the many ways in which taxes may be conserved; businesses and businessmen should not hesitate to use every legal means of minimizing their tax bill.

12

Dividend Policies

The owners of unincorporated firms are not concerned with dividend policies, since the earnings of the business are considered to be the personal income of the owners. This is not true of corporate businesses, since the firm earns the income; it does not become the property of the shareholders until the directors pass a resolution declaring a dividend. The factors that directors consider when making the decision to pay out earnings are many and varied; moreover, in many cases each factor varies with changes in the economy. Therefore, not only is dividend policy complicated by variables, but it is dynamic in that it must be changed whenever the economy changes. Before considering the variables that influence payout policies, we must first discuss (1) the types of dividends and the effects that each has on the accounts of the corporation, and (2) the mechanics of dividend payout.

CLASSIFICATION OF DIVIDENDS

Dividends may be classified according to the source from which they are derived, the medium in which they are distributed, and the regularity with which they are paid. Dividends are derived from two sources: income after taxes and capital. The reader will recall from accounting that each corporation periodically determines its income and, more important, that the level of reported profits is influenced by the firm's accounting policies. For example, the level of income is influenced by the way in which (1) depreciation is charged off,[1] (2) inventories are valued, (3) losses are charged off, and (4) intangible assets are valued.

The purpose of this chapter is not to discuss the ways in which accounting practices influence corporate income; the subject is mentioned only because a firm may report a profit and yet actually be operating at a loss. If dividends are paid under such circumstances, the firm's capital may be impaired, and, as will be pointed out later, dividends should not be paid if such a payment impairs the firm's capital.

In addition to paying dividends out of income after taxes, a firm may distribute its capital to its shareholders. Such a classification is important, since taxes are not paid on dividends paid out of capital.

Dividends may also be classified according to the medium in which they are paid. The two most important types of dividends are cash and stock, but dividends may also be distributed in the form of scrip or property.

Generally speaking, when cash dividends are paid, the retained earnings account is reduced by a like amount; however, there are times when cash dividends are paid from paid-in or capital surplus. The student is aware that the cash account and the retained earnings account are two entirely different accounts. As a matter of fact, there may be times when the firm will have sufficient retained earnings to declare dividends but insufficient cash to pay dividends and at the same time meet the firm's other obligations. In such a case, the firm may borrow the necessary cash to pay the dividend. The important thing to remember is that if the liability created by borrowing will cause insolvency, management should not pay dividends.

If a firm wishes to finance its assets from internal sources and still pay a dividend, it may distribute stock rather than cash. When stock is used, it is distributed on a pro rata basis. For example, South Jersey National Bank paid a 5 percent stock dividend in 1970. In this case, shareholders who held common stock received a share of common stock for each 20 shares owned.

A stock dividend is usually charged against retained earnings; that is to say, the retained earnings account is capitalized by the amount of the stock dividend. Incidentally, if the firm does not have sufficient shares of stock authorized and unissued to meet the stock dividend requirement, shareholders must authorize additional shares before a declaration can be made. Like cash dividends, stock dividends are usually charged to the paid-in or capital surplus account. We should point out, however, that any stock dividend distributed from paid-in surplus or unrealized appreciation requires that a full disclosure of the sources be made to the stockholders.

The net effects of a stock dividend are to increase the number of outstanding shares and to reduce the book and market values of the outstanding stock. These

---

[1] Until June, 1972, corporations will be allowed to use any acceptable method in figuring earnings and profits, but after this date only the straight-line method (or other ratable deduction over useful life) may be used.

results may be desirable, particularly when the price of the stock is considered to be "high." In addition, a stock dividend tends to broaden the ownership base, since it is presumed that some shareholders will sell some of their stock in order to obtain cash.

The most obvious effect of a stock dividend is that it allows firms to conserve cash. This is particularly significant to growth companies, since as a general rule they are constantly short of cash. Not only does it allow the firm to conserve cash, but it permits the firm to secure funds for expansion purposes from internal rather than external sources. In many instances, internal financing is both cheaper and more convenient than raising funds from external sources.

MECHANICS OF
DIVIDEND DISTRIBUTION

Undeclared dividends, unlike interest payments, are not liabilities of the corporation. In fact, it is for this reason that stocks are classified as riskless from the corporation's point of view. In order for a dividend to become a liability, it is necessary for the board of directors to adopt a resolution declaring that a dividend will be paid to stockholders of a certain record date. Such a resolution normally includes the (1) date of record, (2) rate or amount to be paid, (3) class or classes of shareholders to which the dividend will be paid, (4) date when the dividend will be paid, and (5) medium by which the dividend will be paid.

The following announcement appeared in the June 18, 1970, edition of *The Wall Street Journal*:

Gleason Works declared a quarterly dividend of 10½ cents, payable July 31 to holders of record July 10. This is equivalent to 21 cents on shares prior to a two-for-one split. The maker of production equipment for power transmissions paid 19 cents before the split.

An examination of the announcement reveals that each of the items listed above is included in the action of the board of directors of Gleason Works. First, the board authorized a quarterly divident of 10½ cents to be paid to the owners of common stock. Second, only those shareholders whose names appeared on the record books as of July 10, 1970, were entitled to receive the dividend. This means that the stock went ex-dividend as of that date; in other words, persons who purchased stock after that date were not entitled to receive this particular dividend. As a general rule, the price of the stock will decline approximately the amount of the dividend one day following the ex-dividend date. Third, the announcement stated that dividends would be paid on July 31, 1970. (The owners of common stock became general creditors of the company in the amount of their dividends as of the date of the resolution, but these claims were not collectible until July 31.) Fourth, the board declared that the dividend would be paid in cash rather than in stock, scrip, or some other medium. Finally, the announcement also revealed that the firm increased its regular quarterly dividend the equivalent of 2 cents per share.

Several generalizations may be made with respect to the mechanics of paying dividends. First, most large companies have a transfer agent to prepare the list of shareholders who will receive dividends. The information regarding the date of record is derived directly from the resolution, and the transfer agent may issue the dividend check directly to the shareholder. If the disbursing agent does not require the firm to deposit the funds in advance, the agent will pay the dividends and the amount paid will become a liability of the firm.

Second, dividends on common stock are usually paid quarterly rather than annually. For example, 36 of the 41 companies reporting dividends in *The Wall Street Journal* of June 18, 1970, paid quarterly dividends. Finally, the majority of firms listed on the New York Stock Exchange pay cash rather than stock dividends.

DIVIDEND POLICY

A firm's dividend policy incorporates all aspects of payout, such as percentage of payout, stability of dividends, timing of dividend payments, changes in the levels of payout, payment of extra dividends, and methods of payment. Formulating a policy that covers each of these important areas requires careful consideration not only of the needs of the business enterprise but of the requirements of the shareholders as well. Factors that should be considered may logically be divided into the following categories: (1) economic and moral considerations, (2) factors affecting the relative welfare of the firm, and (3) factors affecting the welfare of the shareholders.

Economic and Moral Considerations

Several economic and moral arguments have been advanced opposing management's right to retain the profits of the corporate enterprise. No effort is made here to set forth all these arguments, but students will be better informed if a few of the better-known ones are discussed.

The first argument is economic in nature and states generally that there is a distinct possibility that retained earnings result in a maldistribution of resources because management often invests them unwisely. That is to say, managers should distribute all earnings in the form of cash dividends unless they can invest the funds more advantageously than the shareholders could. A weakness of this argument is the assumption that, on the average, stockholders have the necessary training and experience to consistently seek out advantageous investments and that they would, therefore, prevent a maldistribution of resources. It is true that some firms retain funds when they have no legitimate investment proposals available to them, and in such cases managers are hard put to justify their action. To illustrate, Polaroid held 43.2 percent of its total assets in the form of cash and short-term securities in 1969. If the company had paid 50 percent out in the form of dividends, its return on investment would have amounted to 19.8 percent rather than the 14.9 percent it did earn.[2]

A second economic argument is that since large firms rely more heavily on retained earnings to satisfy the majority of their capital requirements, there are fewer obligations available for investment; consequently, individuals and institutional investors are bidding up the prices of existing securities or investing in poorer-quality securities. In either case, economic resources are wasted. Offsetting this argument is the practice of firms retaining large sums of capital of splitting their stock or issuing stock dividends, thus increasing the number of shares available for investment.

One of the better-known moral arguments says in effect that shareholders' rights are deprived when earnings are retained. One answer to this is that most shareholders knew the dividend policies before they made their investment, and they would not have selected the stock of a firm whose policies were in conflict with their investment objectives. Moreover, there is much to be said for the counterargument that a large-scale corporate enterprise is responsible to more than one group—the shareholders; for example, a major corporation is responsible to the public, to labor, and to its customers, to name only a few. To fulfill its obligations to these groups may require that it retain rather than pay out earnings.

The writer feels that there is logic behind these economic and moral arguments and that they should be considered when dividend policy is being formulated. That is, the welfare of the shareholders should definitely be considered when the dividend policy is developed. It should be remembered, however, that occasionally there are differences of opinion between managers and owners regarding the most effective way to maximize the shareholders' welfare. By carefully analyzing the following factors, management can develop a sound dividend policy, capable of recognizing the rights of the majority of the shareholders, but at the same time able to provide funds for legitimate purposes.

Factors Influencing the Welfare of the Firm

Directors cannot pay dividends in violation of the provisions of outstanding debt contracts, charter and bylaws, and state statutes. State laws prevent firms from paying dividends when the firm is insolvent or if insolvency will result from such payment. In addition, the laws dictate the sources from which dividends can be paid; that is, some state laws say that dividends can be paid only out of current or retained earnings, whereas others permit dividends to be paid out of surplus regardless of its source.

The provisions of debt contracts should be carefully examined, since most indentures contain provisions that either prevent the payment of dividends entirely or disallow their payment until certain conditions are met. Needless to say,

---

[2] See Table 16-2, p. 163.

the finance officer should make available to all board members a brief of all contractual provisions that affect dividends in any way.

In addition to contractual provisions, management must recognize and observe any charter or bylaw provision that affects dividends. As a general rule such provisions are not restrictive in nature; rather, they govern such matters as how often dividends are to be paid and the date when they are to be paid.

A second group of factors that influences dividend policy pertains to internal affairs. Each factor must be analyzed in the light of the particular firm involved, since a dividend policy that is effective in one company may not be effective in another. The first and foremost of these factors is the need for fixed and working capital. A firm should have a strong cash position at all times in order to meet its maturing obligations and to finance its working capital (inventories and receivables) requirements. Therefore, adequate funds to meet these requirements should be set aside before dividends are declared. Any firm that weakens its working capital position by paying dividends not only undermines its entire capital structure, but may very well cause creditors and investors to raise the "price" of their funds. In such cases, the interests of existing stockholders are harmed rather than helped.

By and large, investors are interested principally in dividends; however, many investors are perfectly willing to forfeit dividends in the short run provided there is a reasonable chance of receiving a larger return in the future. Companies whose shareholders have this attitude can adopt a policy of financing fixed-capital needs from retained earnings. The student should remember, however, that if future yields' are not higher than current yields, the market price of outstanding stock will experience a downward movement. An example of this was the decline in the price of the stock of Texas Instruments from $256 per share to approximately $90 ($75 after a 25 percent stock dividend) when earnings failed to grow at the rate anticipated by the shareholders.

Tracor, Incorporated, has adhered to a policy of financing much of its expansion (fixed- as well as working-capital requirements) from retained earnings. The firm's dividend policy was formulated in the light of its capital needs. During 1969, the price of its stock reached $60, which represented a price-earnings ratio of 48 to 1. However, if shareholders had not expected earnings to continue to improve, the price would probably have declined to around $18.75 per share, or a 15 to 1 price-earnings ratio, rather than 48 to 1. Moreover, if the firm had not expected to improve its future earnings, it should have discontinued the expansion program, thereby eliminating the need for retained earnings. In that event the firm could have begun paying dividends.[3]

A third factor to be considered when establishing dividend policy is the firm's cost of capital; that is to say, a firm should obtain capital from the

---

[3]In general, this idea adheres to concepts set forth in James E. Walter, "Dividend Policies and Common Stock Prices," *Journal of Finance*, Vol. XI (March 1956), 29-41. The decline in the stock price during 1969 and 1970 did not stem from a change in Tracor's expansion policies, but resulted primarily from the depression in the stock market.

cheapest possible source, since the desirability of the investment proposal is in direct relation to a firm's cost of capital. The lower the cost, the more desirable is the proposal, and vice versa. Many small firms are unable to receive an adequate market price because the stock is not known to the investing public. Furthermore, the cost of flotation is directly related to the size of the issue. Thus unless a firm intends to raise a large sum from the sale of stock, it may find it cheaper to secure the funds from internal sources rather than raising the firm's cost of capital to a point where the proposed investment becomes undesirable.

As a general principle, a firm should not use retained earnings to meet its requirements unless the use of these funds will enhance the present value of the firm's net worth.

Factors Affecting the Welfare of Shareholders

It is difficult, if not impossible, to adopt a dividend policy that will serve the interest of all shareholders, because of the conflict of interest among shareholders. Also, their desires and wishes are sometimes difficult to determine—and those of shareholders of large corporations are particularly hard to ascertain. Recognizing that these problems do exist, directors must necessarily make a policy that will serve the best interest of the owners. To do so requires consideration of several factors of importance to shareholders. Although many variables are important to individual stockholders, two factors affect all shareholders—income taxes and current income requirements.

Unquestionably the tax positions of shareholders of small or closely held corporations influence dividend policy. That is, if the owners are in high income-tax brackets, they will request that directors follow a policy of paying out only a small percentage of earnings. Such a policy allows them to take their earnings out in the form of capital gains, which, of course, are taxed at a lower rate. On the other hand, if the owners' preference is for current income rather than tax savings, their request will be for a high payout. Also, if the firm prospers, there is a good possibility that these same owners' desires and needs may shift and they will request a change in dividend policy. In the case of small or closely held companies, directors are able to assess the wishes of the owners, and as long as these preferences are not in conflict with sound financial practices, directors will adhere to them when formulating dividend policy.

Directors of large corporations cannot ascertain the wishes of their shareholders, and even if they could, there would not be one common need. Therefore, they must select the dividend policy that serves the needs of the corporation, since it is believed that this is the best way to serve the interest of all owners. In general, three philosophies guide directors of large corporations in making dividend policies.

First, corporate directors adopt a high-payout policy with the idea that such a policy will attract shareholders whose primary need is current income. They believe that when the firm needs additional capital, it can be secured by selling new issues of stock to existing shareholders as well as to new stockholders whose needs are similar to those of the old. The dividend policy of the American Telephone & Telegraph Company follows this basic concept.

Some corporations adhere to the philosophy that many shareholders want capital appreciation rather than current income and are willing to forego the latter provided retained earnings are reinvested in projects with a high return. As a result, directors follow the policy of retaining all or a major part of the firm's earnings instead of paying them out in the form of dividends. In order for this type of dividend policy to be successful, a firm must have a good growth potential plus a reasonably good growth record in earnings. IBM and Xerox have this philosophy as a basis for their dividend policies.

Finally, there are companies that compromise between these two positions and follow the policy of paying out approximately 50 to 60 percent of their earnings in the form of cash dividends, in the belief that such a policy will attract the in-between type of investors who want current income but who will accept a smaller amount in order to receive capital appreciation.

Ideally, management should survey the needs and desires of shareholders and use them as a basis for dividend policy, provided this is within the bounds of good financial practice. Of course, in the case of firms for which this is not practical, the next best thing is to adopt dividend policies that match their best interest, and here the primary problem facing directors would be finding a policy that will meet the needs of the business enterprise. Once the policy has been determined and adopted, it should not be changed until the firm's needs have changed.

13

Short-Term
Capital

The subject of capital procurement policies may be approached in several different ways. For example, they may be studied from the standpoint of internal versus external sources and debt versus equity financing, or they may be viewed in respect to the length of time that the capital remains in use by the firm before it is returned to the supplier. The latter method is generally preferred because the approach it represents is familiar to both the supplier and user. From the standpoint of the user, financial managers have specific uses for short-, intermediate-, and long-term capital and develop definite policies in regard to the time the capital is used. Suppliers, on the other hand, tend to specialize in either long- or short-term capital; to illustrate, banks, commercial finance companies, factors, and commercial paper houses specialize in relatively short-term capital.

There are several disadvantages to this approach. Among the more important are these: First, each category tends to merge into the next; that is to say, short-term loans may really be long-term loans because of a prearranged contract between the supplier and user. Second, no clear line of demarcation exists between the various categories. One financial institution may classify all term loans as intermediate-term capital, and yet some may be for a 5-year period and others may have a 10- to 20-year maturity.

IMPORTANCE OF SHORT-TERM CREDIT

Short-term credit plays a vital role in the business process, since all firms regardless of type or size employ this method of financing assets. This impor-

tance is depicted in Table 13-1, which reveals the sources and relative importance of the various types of funds used by all manufacturing corporations
except newspapers. An examination of these data reveals several very interesting
facts. First, funds secured from short-term sources are used to finance approximately 25 percent of all assets. Second, the relative importance of these funds
has undergone little or no change during 1968-1969. Because of these two
characteristics, finance officers are faced with the continuous job of supplying
short-term credit, and more important, they must secure larger amounts each
year. A third point of general interest is that in each of the two years, short-term
debt accounted for approximately 55 percent of the total debt used in the
financing process.

Turning our attention to the relative importance of the various components
of short-term debt, the following facts are discernible. First, trade accounts and
notes payable (trade credit) are by far the most important source of short-term
credit, and their relative importance has remained stable. Second, other current
liabilities (loans from financial institutions other than commercial banks) constitute the next most important source of short-term credit. This may come as a
surprise, since many students think of banks as being the major source of all
short-term capital. Third, short-term loans from banks rank third in importance;
nearly 5 percent of all assets are financed in this manner.

An analysis of the financing habits of firms of various sizes reveals that
smaller firms employ relatively more short-term credit than do larger firms. In
1969, current liabilities accounted for approximately 70 percent of all debt in
manufacturing firms with assets of less than $1 million, but in firms with more
than $1 billion in assets, they amounted to about 52 percent of the total. One
explanation is that many small manufacturing firms have less access to the
capital markets than larger firms; thus they are forced to look to local institutions such as banks for their capital needs.

The size of the trade credit account also allows smaller firms to have a larger
percentage of their debt in current liabilities than larger firms have; in fact, the
relative importance of trade credit decreases as the size of the firm increases.
Obviously, the answer here is that the inventory accounts in smaller firms are
relatively more important than in larger firms. This will be discussed more fully
under the subject of trade credit.

FACTORS INFLUENCING THE USE
OF SHORT-TERM DEBT

Some students and businessmen have erroneously gained the impression that
working capital should be financed with short-term liabilities and fixed assets
should be financed with long-term and intermediate-term capital. A relation does
exist between the amount of current liabilities and the volume of current assets
that a firm maintains, but it should be emphasized that many other factors are
of greater importance in determining the types of capital to be used in the
capital structure.

The first factor of major importance is the variation in the level of assets. Short-run variations in the volume of assets held by a firm result largely from changes in the level of current assets that the firm maintains rather than changes in the volume of fixed assets. This is because fixed assets are determined insofar as possible by the anticipated optimum level of output and are seldom changed, whereas current assets vary with changes in the rate of production and may undergo radical changes in some firms. In addition to changes in production, current asset levels are also influenced by changes or expected changes in the supply of current assets. For example, a firm using large amounts of steel will increase its inventory if the output of steel is expected to be adversely affected in the short run.

As a general rule, temporary changes in the level of current assets should be financed by short-term credit; it follows that changes in production caused by seasonal variations and short-term business cycles should be financed with short-term capital. Changes that are secular in nature should be financed from permanent funds. Although this is theoretically true, it is difficult at times to tell exactly which changes are permanent and which are temporary in nature; consequently, it is wise to finance any changes in current assets with short-term capital until the demand for these funds is deemed to be permanent.

Another factor influencing the use of short-term funds is the nature of interest rates. During the last decade, interest rates experienced considerable movement, and they are expected to vary even more widely in the future, since it is presumed that financial tools will be used to counteract inflationary and deflationary conditions. Therefore, financial officers will be called upon to establish and follow interim financing policies in order to take advantage of the savings that occur in interest rates. To illustrate, suppose the decision to commit capital for expansion purposes is made by the board during the peak of the interest-rate cycle. Although the capital is to be committed for permanent purposes, it should be obtained from short-term sources until interest rates have returned to a more favorable level. When this occurs, long-term funds can be substituted for short-term capital.

The process of interim financing can also be used to supply current assets during periods of growth. In many instances management does not know whether the expansion in output will be temporary or permanent. Until management is satisfied that the increase is permanent, it would be wise to finance the increase from short-term sources.

The interim financing technique can be used effectively to reduce the cost of raising funds from external sources. Because of the cost involved in raising small amounts of long-term funds, a company may choose to use short-term capital for permanent purposes until its requirements are large enough to justify the use of the capital market.

Another factor influencing the source of capital is the costs involved. We should remember that certain types of short-term capital have no cost except under special circumstances; for example, trade credit has no cost except when discounts are ignored or when the supplying firm raises the price of the product.

For this reason, a firm should employ as much trade credit as possible. This recommendation is made because the prices charged for goods are usually the same whether the goods are purchased for cash or credit. It should be remembered that the savings occur only when purchases are paid for by the last day of the discount period; otherwise trade credit can become expensive.

We should also recall that it is cheaper for local and regional firms to employ short-term or intermediate-term capital than long-term funds. The principal reason for this is that the borrower is more likely to be well known to the supplier of short-term funds and may receive a more favorable interest rate, whereas he may not be known in the capital market and will be charged a higher interest rate.

TRADE CREDIT

Trade credit is characteristically different from other forms of short-term credit, primarily because it is not associated with a financial institution. For this reason trade credit is covered in this chapter and all other types are discussed in the following chapter. The relative importance of trade credit is indicated in Table 13-1, and the importance of the dollar volume of trade credit is depicted in Table 13-2. Note that trade credit accounts for approximately 41 percent of all current liabilities used by all manufacturing corporations (except newspapers). The data contained in Table 13-3 are even more significant in that they show the relative importance of trade credit in various sizes of business firms. It is interesting to note that small firms use more trade credit than larger ones. For example, firms with assets of $1 million or less financed 2.33 times more assets with trade credit than firms whose assets exceeded $1 billion. As firms continued to grow in size, trade credit became relatively less important as a source of funds. The use of trade credit by various industries is shown in Table 13-4. An examination of this table shows that trade credit not only is important in the aggregate, but it constitutes the major source of short-term credit for all industry groups. Also, in the majority of cases, the funds provided by trade credit exceeded by far the funds obtained from banks and other sources.

Characteristics of Trade Credit

Trade credit differs from the other types of short-term credit in several significant ways. First, and probably most important, trade credit is granted on an informal basis. That is, there are usually no documents representing the debt; instead, the credit is in the form of an open-book account. As a result, the "borrower" is not required to secure the loan with tangible assets or cosigners, although occasionally firms require a promissory note to be signed by the purchaser. As a general rule, the only evidence that credit has been extended is an entry in the accounts-receivable ledger, as well as the invoices that describe the items delivered, prices, and credit terms.

TABLE 13-1

ALL MANUFACTURING CORPORATIONS
EXCEPT NEWSPAPERS—FINANCIAL
STATEMENT, PERCENT OF
TOTAL ASSETS

	Fourth Quarter, 1968	Fourth Quarter, 1969
LIABILITIES AND STOCKHOLDERS' EQUITY		
Short-Term Loans from Banks (original maturity of 1 year or less)	3.9	4.5
Advances and Prepayments by U.S. Government	1.3	1.3
Trade Accounts and Notes Payable	8.5	8.8
Federal Income Taxes Accrued	2.5	2.1
Installment, Due in 1 Year or Less, on Long-Term Debt		
Loans from banks	0.5	0.6
Other long-term debt	0.6	0.8
Other Current Liabilities	6.7	6.9
Total Current Liabilities	23.9[a]	24.9[a]
Long-Term Debt Due in More Than 1 Year:		
Loans from banks	3.2	3.7
Other long-term debt	13.1	13.0
Other Noncurrent Liabilities	3.6	3.7
Total Liabilities	43.8	45.4
Reserve Not Reflected Elsewhere	0	0
Capital Stock, Capital Surplus, and Minority Interest	19.2	18.7
Earned Surplus and Surplus Reserves	37.0	35.9
Total Stockholders' Equity	56.2	54.6
Total Liabilities and Stockholders' Equity	100.0	100.0
OPERATING RATIOS		
Annual Rate of Profit on Stockholders' Equity at End of Period:		
Before federal income taxes	21.8	19.3
After taxes	12.8	11.3
Current Assets to Current Liabilities	2.14	2.01
Total Cash and U.S. Government Securities to Total Current Liabilities	0.28	0.23
Total Stockholders' Equity to Debt	2.65	2.45

[a]Figures have been rounded.

Source: Federal Trade Commission–Securities and Exchange Commission, *Quarterly Financial Reports for Manufacturing Corporations*, 4th Quarter, 1969 (Washington, D.C., 1970), p. 12.

A second important characteristic is that there is no computable cost associated with trade credit unless a discount is made a part of the credit terms. This is important because, as a general rule, the cost of not taking this discount is quite high when compared to other forms of short-term credit.

A final characteristic of trade credit is that it is used to finance inventories, whereas other kinds of short-term credit may be used to finance fixed assets as

TABLE 13–2

BALANCE SHEET DATA OF ALL
MANUFACTURING CORPORATIONS
EXCEPT NEWSPAPERS, 1968 AND 1969
(in billions)

LIABILITIES AND STOCKHOLDERS' EQUITY	FOURTH QUARTER	
	1968	*1969*
Short-Term Loans from Banks (original maturity of 1 year or less)	$ 18.7	$ 24.6
Advances and Prepayments by U.S. Government	6.4	7.3
Trade Accounts and Notes Payable	41.3	47.6
Federal Income Taxes Accrued	11.9	11.6
Installments, Due in 1 Year or Less, on Long-Term Debt:		
Loans from banks	2.3	3.0
Other long-term debt	3.1	4.2
Other Current Liabilities	32.7	37.3
Total Current Liabilities	$116.3[a]	$135.5[a]
Long-Term Debt Due in More than 1 Year:		
Loans from banks	$ 15.6	$ 20.1
Other long-term debt	63.5	70.6
Other Noncurrent Liabilities	17.3	20.4
Total Liabilities	$212.7	$246.6
Reserves Not Reflected Elsewhere	0	0
Capital Stock, Capital Surplus, and Minority Interest	93.4	101.9
Earned Surplus and Surplus Reserves	179.8	195.2
Total Stockholders' Equity	$273.2	$297.1
Total Liabilities and Stockholders' Equity	$485.9	$543.7

[a] Figures have been rounded.

Source: Federal Trade Commission–Securities and Exchange Commission, *Quarterly Financial Report for Manufacturing Corporations,* 4th Quarter, 1969 (Washington, D.C., 1970), p. 34.

well as current assets. As a result, trade credit is relatively more important to firms whose inventories constitute a larger percentage of total assets. Table 13-5 shows the relative size of accounts payable and inventory accounts of selected industries. Note the direct relation between the size of inventory and the amount of trade credit outstanding.

Cost of Trade Credit

As a general rule, businessmen use trade credit for two reasons. First, it is more convenient to purchase goods and services on an open-book account than to pay cash at the time of the purchase. Second, unless the discounts that are often given by the firms supplying the credit are not taken, there is no measurable cost for the use of the credit. The first of these arguments is sound and cannot be refuted. However, there is some question with respect to the concept that trade credit is free even when discounts are taken. Let us examine the cost of trade credit.

It is commonly understood by businessmen and students of finance that

TABLE 13-3

CURRENT LIABILITIES OF ALL
MANUFACTURING CORPORATIONS EXCEPT
NEWSPAPERS, 1969, BY SIZE OF FIRM
(Percent of total assets)

	Under $1 Mil.	$1 Mil. to 5 Mil.	$5 Mil. to 10 Mil.	$10 Mil. to 25 Mil.	$100 Mil. to 250 Mil.	$1 Billion and Over
Short-Term Loans from Banks (original maturity of 1 year or less)	5.7	6.9	7.6	7.3	6.5	2.8
Advances and Prepayments by U.S. Government	0	0.1	0.3	0.1	0.8	2.0
Trade Accounts and Notes Payable	17.7	14.0	12.0	9.6	7.8	7.6
Federal Income Taxes Accrued	2.7	2.8	2.1	2.1	2.1	1.9
Installments, Due 1 Year or Less on Long-Term Debt:						
Loan from banks	1.3	1.1	1.0	0.9	0.6	0.3
Other long-term debt	1.9	1.2	1.0	1.1	0.7	0.6
Other Current Liabilities	6.2	5.8	5.6	5.7	5.8	7.8

Source: Federal Trade Commission-Securities and Exchange Commission, *Quarterly Financial Report for Manufacturing Corporations,* 4th Quarter, 1969 (Washington, D.C.:, 1970), pp. 28-33.

there is a definite cost of foregoing discounts. For various reasons, many firms offer a discount to their customers if they pay cash within a certain period of time. If payment is not made within the stipulated period, the customer is required to pay the full amount of the bill; in other words, he is paying the amount of the discount for the number of days between the end of the discount period and the end of the net period. An example will illustrate this statement.

Suppose company A places an order for inventory in the amount of $5,000 with Company B. Company B's credit terms to their regular customers are 2/10, net 30. This means that if company A pays the full amount of the bill within 10 days after the purchase date, it will receive a 2 percent discount; that is, company A will pay only $4,900 instead of $5,000, saving $100. However, if it fails to pay within the discount period, it will be required to pay the full $5,000 by the end of 30 days. The net effect of this is that company A will pay 2 percent for the use of $5,000 for 20 days. Translated to an annual rate of interest, the cost of not taking the cash discount is roughly 36 percent per year. The size of the annual interest cost is determined by the size of the discount and the length of time between the end of the discount period and net period (see Table 13-6).

We can easily see that it is advisable for financial managers to borrow from financial institutions and take the discount. For example, the finance officer could have saved about $75 if he had borrowed $5,000 for 30 days at 6 percent simple interest and taken the discount.

The cost of not taking a discount is easy to see and measure, but there may be a cost even when discounts are not part of the credit terms. There is no

TABLE 13-4

USE OF TRADE CREDIT BY INDUSTRY
GROUPS, 1969 (Percent of total assets)

	SHORT-TERM LOANS FROM BANKS	TRADE CREDIT	OTHER CURRENT LIABILITIES
Durable Goods Industries			
Transportation Equipment	4.6	10.9	9.5
Motor vehicles and equipment	4.2	11.2	9.6
Aircraft and parts	5.0	10.2	9.8
Electrical Machinery, Equipment, and Supplies	6.6	8.7	. 10.9
Other Machinery	6.6	8.4	7.2
Metal working machinery and equipment	6.5	9.1	6.1
Other Fabricated Metal Products	5.2	9.9	8.8
Primary Metal Industries	2.0	7.2	5.7
Primary iron and steel	1.3	7.7	6.5
Primary nonferrous metals	2.8	6.5	4.6
Stone, Clay, and Glass Products	2.6	6.8	4.6
Furniture and Fixtures	5.7	11.3	6.5
Lumber and Wood Products, Except Furniture	3.7	6.9	5.5
Instruments and Related Products	4.8	6.5	8.5
Miscellaneous Manufacturing and Ordnance	9.1	11.1	6.3
Nondurable Industries			
Food and Kindred Products	8.4	10.7	5.5
Dairy products	3.4	14.1	5.1
Bakery products	2.3	11.6	5.4
Alcoholic beverages	8.5	5.4	7.4
Tobacco Manufacturers	8.5	4.7	5.7
Textile Mill Products	6.2	11.4	4.0
Apparel and Other Finished Products	11.3	19.2	6.7
Paper and Allied Products	3.5	7.0	4.0
Printing and Publishing, Except Newspapers	3.0	9.1	6.5
Chemicals and Allied Products	3.1	6.8	6.4
Basic chemicals	2.2	5.8	6.5
Drugs	3.9	6.4	8.2
Petroleum Refining and Related Industries	0.6	7.5	5.1
Petroleum refining	0.5	7.5	5.1
Rubber and Miscellaneous Plastics Products	8.1	9.1	6.3
Leather and Leather Products	10.4	12.0	4.6

Source: Federal Trade Commission-Securities and Exchange Commission, *Quarterly Financial Report for Manufacturing Corporations*, 4th Quarter, 1969, (Washington, D.C., 1970), pp. 13-27.

question that when credit terms are given, the supplier is providing the buyer with funds for the period set forth in the credit terms. Unless the supplier is receiving these funds free of charge, which is unlikely, his cost of doing business is greater than it would have been had he not financed the buyer of the goods. It is assumed that the cost of the financing is hidden in the price of the goods. This idea is difficult to prove, since in the majority of cases everyone in a particular industry gives the same terms. That is, one supplier will not be selling for cash while everyone else is giving credit terms; therefore, a comparison of prices is not

TABLE 13-5

RELATION BETWEEN TRADE CREDIT AND
INVENTORIES IN SELECTED
INDUSTRIES, 1969

	INVENTORY, % OF TOTAL ASSETS	CURRENT ASSETS, % OF TOTAL ASSETS	TRADE CREDIT, % OF TOTAL ASSETS
Durable Goods Industries			
Primary Iron and Steel	17.7	38.5	7.7
Stone, Clay, and Glass Products	15.6	42.0	6.8
Furniture and Fixtures	31.6	68.8	11.3
Aircraft and Parts	49.3	70.0	10.2
Nondurable Goods			
Paper and Allied Products	15.9	36.1	7.0
Drugs	21.4	56.9	6.4
Leather and Leather Products	37.1	73.6	12.0
Apparel and Other Finished Goods	38.0	78.9	19.2

Source: Federal Trade Commission-Securities and Exchange Commission, *Quarterly Financial Reports for Manufacturing Corporations*, 4th Quarter (Washington, D.C., 1970), pp. 13-27.

TABLE 13-6

VARIATION OF COST WITH
CREDIT TERMS

Credit Terms	Annual Cost (percent)
1/10, net 30	18.0
2/10, net 30	36.0
3/10, net 30	54.0
1/10, net 60	7.2
2/10, net 60	14.4
3/10, net 60	21.6

usually possible. We may conclude that there is a definite cost of trade credit when discounts are available and not taken, and there is a good possibility that a cost exists even when discounts are not available, although these costs may be hidden and impossible to measure.

Terms of Trade Credit

The length of time for which a firm receives trade credit is determined largely by the industry in which it operates; Chapter 8 provides a detailed discussion of credit terms. Over the years standard terms for the various industries have been established. The cash-flow cycle of the selling firm also influences the length of time that trade credit can be extended. Normally a firm attempts to synchronize the flow of cash into the firm with its outflow; in other words, it gives the same terms that it receives. In addition to these considerations, credit terms are influenced by the buyer's characteristics. If the buyer's purchases are smaller than the average, there will be a tendency for the seller to shorten the terms. The terms will be much shorter, and in some cases nonexistent, for those customers who do not have a good credit rating. Finally, the status of the seller also influences the credit terms. If the seller is weak financially, he will attempt to grant the shortest terms possible, or in lieu of this, he will offer an attractive cash discount.

Needless to say, trade credit is an advantageous and important source of credit. The financial manager should be careful to use it wisely, since the trade credit that he receives will influence the amount of trade credit that he gives.

14

Short-Term Credit,
as Supplied by
Financial Institutions

The data depicting the sources and uses of corporate funds for the years 1967-1969 (see Table 9-1, p. 83) reveal several interesting facts concerning short-term credit. First, the need for short-term credit varies sharply, requiring constant attention on the part of financial management. Second, the volume of short-term credit supplied by financial institutions fluctuates more widely than the volume supplied by trade credit. Third, although banks are the largest group of financial institutions supplying short-term credit, other financial institutions also play a major role in this type of lending. The purpose of this chapter is to explore the characteristics of lending habits pertaining to short-term credit supplied by various financial institutions.

COMMERCIAL BANKS

Traditionally, banks have been one of the major sources of short- and intermediate-term capital for business firms. At the end of 1969, total outstanding commercial and industrial loans stood at an all-time high of $276.2 billion (see Table 14-1). Although the bulk of the funds supplied by banks consists of short- and intermediate-term capital, it is impossible to ascertain to what extent these funds are used to finance working capital, since many firms use both types of capital to finance fixed assets. Financing of fixed assets with short-term capital is accomplished by an arrangement between the owner or finance officer and the banker, whereby a short-term loan is contracted with the understanding that upon maturity partial payment will be made and the balance renewed. In some cases a business firm will rotate loans among banks; that is, it borrows from bank B to repay an outstanding loan at bank A at the end of the first year, and then borrows from bank C the following year to repay bank B. This, of course, is necessitated by the so-called clean-up rule that some banks follow; that is, borrowers are required to pay the entire amount of the loan each year. When these loans are used to finance assets that are not self-liquidating within the contract period, the firm must resort to this course of action. This type of borrowing is being replaced by term loans.

Short-term business loans made by banks are more important from the standpoints of amount and of number of loans outstanding than either term loans or long-term loans. Loans in this category make up roughly two-thirds of outstanding bank loans, by dollar amount. We should point out, however, that term loans have increased in importance during the past several years at the expense of short-term loans.

Banks have traditionally supplied capital to all kinds and sizes of business firms. For example, although 91 percent of the total number of short-term loans outstanding as of October 1957 were held by firms with assets of $1 million or less, the same group held only 31 percent of the dollar volume outstanding. In other words, firms with assets exceeding $1 million borrowed more than two-thirds of the dollar amount of all business loans made by commercial banks in 1957. We can assume that these ratios have changed somewhat since 1957, but it is doubtful that they have experienced substantial alteration.[1]

As may be expected, the size of the short-term loan varies with the size of the borrower. For example, in 1957 the average size of the loan made to firms with assets of less than $50,000 amounted to $3,000, but the average for firms with assets of $100,000,000 was about $1,363,000. This, of course, is one reason why large firms receive a lower interest rate than small firms.

The security behind every business loan is earnings, but the future of any business is fraught with uncertainties; therefore, banks require many businesses to secure loans with various types of collateral. As a matter of fact, many loans are described by their security—for example, inventory loans. Small businesses are called upon to provide specific security more often than large firms. For example, some years ago a survey revealed that 78 percent of the loans made to businesses with assets of less than $50,000 were secured, but only 17.5 percent of the loans made to firms with assets exceeding $100 million were secured.[2] It is not accurate to describe loans as being unsecured, since these so-called loans are backed by the general credit of the firm, and any assets not specifically pledged as security for other liabilities are considered security for so-called unsecured loans.

---

[1] "Member Bank Lending to Small Business," *Federal Reserve Bulletin*, April 1958, pp. 400-401.

[2] *Ibid.*, p. 403.

TABLE 14-1

LOANS AND INVESTMENTS, ALL
COMMERCIAL BANKS (in billions)

| YEAR | TOTAL | LOANS | SECURITIES | |
			U.S. Govt.	Other
1965	$294.4	$192.6	$ 57.1	$ 44.8
1966	310.5	208.2	53.6	48.7
1967	346.5	225.4	59.7	61.4
1968	384.6	251.6	61.5	71.5
1969	398.6	276.2	51.8	70.5

Source: Federal Reserve Bulletin, May 1970, p. A23.

The cost of short-term credit at banks is determined by several factors, three of which are: the state of the economy at the time of the loan, the credit status of the firm, and the cost of processing the loan. Generally speaking, the firm pays a simple rate of interest; for example, a firm that borrows $500 at 5 percent for 12 months pays $25 in interest charges. In some cases banks will discount the loan; that is, they collect the interest in advance. If the 5 percent in the above were discounted, the effective rate of interest would be 5.28 percent ($25 ÷ $475). Smaller firms are often required to repay their loans periodically—for example, monthly. If the interest is paid at maturity and is not based on the declining balance, the effective rate will be about twice the size of the contract interest rate. Generally, interest charged to smaller firms is higher than that charged to larger firms. For example, in February 1970, 84.9 percent of the dollar amount of all loans of $1 million and over carried rates of 8.99 percent or less, but only 31.3 percent of all loans of $10,000 or less were for rates of 8.99 percent or less. Stated differently, 68.7 percent of all loans of less than $10,000 were made for 9 percent or more, whereas only 15.1 percent of the loans exceeding $1 million were for rates of 9 percent or more (see Table 14-2). This does not mean that size is being penalized, but rather that small firms are usually more risky. Moreover, the higher unit cost of processing small loans contributes to the higher interest charge.

It is also interesting to note in Table 14-3 that during February 1970, only 8.9 percent of the dollar amount for all business loans went for loans of $100,000 or less, but 58.8 percent was for loans of $1 million or more. The opposite was true with regard to the number of loans made; 42.1 percent of all loans were for less than $100,000, whereas only 3.6 percent were for $1 million or more. It may be concluded that the numerical majority of all loans—79.2 percent in February 1970—went to small and middle-sized businesses, but the bulk of the loans from a dollar standpoint went to large businesses.

Many banks follow the practice of requiring that a business firm maintain a minimum balance at all times when a loan is outstanding. This policy affects the firm by (1) increasing the effective rate of interest, (2) causing it to borrow more funds than are actually needed, and (3) lowering the firm's investment turnover, which has the effect of reducing its rate of return on investment. To illustrate,

TABLE 14-2

RATES ON SHORT-TERM BUSINESS LOANS
OF BANKS, FEBRUARY 1970
(size of loan in thousands)

Interest Rate (percent per annum)	All Sizes	$1-9	$10-99[a]	$100-499[a]	$500-999[a]	$1 million and Over
Less than 8.50	2.8	19.3	8.1	4.9	2.1	1.2
8.50	47.2	3.6	8.4	21.8	37.4	63.8
8.51-8.99	21.1	8.4	12.9	22.6	26.2	20.9
9.00	7.9	10.8	14.2	13.1	10.9	4.6
9.01-9.49	7.0	12.0	15.9	12.9	6.5	3.9
9.50	5.4	14.1	13.0	8.5	6.2	3.0
9.51-9.99	3.2	13.9	9.9	6.2	4.2	0.9
Over 10.00	5.4	17.9	17.5	10.2	6.4	1.8
Total	100.0	100.0	100.0	100.0	100.0	100.0
Total loans:						
Dollars (millions)	4,502.3	44.1	399.0	810.7	598.9	2,649.6
Number (thousands)	30.2	11.2	12.7	4.2	1.0	1.1

[a]Column does not total 100.0 because figures have been rounded.
Source: Federal Reserve Bulletin, May 1970, p. A23.

suppose a firm borrows $1 million at 5 percent with the condition that it maintain a compensating balance of 20 percent. In this case the borrower has the use of $800,000 instead of $1 million, and the effective cost of the $1 million is 6.25 percent rather than 5 percent; if the firm actually needs $1 million, it will have to borrow $1.25 million. Finally, the firm's investment turnover is reduced because $250,000 is not gainfully employed.

One of the primary ways in which a firm can lower its investment is to establish a line of credit with its bank. Specifically, a line of credit is an indication that a bank is willing to loan up to a certain amount during a particular period of time provided the firm's financial condition does not undergo a substantial change. During this period the firm can draw against the line of credit. In many cases there is no charge for the line of credit; that is, interest is charged only for the amount of funds that is borrowed. Some banks, however, charge a small fee for the unused portion of the line.

The selection of the firm's banking facilities is one of the financial manager's more important functions, since the ability to obtain funds at a proper cost affects not only the firm's profitability, but also its ability to compete effectively with other firms in the industry. Many excellent discussions are available to the student concerning ways and means of selecting the bank; it is recommended that one be read and studied.

The volume of credit made available to business firms by banks indicates that many advantages accrue to users of this source. Following are the advantages normally associated with bank borrowing:

1. Advice and counsel can be obtained from experts in finance.
2. Credit information is available.

TABLE 14-3

SHORT-TERM BUSINESS LOANS OF BANKS—
NUMBER AND DOLLAR AMOUNTS, BY
VARIOUS SIZES
(for the month of February, 1967-1970)

SIZE OF LOAN (in thousands)

Period		All Sizes	$1-9 Amount	$1-9 Percent	$10-99 Amount	$10-99 Percent	$100-499 Amount	$100-499 Percent	$500-999 Amount	$500-999 Percent	$1 million and over Amount	$1 million and over Percent
Feb. 1967	Amount	3,790.8	56.2	1.5	435.0	11.5	858.5	22.6	549.2	14.5	1,891.8	49.9
	Number	35.9	15.5	43.2	14.3	39.8	4.5	12.5	.9	2.4	.8	2.1
Feb. 1968	Amount	3,576.5	58.5	1.6	455.9	12.7	833.0	23.3	536.6	15.0	1,692.4	47.3
	Number	36.6	15.6	42.6	15.1	41.3	4.4	12.0	.9	2.4	.7	1.9
Feb. 1969	Amount	3,880.5	49.3	1.3	421.6	10.9	793.3	20.4	498.2	12.8	2,118.2	54.6
	Number	32.2	12.8	39.8	13.6	42.2	4.1	12.7	.8	2.5	.9	2.8
Feb. 1970	Amount	4,502.3	44.1	1.0	399.0	8.9	810.7	18.0	598.9	12.9	2,649.6	58.8
	Number	30.2	11.2	37.1	12.7	42.1	4.2	13.9	1.0	3.3	1.1	3.6

Source: Federal Reserve Bulletin, May 1967, May 1968, May 1969, and May 1970.

3. Banks are a source of information regarding potential mergers and consolidations.
4. Aid with regard to future financing is obtained.
5. Banks provide contact with other sources of capital.
6. Banks are major sources of both short- and intermediate-term capital.

Several disadvantages are also associated with bank borrowing; the most
important are:

1. Confidential information must be revealed if loans are to be secured.
2. Firms are compelled to maintain compensating balances, and this increases the cost of funds.
3. Periodic reports are usually required by banks.
4. Banks often demand that they be allowed to ratify managerial decisions.

COMMERCIAL PAPER HOUSES

Commercial paper consists of short-term promissory notes that are discounted directly or through dealers to large corporations, college endowment
funds, pension funds, insurance companies, and banks. Although commercial
paper is one of the oldest means of obtaining short-term funds, the present
techniques for its use were developed in the early part of the twentieth century.
During the 1920s and early 1930s, almost all commercial paper was placed
directly through dealers, but since the mid-1930s the volume of paper sold
directly to the investor has increased tremendously; for example, between the
years 1963 and 1970, the volume of paper sold directly ranged from a high of
79 percent in 1965 to a low of 63 percent in 1969.

It is worthy of noting that since 1965 the volume of paper sold by commercial paper houses has progressively increased from 21 percent to 37 percent
of the total. The explanation of this change is the increasing importance placed
by business firms on commercial paper as a source of short-term funds. In the
period 1964-1969 all commercial paper rose $22.3 billion, an increase of
278 percent. Paper sold through dealers increased nearly twice as much as that
sold directly by the firm using the capital, 432 percent compared to only
222 percent. The student knows that consumer finance companies place the
greatest majority of the paper placed directly, whereas business firms rarely sell
paper directly (see Table 14-4).

Although investors in commercial paper are located in every section of North
America, the majority are concentrated in the eastern part of the United States.
As a result, the borrowers are also found in and around the large money markets
of the East. The borrowers are largely manufacturers and finance companies, and
all are characterized by their size and their outstanding credit records.

The length of maturity of commercial paper, regardless of whether it is sold
directly or through dealers, usually ranges from one to twelve months, with the

TABLE 14-4

COMMERCIAL AND FINANCIAL
COMPANY PAPER
(in millions)

End of Period	Total	PLACED THROUGH DEALERS		PLACED DIRECTLY	
		Bank-Related	Other	Bank-Related	Other
1964	$ 8,361	NA	$ 2,223	NA	$ 6,138
1965	9,058	NA	1,903	NA	7,155
1966	13,279	NA	3,089	NA	10,190
1967	16,535	NA	4,901	NA	11,634
1968	20,497	NA	7,201	NA	13,296
1969	31,624	$1,216	10,601	$2,993	16,814

Source: *Federal Reserve Bulletin,* May 1970, p. A37.

most common maturity being about six months. The notes are usually in multiples of $5,000 and generally range in size from $5,000 to $1 million. Very rarely do borrowers renew the paper, and the delinquency rate is extremely low. For these reasons the users of commercial paper enjoy low borrowing costs.

The rate on paper placed directly by finance companies is usually about 50 to 100 basis points higher than the rate on prime paper sold through dealers. Incidentally, the rate paid by finance companies ranges about 25 to 75 basis points below the prime rate charged by banks.

The financial officer of a business firm should carefully consider this method of raising short-term funds for the following reasons. First, funds can be secured more economically from the sale of commercial paper than by any other means. Second, the borrower is not required to seek several sources, as he may in the case of bank borrowing. Owing to the 10 percent rule, a bank is often unable to supply the entire short-term capital needs of a borrower. Third, compensating balances are not required, thus further reducing the cost of borrowing. Fourth, raising funds through the sale of commercial paper allows the firm to improve its image, since only those companies with the highest credit status have access to these funds. The principal shortcoming of commercial paper is the impersonal attitude of the lender. The borrower seldom if ever receives any consideration from the lender in the event of financial embarrassment. However, if the lender is a bank or some other financial institution, the borrower is usually granted a period of time to work out a satisfactory solution.

BUSINESS FINANCE COMPANIES

Three principal types of finance companies have developed in this country: consumer finance companies, sales finance companies, and business finance companies. The first type provides funds to consumers in the form of small loans repayable periodically. Sales finance companies purchase installment sales contracts from retailers of consumer durable goods, such as autos, appliances, and house trailers. Whereas the consumer finance company and sales finance company supply capital to consumers, business finance companies supply capital to business firms for working-capital purposes. In a few cases, they also supply funds to finance fixed assets.

Generally the business finance company is a specialized company whose primary function is to supply funds to small and middle-sized companies. In general they provide funds for (1) the purchase of commercial, industrial, and farm equipment; (2) financing commercial accounts receivable; (3) factoring; (4) the purchase of commercial vehicles and auto dealers' vehicle inventories; (5) leased equipment; and (6) rediscounting for other finance companies. Table 14-5 depicts the type of business as well as the relative importance of each type of financing done by business finance companies.

Although it is impossible to describe the size characteristics of business finance companies, it is reasonable to conclude that the great majority are relatively small. A survey made in 1965 revealed that of the 571 companies that reported, only 12 had assets in excess of $100 million, and 133, or 23.3 percent, had less than $100,000 in assets (see Table 14-6, on pages 138-39).

In respect to volume of business, wholesale and retail equipment financing is by far the most important function of business finance companies, accounting for 69 percent of all receivables. Loans on commercial accounts receivable,

TABLE 14-5

BUSINESS RECEIVABLES OF FINANCE
COMPANIES, JUNE 30, 1965

Type of Receivable	Amount (in millions)	Percentage Distribution
Wholesale Loans	$ 4,242	35.4
Automobiles	2,897	24.2
Other consumer goods	318	2.7
Other, including inventory loans	1,026	8.6
Retail Loans	4,034	33.7
Commercial vehicles	1,614	13.5
Business, industrial, and farm equipment	2,419	20.2
Lease Paper	843	7.0
Business equipment and motor vehicles	818	6.8
Other	25	0.2
Other Business Credit[a]	2,867	23.9
Commercial accounts receivable[b]	1,036	8.7
Factored accounts receivable[c]	608	5.1
Advances to factored clients	200	1.7
Rediscounted receivables[b]	305	2.5
Other[d]	717	6.0
Total business receivables	$11,986	100.0

[a] Includes export–import credits.
[b] Net of balances withheld.
[c] Less liability to factored clients.
[d] Includes loans on open credit, dealer capital loans, small loans for business or farm purposes, and all other business loans not elsewhere classified.

Source: *Federal Reserve Bulletin*, October 1968, p. 816.

factored accounts receivable, advances to factored clients, rediscounted receivables, and other loans accounted for 33.5 percent of the total credit granted by the 571 companies included in the survey.

Business finance companies trade heavily on their equity in order to increase their return to equity. To illustrate, 83 percent of all capital was from debt sources, and of this total approximately 65 percent was obtained from short-term sources. The unusually large amount of short-term capital reflects both the high ratio of short-term loans in their portfolios and the seasonal and cyclical nature of the demand for funds from these companies.

FACTORS

The factor is one of the oldest financial institutions, and yet it is probably one of the least known. Its origin can be traced back for centuries; for example, Shakespeare spoke of the factor in *Richard III, Henry IV, Antony and Cleopatra*, and *The Comedy of Errors*. During the fifteenth and sixteenth centuries, England, France, and Spain were engaged in shipping large quantities of goods to their colonies. Because of the distances and because of inadequate communication and transportation facilities, factors were appointed by manufacturers to arrange for the sale and distribution of their goods. Factors never received title but were responsible for the safekeeping of the goods as well as the proceeds of the sale. They investigated the credit standing of potential customers and advanced funds to their principals. During the nineteenth and twentieth centuries, the functions of the factor changed somewhat in that the manufacturer retained the distribution function but transferred the financing and credit and collection functions to the factor.

The modern factor has experienced unusual growth during the past three decades; moreover, factors have expanded their operations both horizontally and vertically. Whereas the early factor operated at the manufacturing level in the textile industry, the contemporary factor has expanded into such industries as lumber, leather, furniture, plastics, toys, and sportswear. Furthermore, factors are currently operating at the wholesale and distribution levels as well as at the manufacturing level.

Factors perform three primary functions for their clients: (1) purchasing accounts receivable, (2) selecting credit risks and collecting receivables, and (3) providing advisory services. The purchase of accounts receivable without recourse is the method employed by factors to supply funds to business firms. The procedure is generally as follows: The client, upon receipt of an order, submits it to the factor for credit approval. After approval, the shipment is made and the invoice is sent, along with the shipping documents, to the factor. The amount of the invoice is credited to the account of the client, who may withdraw his credit balances, less a reasonable reserve, at any time. This reserve is held in anticipation of (1) merchandise that may be returned and (2) any claim that may be made against the client by a customer.

TABLE 14-6

BUSINESS RECEIVABLES OF 571
BUSINESS FINANCE COMPANIES,
JUNE 30, 1965

SIZE OF COMPANY (BUSINESS RECEIVABLES, IN THOUSANDS)

Type of Receivable	Total	$100,000 and Over		$25,000-99,000		$5,000-24,999		$2,500-4,900		$1,000-2,499		$500-999		$250-499		$100-249		Under $100	
		$	%	$	%	$	%	$	%	$	%	$	%	$	%	$	%	$	%
Total	$4,624	$2,897	62.7	$842	18.2	$603	13.0	$81	1.8	$81	1.8	$40	0.9	$57	1.2	$16	0.3	$6	0.1
Wholesale Paper	954	765	80.2	94	9.9	75	7.9	11	1.2	5	0.5					3	0.3	1	0.1
Automobiles	142	140	98.6			*	*	*	*							1	0.7	1	0.7
Other consumer goods	41	1	2.4	2	4.9	23	56.1	10	24.4	4	9.8					1	2.4		
Other, including inventory loans	770	623	80.9	92	11.9	52	6.8	1	0.1	1	0.1					1	0.1		
Retail paper	1,778	1,279	72.0	221	12.4	211	11.9	24	1.4	18	1.0	3	0.2	16	0.9	4	0.2	2	0.1
Commercial vehicles	838	797	95.1	11	1.3	13	1.6	6	0.7	5	0.6			5	0.6	1	0.1		
Business, industrial, and farm equipment	939	482	51.3	210	22.4	197	21.0	18	1.9	13	1.4	3	0.3	11	1.2	3	0.3	2	0.2
Lease Paper	341	64	18.8	111	32.6	154	45.2	2	0.6	9	2.6							1	0.3
Business equipment and motor vehicles	330	60	18.2	107	32.4	152	46.1	2	0.6	8	2.4							1	0.3
Other	11	4	36.4	4	36.4	2	18.2			1	9.1								
Other Business Credit[a]	1,551	790	50.9	416	26.8	163	10.5	44	2.8	49	3.2	37	2.4	41	2.6	9	0.6	2	0.1
Loans on commercial accounts receivable[b]	624	352	56.4	126	20.2	42	6.7	32	5.1	28	4.5	26	4.2	15	2.4	3	0.5	*	*

TABLE 14-6 (cont.)

SIZE OF COMPANY (BUSINESS RECEIVABLES, IN THOUSANDS)

Type of Receivable	Total	$100,000 and Over		$25,000-99,000		$5,000-24,999		$2,500-4,900		$1,000-2,499		$500-999		$250-499		$100-249		Under $100	
		$	%	$	%	$	%	$	%	$	%	$	%	$	%	$	%	$	%
Factored accounts receivable[c]	324	110	34.0	165	50.9	31	9.6			9	2.8			6	1.9	2	0.6	1	0.3
Advances to factored clients	88	33	37.5	48	54.5	7	8.0	*	*	*	*								
Rediscounted receivables[b]	158	87	55.1	35	22.2	30	19.0	*	*	*	*	5	3.2			1	0.6		
Other[d]	357	208	58.3	42	11.8	53	14.8	12	3.4	12	3.4	6	1.7	20	5.6	3	0.8	1	0.3
CUMULATIVE DATA																			
Number of Companies and Percentages of Total		12	2.1%	18	3.2%	40	7.0%	25	4.4%	55	9.6%	63	11.0%	139	24.3%	86	15.1%	133	23.3%

a Includes export–import credits.
b Net balances withheld.
c Less liability to factored clients.
d Includes loans on open credit, dealer capital loans, small loans for business or farm purposes, and all other business loans not elsewhere classified.
* Less than $500,000 or less than half of 1 percent.

Source: *Federal Reserve Bulletin*, October 1968, p. 819.

139

Some Advantages of Factoring

Certain advantages accrue to firms that factor their receivables. First, cash is received for the majority of the outstanding receivables immediately after the sale has been made. Second, factoring permits the firm to improve its financial position. A simple example will explain this point. Assume that before factoring, a firm's current assets and liabilities consist of the following: cash $5,000, receivables $50,000, and inventory $7,500; accounts payable $5,000, notes payable $37,500; and accrued taxes $6,500. The current ratio under these conditions is 1.3 to 1. Now assume that the firm factors its receivables and receives $45,000 in cash; the remaining $5,000 is held in reserve, appearing on the balance sheet as "due from factor." Accounts payable and notes payable are reduced, and the remaining $2,500 is transferred to the firm's cash account. The current ratio after factoring is 3.07 to 1, and the cash account has been improved. Finally, factoring accounts receivable reduces the amount of working capital required for a particular volume of sales, thus improving investment turnover. If the cost of factoring does not exceed the economies accruing to the firm, then factoring is advantageous. This will be examined later.

The second function mentioned is that of credit and collection. Pursuant to agreement between a business firm and a factor, the credit-and-collection function and all expenses associated with the function are assumed by the factor. Among the more important advantages gained by small and middle-sized firms by transferring this function to a factor are: (1) the firm receives a superior service, since the function is placed in the hands of a specialist; (2) the function is accomplished more cheaply, since the factor is able to pass on the cost of maintaining complete credit records to the many different firms; and (3) the firm is able to reduce its credit and collection expense to a fixed percentage of net credit sales.

The third important function that factors perform is to provide advice on marketing, finance, and production. The factor is in position to provide information concerning product design, prices, market conditions, and economic prospects, areas in which many firms are unable to do effective research because they have neither the funds nor the skills. The benefits obtained from such services are difficult to evaluate, but in many cases the economies gained tend to offset the cost of factoring.

Although the primary financing function performed by factors is the purchase of accounts receivable without recourse for credit losses, factors also make secured and unsecured loans to their clients. However, when such financing is performed, the factor is acting in the capacity of the commercial finance company.

The factor's charge includes two major components: first, a fee for performing the credit-and-collection function and for purchasing the firm's receivables without recourse for credit losses; and second, an interest charge on funds loaned to the business firm.

The first of these costs, the commission rate, is determined through negotiation; it is influenced by several considerations: (1) type of industry, (2) volume of sales, (3) average size of sale, (4) average annual sales volume per customer, (5) credit standings of the firm's customers, and (6) credit terms offered by the firm.[3] The commission rate is expressed as a percentage of the full net face value of the receivables sold; it generally ranges from 1 to 2 percent.

In addition to the commission or fee, the factor charges an interest rate on the funds advanced. This is usually a simple interest charge and not a discount rate.

In deciding whether to use a factor, the finance officer must compare the cost of shifting the credit-and-collection function to a specialist with the cost of operating it as a part of the finance function. In some cases, particularly for small and middle-sized companies, it is cheaper to use the factor, but in other cases this may be an expensive way of raising capital.

MISCELLANEOUS SOURCES

Business firms, particularly small firms, occasionally obtain funds from officers, employees, relatives, and friends. As a general rule, loans of this nature are subordinated to any claims held by financial institutions; that is, capital secured from such sources may be considered quasi equity. Neither the terms nor the cost of these funds follows any set pattern; they are usually fixed in direct relation to need.

Customers occasionally provide debt capital to business firms in the form of advances and/or prepayments. Although loans of this kind are rather common in the construction industry, they are not very popular in other areas of business. An exception, however, is provided by firms doing business with the U.S. government (see Table 13-1, p. 123).

Another source of short-term credit is the supplier—for example, the advances to customers by major oil companies through the credit-card device.

The miscellaneous sources mentioned here are, of course, not important when funds or credit obtained through them is compared to loans made by financial institutions and suppliers.

---

[3] Clyde Phelps, *Role of Factoring in Modern Business Financing, Studies in Commercial Financing No. 1* (Baltimore: Commercial Finance Company, 1952), p. 53.

15

Intermediate
Financing

The two previous chapters were concerned with a discussion of short-term financing; that is, credit that is repaid or renewed within one year from the date of the loan. This chapter deals with intermediate credit, which may be defined as credit extended for periods longer than one year but not long enough to permit a classification as long-term credit. Although intermediate credit is secured in many ways and is evidenced by many different credit instruments, it is generally conceded that its major source is through the use of the term loan. Leasing is another major source of capital, and if data were available on total leasing, it is entirely possible that it would rank as the most important source from a volume standpoint; therefore, leasing as a method of financing will be included in this chapter.

THE NATURE AND IMPORTANCE
OF TERM LOANS

The term loan as we know it today is a relatively new type of credit-granting device, even though it has been employed in principle for many years in the form of extended and renewed short-term loans. The data concerning the dollar volume and number of term loans made by banks are irregular and imcomplete, but there is sufficient evidence to indicate that credit granted in this manner has grown at a rather rapid rate during the past two decades. To illustrate, the dollar volume of term loans made by all member banks rose from $4.5 billion in 1946 to $15.4 billion in 1957, an increase of 243 percent.[1] Data for subsequent term loans are not available for all banks, but they are available for the New York banks. These data indicate that term loans rose from $3.5 billion in 1962[2] to $6.8 billion in April 1964.[3] In 1965, the "weekly reporting banks in New York City increased their term loans to businesses by well over $2 billion . . . . "[4]

In seeking out the primary reasons for the importance that has been achieved by term loans, it was observed that the increase originated from users as well as suppliers, although financial literature tends to emphasize the reasons associated with the latter. One important reason was that during the late 1930s and 1940s banks discovered that they were holding large free reserves, averaging around $3.25 billion. Since traditional investments provided low yields, banks began seeking new types of loans that would provide higher yields, and term loans seemed to answer this need.

A second reason for the increased importance of term loans was the decision of regulatory agencies' examiners to delete the "slow" classification for term loans and to evaluate them on their "probable collectibility" rather than on maturity. Third, commercial banks were encouraged by favorable experience to participate in term loans with the Reconstruction Finance Corporation and the Federal Reserve. Fourth, commercial banks moved from the discount theory, which in essence required loans to be self-liquidating during short periods, to the anticipated income theory—the idea that a loan may be liquidated from future income rather than from existing earnings or assets.

It is obvious that there will be no demand for a particular type of loan unless the user benefits from the use of it; therefore, it is presumed that all types of businesses benefit from the use of term loans since all types of businessmen use them to some degree. In analyzing the reasons for the demand for term loans, the following seem to be the most important. First, since the mid-1930s the federal income tax has increased considerably, thus creating at least one reason for management to retain a greater proportion of its earnings. It should be remembered that businesses are required to pay a penalty tax on funds that are retained in excess of their needs. Financial managers concluded that the periodic repayment of term loans certainly qualified as a legitimate need; therefore, it may logically be concluded that the income tax contributed much to the rapid rise in term loans.

Second, during this period the cash flow of businesses experienced substan-

---

[1] Carl T. Arlt, "Term Lending to Business," *Federal Reserve Bulletin*, April 1959, pp. 357-62.

[2] "Term Lending by New York City Banks," *Monthly Review* (New York: Federal Reserve Bank of New York), Vol. 43, No. 2 (December 1961), 30.

[3] George Budzeika, "Term Lending by New York City Banks," *Essays in Money and Credit* (New York: Federal Reserve Bank of New York, 1964), p. 64.

[4] William F. Treiber, "Recent Trends in Commercial Banking Lending and Borrowing," *Monthly Review*, Vol. 48, No. 2 (February 1966) (New York: Federal Reserve Bank of New York), p. 29.

tial growth, providing an excellent source of funds required to retire term loans. Third, term loans prevent banks from canceling credit to the borrower on short notice, since they are, in effect, long-term loans. Fourth, as a general rule most businesses in their early years cannot finance capital requirements internally or from short-term credit, yet they are not mature enough to go to the public for debt capital. In such cases it is normal for them to resort to such sources as commercial banks and insurance companies for intermediate funds in the form of term loans. Undoubtedly businesses employ term loans for other reasons as well, but these appear to be the most important.

Characteristics of Term Loans

The characteristics of term loans, like those of other loans, vary with the economy; therefore, any descriptions of loan characteristics should be considered in the light of existing economic conditions. Nevertheless, a brief discussion is given here in order to familiarize the reader with this type of credit.

The following description of term loan characteristics is taken primarily from an article prepared by Carl T. Arlt for the Federal Reserve Board.[5]

Approximately three-fourths of all term loans have maturities of one to five years; however, it is interesting to note that approximately 60 percent of these loans are made for less than three years and only 5 percent for more than ten years. Furthermore, these proportions have remained fairly constant since 1946. From a volume standpoint, loans of one to five years have increased in importance. In 1946, they amounted to 40.2 percent of the total, but by 1959 their importance had increased to 50 percent.

Interest on term loans may be charged either on the original amount or on the outstanding amount of the loan. If charged on the outstanding amount, the interest charge declines as the loan is repaid. If charged on the original amount, the effective interest rate is approximately twice the amount of the stated rate. This latter method of computing interest was employed in about 40 percent of the total number of loans outstanding and for approximately 10 percent of the amount of the loans outstanding in 1957. In the main, this method of charging interest was used in computing interest charges for small borrowers. Firms of such size that several sources of credit are available not only pay a much smaller interest rate, but the rate is computed on the unpaid balance rather than being discounted.

The survey also revealed that approximately 60 percent of the volume and 90 percent of the number of term loans made in 1955 by member banks were secured. Again, the smaller firms were required to secure the majority of their loans; the larger firms were able to obtain funds without providing specific security. Fixed assets, such as plants, other real estate, and equipment constituted the most important type of security. Next in importance was assignment

---

[5] Arlt, "Term Lending to Business."

of claims such as accounts receivable or liens on revenue. Finally, stocks and bonds also served as security.

As one might guess, the larger banks tend to make the larger loans; for example, in 1957, banks with assets exceeding $1 billion in deposits held 54 percent of the dollar volume of term loans outstanding, but this amounted to only a small percentage of the number of loans outstanding. The opposite is true with smaller banks. For example, banks with deposits of less than $100 million held more than one-half the total number of loans outstanding, amounting to only one-fifth of the dollar amount. The survey also revealed that nearly one-third of the dollar volume of loans outstanding involved participation by two or more banks. Also interesting to note is that small banks seldom, if ever, use participating arrangements; rather, it is the larger banks that join together to make loans.

Term loans are made available by several financial institutions, but banks supply the bulk of this type of credit. For example, between the years 1955 and 1957, the volume of term loans outstanding held by member banks increased from $10.5 to $15.4 billion, or 47.5 percent. The dollar volume in the years from 1946 to 1957 experienced a phenomenal 235 percent growth—that is, from $4.6 to $15.4 billion.[6]

Life insurance companies and commercial and sales finance companies also supply term loans to business firms. Unfortunately, financial data are not available to indicate the number and volume of term loans that are made by these institutions each year.

Term Loans as a Financing Device

Although financial managers employ term loans for many valid reasons, there are certain conditions when these loans may create some operational problems. First, the use of term loans may "disturb" a firm's optimum capital structure, which could adversely affect earnings on equity and cost of capital. To illustrate, assume the following: Company A negotiates a term loan in the amount of $2.5 million, repayable in equal installments over a five-year period. The balance sheet data in Table 15-1 depicts A's capital mix at the time the term loan is made, and after the loan is repaid.

Table 15-2 depicts the changes that take place in the firm's capital structure when a term loan is used to raise funds. Note that in the beginning the ratio of debt increases sharply, but as the loan is retired out of current earnings, the ratio declines. The net effect of the increase in debt is to increase the return on equity capital, but in so doing financial risk is also increased. The student remembers that K_e increases as additional financial risk is incurred, and should the term loan add too much financial risk to the capital structure, the cost of capital (K_o) will rise.

As the term loan is paid off with earnings, financial risk decreases, causing a

---

[6] Arlt, "Term Lending to Business," p. 357.

TABLE 15-1

BALANCE SHEET DATA,
COMPANY A

	Time Loan Made	After Loan Repaid
Current Liabilities		
Trade credit[a]	$ 400,000	$ 400,000
Notes payable[b] (6%)	500,000	500,000
Other	100,000	100,000
Term Loan[c]	2,500,000	0
Long-Term Debt[d] (6%)	1,500,000	1,500,000
Common Stock[e]	5,000,000	5,000,000
Retained Earnings	0	2,500,000

[a] For simplicity, trade credit remains constant and has no cost.
[b] Assume company maintains a constant short-term balance of $600,000.
[c] Interest at 6 percent.
[d] Interest on long-term debt is 6 percent; however, interest rises as additional leverage is employed.
[e] Cost of equity rises as additional debt is added, and vice versa.

decline in both the cost of equity and the cost of capital. It should be noted that after the term loan is completely repaid (out of equity) the firm's debt-equity ratio is smaller than it was when the loan was undertaken. In the above example, debt constituted 33 percent of the total capital before the loan was made, but after the loan was repaid, it accounted for only 25 percent of the total. In other words, the firm's capital structure is no longer at its optimum, its cost of capital has increased, and return on equity has declined—assuming that the firm is at its optimum capital structure, where debt amounts to 33 percent of total capital. In all probability the market value of the firm's stock would also have declined.

A term loan can avoid distorting earnings per share, cost of capital, and market value of stock if it is not very large relative to other debt and if installments are paid with debt rather than equity capital. This is not to suggest that term loans should be avoided; rather, it suggests that *care* should be exercised when term loans are used in the financing process.

THE NATURE AND IMPORTANCE
OF LEASING

Leasing as a method of procuring assets is probably the most significant development that has taken place in the field of finance during the past three decades. Originally the emphasis was on real estate leasing, but during the past several years, firms have been able to lease almost any type of fixed asset. Although there are no figures measuring the amount of leased equipment presently in use, we may safely conclude that lease financing is one of the major methods of external financing being used in many industries. Although a firm would probably never lease all its fixed assets, there is a definite trend toward owning less and leasing more. It is difficult to say whether the increased impor-

TABLE 15-2

CHANGES IN BALANCE SHEET AS TERM
LOAN IS REPAID
(in millions)

Year[a]	Equity		Long-Term Debt		Notes Payable		Other		Term Loan		Total	
	Amount	Percent	Amount	Percent	Amount	Percent	Amount	Percent	Amount	Percent	Amount	Percent
0	$5.0	66.7	$1.5	20.0	$0.6	8.0	$0.4	5.3	$0	0	$ 7.5	100.0
1	5.5	55.0	1.5	15.0	0.6	6.0	0.4	4.0	2.0	20.0	10.0	100.0
2	6.0	60.0	1.5	15.0	0.6	6.0	0.4	4.0	1.5	15.0	10.0	100.0
3	6.5	65.0	1.5	15.0	0.6	6.0	0.4	4.0	1.0	10.0	10.0	100.0
4	7.0	70.0	1.5	15.0	0.6	6.0	0.4	4.0	0.5	5.0	10.0	100.0
5	7.5	75.0	1.5	15.0	0.6	6.0	0.4	4.0	0.0	0	10.0	100.0

[a] End-of-year data.

tance of leasing is a result of the financial officer's desire to conserve funds or whether it results from increased effort on the part of leasing companies.

Prior to discussing the pros and cons of lease financing, we should first examine briefly the two principal techniques of leasing, which are (1) leasing rather than purchasing the asset, and (2) the sale and leaseback of an asset that has been previously acquired and financed out of the firm's own funds. In the first instance, a business firm contracts to "rent" an asset from another firm. In most instances the contract includes the following terms: (1) a basic term during which the lease is noncancellable; (2) periodic rental payments that will produce over the life of the lease the original investment plus a predetermined rate of return; (3) the inclusion of costs of maintenance, taxes, insurance, and the like, as part of the rental price; and (4) an agreement that will permit the firm to continue to use the asset after the basic lease term.[7]

The sale-and-leaseback technique involves nothing more than transferring the title of the asset owned by the firm to another party in exchange for a price that reflects the market value of the property, following which the asset is leased by the original owner. The net effect of the transaction is for the firm to "trade" a fixed asset for a current asset.

Advantages and Disadvantages of Leasing

An examination of the literature in the fields of lease financing reveals that unanimity of opinion about the advantages and disadvantages of lease financing does not exist. The student of finance should know by this time that authorities will never agree completely; therefore, we will list those advantages that have not been questioned and then list those that have been set forth and have been discredited.

The following advantages are currently acknowledged as being valid:[8]

1. Permits a lessee to obtain the use of property that he cannot acquire in any other way
2. Provides facilities that are needed only temporarily
3. Avoids the risk of obsolescence
4. Relieves the user of maintenance, service, and administrative problems
5. Provides an additional source of financing
6. Gives the lessee flexibility

Advantages as obvious as these do not require individual explanations. It should be pointed out, however, that given certain conditions, it is possible to question one or more of them. In the past, various attempts have been made to

---

[7] Donald R. Gant, "Illusion in Leasing Financing," *Harvard Business Review*, Vol. XXVII (March-April 1959), 123.

[8] Henry G. Hamel, *Leasing in Industry* (New York: National Industrial Conference Board, 1968), p. 9.

establish the beneficiality of four alleged advantages, although recent literature has discredited them. The more important of these are that leasing (1) frees working capital, (2) yields a tax saving, (3) improves the lessee's apparent financial position, and (4) spares management the need to review capital expenditures.[9]

The most frequently mentioned disadvantages of leasing are: (1) high cost; (2) loss of residual values; (3) the possibility that a premium will be demanded for vital equipment unless adequate care is taken when the lease is negotiated; (4) inadequate evaluation due to habitual leasing; (5) the lack of accumulation of equity, which could have some adverse effects on future financing; and (6) the possibility that control of the facility may be lost at the end of the lease period.

The validity of each of these disadvantages depends upon the alternatives and the care exercised when negotiating the lease agreement. To illustrate, the cost of a lease may or may not exceed the cost of alternative sources. There are several elements that determine whether a lease is more "expensive" than the alternative sources; these include the tax rate, the repayment schedule, the depreciation method used, and the rate of interest charged on the balance of the investment. The importance of each of these elements is illustrated in the following example.

Assume that a company has three alternative sources of funds available to finance a machine that costs $9,000.

Alternative Number 1: Lease the equipment.

Assumptions: cost of leased facilities, $9,000; annual lease payments, $3,600; useful life, 3 years; term of lease, 3 years; residual value, 0; income tax, 50 percent; interest rate, 10 percent on declining balance.

Alternative Number 2: Buy on installments.

Assumptions: Down payment, $2,000; three equal annual installments; interest at 7 percent on declining balance.

Alternative Number 3: Borrow from bank.

Assumptions: Repay principal at end of third year; 7 percent interest paid annually.

The calculations in Table 15-3 depict the present value of the cash outlays that are made in connection with each alternative. Obviously, if all other things are equal, the alternative whose cash outlays have the lowest present value will be the most desirable.

Note that for all practical purposes alternatives 2 and 3 are superior to 1 in that both are "cheaper" when the present value of the cash outlay is used as a basis of comparison. From the standpoint of the number of dollars actually paid out, alternatives 1 and 3 are inferior to 2, but no consideration is given to the tax savings or the time value of funds.

---

[9]*Ibid.*, pp. 11-12.

TABLE 15-3

PRESENT VALUE OF THE CASH OUTLAY
FOR THREE METHODS OF FINANCING

Alternative Number One: Leasing	
$3,600 × 0.50 × 2.487 =	$4,476.60

Alternative Number Two: Installment Plan	
Down payment: $2,000 × 1.00 =	$2,000.00
Interest Payments:	
Year 1 $7,000.00 × 0.07 × 0.909 × 0.50 =	222.70
Year 2 $4,666.66 × 0.07 × 0.826 × 0.50 =	134.91
Year 3 $2,333.34 × 0.07 × 0.751 × 0.50 =	61.33
Principal Payments: $2,333.33 × 2.487 =	5,802.99
Present Value	$8,221.93
Less: Present Value of Depreciation	3,771.00
	$4,450.93

Alternative Number Three: Borrow From Bank	
Down payment =	0
Interest Payments:	
Year 1 $9,000 × 0.07 ⎫	
Year 2 $9,000 × 0.07 ⎬ × 0.50 × 2.487 =	$ 783.40
Year 3 $9,000 × 0.07 ⎭	
Principal Payments: $9,000 × 0.751	6,759.00
Present Value	$7,542.40
Less: Present Value of Depreciation	3,771.00
	$3.771.40

NOTE: Tax rate assumed to be 50 percent; cost of capital equals
10 percent.

Cost of a Lease. Lease payments are determined in many different ways, the most common being the level lease plan. This amount is determined by adding the interest cost to the principal amount and dividing by the number of years the lease will be outstanding. Assume the following: cost of the leased facilities, $9,000; useful life, 3 years; term of the lease, 3 years; scrap value, 0; nominal rate of interest of lease, 10 percent on the declining balance; income tax rate, 50 percent; and depreciation determined by using the sum-of-the-years'-digits method. The annual lease payment equals $3,600, derived by solving the following formula:

$$\frac{\text{Cost of leased facilities} + \text{Interest payments}}{\text{Number of years lease is outstanding}}$$

Substituting the data above into the formula, we have:

$$\$9,000 + \$1,800 \div 3 = \$3,600$$

Once the annual lease payment is known, the cost of the lease may be determined. The most accurate method of ascertaining this is to find the interest rate that discounts the net cash outlay of the lease to the purchased cost of the leased facilities. The following is the calculation of the leased equipment described above (see Table 15-4).

TABLE 15-4

COST CALCULATIONS OF LEASES

END OF YEAR	LEASE PAYMENT		DEPRECIATION SUM-OF-THE-YEARS'-DIGITS		PRESENT VALUE		
	Gross	After Tax	Gross	After Tax	Actual	6%	4%
1	$3,600	$1,800	$4,500	$2,250	$4,050	$3,819	$3,896
2	3,600	1,800	3,000	1,500	3,300	2,937	3,052
3	3,600	1,800	1,500	750	2,550	2,142	2,267
	$10,800	$5,400	$9,000	$4,500	$9,900	$8,898	$9,215

Interpolate: $\frac{\$215}{\$317}$ X 0.02 = 1.36 + 4.0 = 5.36 percent.

The cost of the lease is 5.36 percent, determined by using the following formula:

$$Q_0 - \sum_{t=1}^{N} \frac{C_t}{(1 + k)^t} = 0$$

where Q_0 = purchased price of equipment
C_t = net cash outlay (interest adjusted for taxes plus tax-adjusted depreciation)

SALE AND LEASEBACK

As stated above, sale and leaseback financing is the sale of an asset, generally real estate, that was previously acquired and financed out of the firm's own funds to another party, from whom it is then leased back on a long-term basis, such as 20 to 50 years. Although it is difficult to say precisely why this method of financing has increased in importance during the past several years, the change may be attributable to the growth of financial institutions and their effort to find attractive investments. Also, this technique allows firms to convert long-term investment in fixed assets to current assets. For example, firm A could sell its home office building for $1 million and sign a long-term lease with the purchasing unit. Immediately, its permanent working capital is increased by $1 million without an increase in debt or equity capital.

The following advantages, which accrue to both financial institutions and business firms, reveal why this particular technique has enjoyed such success during the past several years. The advantages for the financial institution are several. First, it is able to obtain a higher yield from such an arrangement than it could by holding high-grade bonds.

Second, it is generally conceded that the lessor is in a relatively safe position, since the types of firms that enter into these agreements have relatively small amounts of debt outstanding. In the event of insolvency, the lessor is not in as strong a position as a general creditor, since the lessee can obtain legal relief from rental obligations; however, until insolvency occurs, the lessor is in a very strong position, since the asset involved is of such character that the lessee cannot operate without it.

Third, the asset will, in many cases, have a value at the expiration of the lease. In this event, several courses of action are open to the investor. First, the lessor may allow the firm to repurchase the property at substantially the amortized value. Since tax problems may result from such a course of action, however, many firms refuse to grant options to repurchase the property. Second, the investor may sell the property and pay a capital gains tax; or third, the lessee may renew the lease at the going market rate, which means that the investor receives an even higher rate of return.

Two advantages most often accrue to the lessee. The first involves the release of capital funds for current use. If a firm can sell its fixed assets and reinvest the funds in current assets, it may improve its return on investment in two ways: First, the funds will be invested in assets that turn over faster; therefore their return will be higher in the long run than it would have been had the funds been invested in assets with a slow turnover. Second, if the firm raises the needed capital from equity sources at a time when the cost of equity capital is high, the earning power of each share will be diluted; therefore, it will benefit the firm to raise the necessary funds by selling its fixed assets instead.

The second major advantage of the sale and leaseback technique is that, under certain conditions, the firm can experience a definite tax saving. For example, suppose a firm sells the land and building that it has owned for the past 10 years for $60,000. The firm paid $20,000 for the building and $5,000 for the land. The economic life of the building is estimated to be 20 years, and depreciation is computed on a straight-line basis. Under these conditions, the transaction yields a net profit of $45,000. Since the firm can pay a capital-gains tax on the profit, the amount of the tax equals $13,500. The firm has increased its current assets by $46,500 and realized a profit on the sale, and it will be allowed to charge off the rental payments as an expense.[10] A sale-and-leaseback arrangement can also result in a tax saving when the value of the property has declined below the original cost.

---

[10]Sale of capital assets by a corporation is governed by complex regulations, but in some cases the profit can be treated as a capital gain. See Sec. 1231 IRC.

The financial manager must weigh several salient disadvantages of leasing against the advantages before making a final decision. The principal disadvantage is that capital secured in this manner often costs more than capital raised from traditional methods. Financial managers may find projects to be unprofitable if the assets are leased because of the differential between the return and the cost of capital raised in this manner. It is the author's opinion that future lease proposals will be examined more carefully now that more emphasis is being placed on the cost of capital. Additional disadvantages of leasing are: (1) inflexibility, resulting from the rigidity of the rental contract; and (2) the uncertain tax status of the sale-and-leaseback technique.

Leasing, which is a means of financing the cost of assets out of future earnings, should be given careful consideration by the financial manager. If, after all things are considered, it appears that the technique will result in a profitable venture, it should be adopted by the company.

16

Internal

Sources of Funds

By now students are aware that when working capital is applied to fixed capital, a flow of funds consisting of profits and noncash expenses is created. Although all these funds are available for use by management in the financing process, the actual amount used is predicated on the payout policies of the firm. Funds remaining in the firm after dividends have been paid are classified as retained profits, depreciation, and depletion, and may be used to finance working and fixed capital requirements.

Relatively, as well as quantitatively, funds from internal sources are more important than those obtained from external sources. For example, during 1967-1969, funds from internal sources never accounted for less than 53 percent—and ran as high as 65 percent—of all funds used by corporations. Comparatively speaking, such funds are roughly three times more important than funds obtained from the sale of long-term equity and debt instruments. The two major components of internal funds—retained earnings and depreciation— will receive particular attention in this chapter.

RETAINED EARNINGS

The relative importance of retained earnings as a source of funds makes it difficult to explain why many writers in the field of business finance have paid little or no attention to this source of capital. Compared to other sources of funds used during the years 1967-1969, retained earnings were exceeded in

TABLE 16-1

SOURCES AND USES OF FUNDS—
NONFARM, NONFINANCIAL CORPORATE
BUSINESS, 1967–1969
(in billions)

	1967		1968		1969	
	Amt.	*Percent*	*Amt.*	*Percent*	*Amt.*	*Percent*
Total Sources	$94.2	100.0	$110.4	100.0	$118.8	100.0
Internal Sources	61.2	65.0	63.1	57.1	62.7	52.8
Undistributed profits	21.2	22.5	22.0	19.9	20.9	17.6
Corporate inventory valuation adjustment	-1.1	-1.2	-3.2	-2.9	-5.6	-4.7
Capital consumption allowances	41.2	43.7	44.3	40.1	47.4	39.9
External Sources	33.0	35.0	47.3	42.8	56.1	47.2
Stocks	2.3	2.4	-.8	-0.7	4.3	3.6
Bonds	14.7	15.6	12.9	11.7	12.1	10.2
Mortgages	4.5	4.8	5.8	5.3	4.4	3.7
Bank loans, n.e.c.	6.4	6.8	9.6	8.7	10.9	9.2
Other loans	1.4	1.5	3.6	3.3	6.2	5.2
Trade debt	2.6	2.8	5.7	5.2	10.9	9.2
Profits tax liability	-4.1	-4.8	3.7	3.3	.8	.7
Other liabilities	5.2	5.5	6.9	6.2	6.5	5.5
Total Uses	86.0	100.0	103.5	100.0	111.7	100.0
Purchase of Physical Assets	72.5	84.3	76.9	74.3	87.5	7.8
Nonresidential fixed investment	63.8	74.2	68.0	65.7	77.2	69.1
Residential structures	2.2	2.6	2.3	2.2	2.9	2.6
Change in business inventories	6.4	7.4	6.5	6.3	7.4	6.6
Increase in Financial Assets	13.5	15.7	26.6	25.7	24.2	2.2
Liquid assets	.0	0	10.1	9.7	2.3	2.1
Demand deposits and currency	-2.2	-2.6	1.3	1.2	.5	.4
Time deposits	4.1	4.8	2.2	2.1	-7.8	-7.0
U.S. government securities	-3.1	-3.6	1.8	1.7	-1.4	-1.3
Open-market paper	1.5	1.7	4.5	4.3	8.7	7.8
State and local obligations	-.4	-0.5	.4	.3	2.3	2.0
Consumer credit	.9	0.1	1.7	1.6	1.3	1.2
Trade credit	8.8	10.2	14.8	14.2	17.3	15.5
Other financial assets	3.8	4.4	.1	.1	3.4	3.0
Discrepancy (uses less sources)	-8.2	-9.1	-6.9	-6.6	-7.0	-6.3

Source: Survey of Current Business (Washington D.C.: May 1970), U.S. Department of Commerce, Office of Business Economics, p. 18.

importance only by depreciation (see Table 16-1). In fact, funds obtained from the public and private sale of stocks and bonds during this three-year period exceeded retained earnings by only $8.6 billion.

Causes for the Increased Use of Retained Earnings

One of the primary reasons for the increased importance of retained earnings is the size of the personal income tax rate relative to the capital gains tax. The personal tax on ordinary income ranges from 14 to 70 percent, and the capital-gains tax amounts to only 50 percent of the personal tax rate with a maximum limit of 25 percent. The effect of this differential is that individuals would pay 14 to 70 percent on income received in the form of cash dividends, but if the earnings are retained, presumably equity capital will increase in subsequent periods by the amount retained plus the amount earned on these funds. If owners wish to receive cash, they can sell the stock and pay a capital-gains tax on the difference between the market price and the price they paid for the stock—assuming, of course, that the stock has been held for at least six months. The majority of firms that follow the practice of retaining large amounts of capital either issue stock dividends or split the stock in order to allow owners to realize cash while at the same time maintaining their original investment in the form of stock. IBM is a good example of a firm following such a policy.

To prevent abuses arising from this practice, the government imposes a tax on any corporation that retains an unreasonable amount of earnings. Such a tax was first passed in the form of an undistributed-profits tax in 1936; the law was repealed in 1940, but Section 531 was added to the *Internal Revenue Code*, imposing a punitive tax on retained earnings that exceeded need. The tax now consists of a surtax of 27.5 percent on the first $100,000 of unreasonably re-tained earnings and 38.5 percent on the remainder. Although need is the basis for the retention of earnings, authorities do not impose the tax on any business that retains less than $100,000. Some firms may take advantage of the govern-ment and retain funds in excess of their actual needs, but it is doubtful that there is widespread violation of the spirit of the law.

A second reason for using internal rather than external sources is the differ-ence in the cost of procurement. Selling securities to the public can be quite expensive, particularly if an underwriter is used and the securities are registered with the Securities and Exchange Commission. As a result, the proprietary in-terest of shareholders is diluted. To illustrate, suppose a firm earning 10 percent on invested capital needs $500,000 for expansion purposes. The flotation costs on $500,000 amount to $50,000 if the funds are raised by selling stock to the public; therefore, the firm is required to raise $550,000. In order for the present shareholders to continue earning 10 percent on their investment, the new capital must earn 11 percent. Had retained earnings been used, the firm would have increased investment by only $500,000 and would have had to earn only 10 percent to protect the interest of existing shareholders.

The retention of earnings is not always advantageous, since under certain circumstances shareholders lose by not receiving the earnings in the form of cash dividends. For example, in many cases the stocks of firms that pay a high rate of dividends have a higher market price than the stocks of companies that retain the majority of their earnings. This is because of the time-value concept; that is, a dollar today is worth more than one received at some later date. In some cases the reverse is true; that is, investors will pay more for the stock if the firm reinvests its earnings. The principal reason for this is that the shareholders believe the firm can earn more than they themselves could if they were to invest the funds received in the form of cash dividends.

Policy Governing Retained Earnings

The financial manager asks the question: What should I do, retain my earnings or pay them out in the form of cash dividends? The considerations regarding dividend policy set forth in Chapter 12 should be taken into account when making retained earnings policy. In addition, several other factors should be considered.

The formulation of retained earnings policy for a large corporation differs greatly from procedures used by small or middle-sized firms. The desires and wants of the majority of the shareholders of large companies are unknown to management and cannot be considered when policy is formulated. This is not true in small and middle-sized corporations. It is suggested, therefore, that whenever possible, management consider the wishes of the shareholders in establishing policy regarding retained earnings.

A second matter to be weighed is *need*. If the firm does not actually need the funds, management should not retain them in the business. Funds invested that are not needed decrease the firm's investment turnover, and all other things being equal, this results in a reduction in the rate of return on investment. Unless offsetting policies are adopted, the market value of the stock will decline. On the other hand, management has every right to invest the earnings of shareholders if there is a need and if the expected earnings from these investments will equal what a shareholder would receive by investing the funds himself.

The cost of flotation should be considered by management when raising equity funds. As we mentioned above, flotation costs are higher for funds raised in the marketplace than for those retained from earnings. This is particularly true for small and middle-sized firms, and careful attention should be given to this factor when capital procurement policies are being formulated.

Finally, we should remember that equity funds serve as a base for debt capital, and the correct proportion of equity should always be maintained.

DEPRECIATION AS A SOURCE OF FUNDS

The reader should now direct his attention again to Table 16-1, in order to observe the role that depreciation plays in the financing process. Note that depreciation is the largest single supplier of funds. During the past several years, considerable argument has taken place among academicians concerning the true nature of depreciation. Is it or is it not a source of funds? The argument is largely semantic and does not warrant long discussion. Yet the number of dollars represented by depreciation is so great that several statements are in order, to support the contention that depreciation is a source of funds.

First, for all practical purposes, by including the depreciation expense in the price of its goods and services, a firm is *selling its fixed assets* piecemeal. Those who contend that depreciation is not a source of funds also argue that the sale of fixed assets results in an increase of funds and is therefore a source of funds.

Using the same argument, it is difficult to see why depreciation is not also considered a source of funds, since the firm is selling its fixed assets in smaller pieces but selling them nevertheless.

Others advance the argument that depreciation cannot be a source of funds since it is an expense. They contend that if depreciation is a source of funds, why are not labor expenses, cost of inventories, cost of supplies, and overhead also considered sources of funds? They argue that these are expenses, and the only true source of funds results from external sources such as (1) the sale of both debt and credit instruments, (2) the sale of fixed assets, and (3) funds received from net sales.

Let us examine this statement. No argument can be advanced against item (1), but (2) and (3) can certainly be questioned, provided the logic used matches that set forth when arguing that depreciation is not a source of funds because it is an expense. That is, unless a profit is received, the sale of fixed assets is nothing more than the return of capital that was previously raised from "true" sources of funds. In the case of (3), the funds received from sales are equal to the total of all costs plus profit. This being the case, the funds representing costs should be classified as the return of funds previously raised, and only profit represents a source of funds.

The above arguments support the contention that the problem is one of semantics. The opinion of the writer is that any funds returned to the business—from depreciation or any other expense—are available for use and, in this frame of reference, constitute a "source" of funds. Terminating this debate, let us now direct our attention to more important facets of the subject.

Depreciation Policy

Good managerial practices require that management protect the owners' investment in working and fixed assets. To accomplish the latter necessitates that the original investment be recovered by the time the assets are "worn out." The method used to recover investment is to include in the prices of the firm's goods and services an amount equal to the wear and tear (depreciation) of the assets used in their production. If the depreciation expense is properly calculated, the original cost minus scrap value will have been recovered by the time the asset wears out. When this occurs, management can replace the asset from the capital that has accumulated from the depreciation charges. In this way the investor's capital has been protected. We should point out that very seldom does management replace worn-out assets with precisely the same funds that have been accumulated from depreciation charges. We can easily see that if the funds were kept idle until an asset needed replacing, management would be inefficient.

The depreciation charge, unlike other expenses, does not represent a cash outlay; consequently, management may use these funds for any valid purpose—for example, to increase cash, inventories, and accounts receivable; to pay taxes, dividends, or wages; or to buy other fixed assets. A simple illustration makes this point clear. Assume that company *A* buys a machine with an economic life of five years for $1,800. Assume further that at the end of five years the machine is scrapped and sold for $300. In order to protect its investment, management will charge off $300 in expenses each year; that is to say, the price of all products produced by the machine during the year will be increased by $300. The machine will not be replaced until the beginning of the sixth year; therefore, the firm's cash flow is increased by $300 annually and is available for use wherever management feels that it will best serve the interests of the company.

The policy determining how much to charge off each year is influenced by many factors. Before entering into a discussion of these, it may be well to mention briefly the various ways of calculating depreciation. Four of the most common of the many diverse ways of computing depreciation are (1) the straight-line, (2) the unit-of-production, (3) the double-rate declining-balance, and (4) the sum-of-the-years'-digits methods.[1]

The straight-line method is the easiest to calculate and is probably the one most widely used today. To ascertain the amount to be charged off during éach period, the number of years of useful life is divided into the original cost minus the scrap value of the asset. The most difficult step of this method is the determination of the asset's useful life. This method presumes that the annual wear and tear of the asset will be uniform. This assumption should be criticized, since in most cases physical wear is greater in the last years of the asset's life.

When the unit-of-production method is used, the depreciation charge is calculated by dividing the estimated units of production into the original cost minus scrap value. This method allows depreciation to be charged in direct proportion to the usage of the asset. That is, the regularity of the expense is dependent upon the regularity of the use of the asset. A weakness of this method is that the wear and tear of the asset may not be associated primarily with its use.

The double-rate declining-balance method of computing depreciation consists of applying a constant depreciation rate to a declining asset value. A simple example illustrates this method. A $1,000 asset with a useful life of 10 years is depreciated as follows: $1,000 × 20 percent = $200; $800 × 20 percent = $160; $640 × 20 percent = $128; and so forth. Note that the value of the asset in each subsequent year is reduced by the amount of the depreciation of the preceding year. The primary advantage of this method is that the depreciation charge is greatest in the first years of the asset's life and decreases thereafter. A disadvantage of this method is that an undepreciated value is always left at the end of the useful life of the asset. To depreciate the asset fully, it is necessary for management to switch back to the straight-line method in the latter years of the asset's life. The commissioner of Internal Revenue will permit this double-rate declining-balance method only if the rate used will not yield an amount exceeding 200 percent of the straight-line method; for example, if the straight-line is 10 percent, the IRS will not allow a rate in excess of 20 percent.

---

[1] For taxable years beginning after June 1972, corporations can use only straight-line (or other ratable deduction over useful life) methods in figuring earnings and profits.

The depreciation resulting from the sum-of-the-years'-digits method is calculated by applying a changing percentage rate of depreciation to a constant base (original cost minus scrap). To illustrate, assume that an asset costs $2,000, has a useful life of five years, and will have a salvage value of $500. Depreciation equals 5/15 of $1,500 in the first year, 4/15 of $1,500 in the second year, 3/15 of $1,500 in the third year, and so on. Computed thus, depreciation amounts to $500, $400, $300, $200, and $100, respectively, over the five years of the asset's life.

Factors Affecting Depreciation Policy

One of the primary functions of management is to see that the funds invested in the firm's assets are protected and that the costs of the fixed assets are returned to the firm by the time the assets have been expended. The government, recognizing this responsibility, allows management to charge off a depreciation charge in each accounting period. It has been noted that management is not bound by any one method of determining the depreciation. The reader will readily see that two of the methods described above allow a larger amount to be charged off during the early years of the asset's life, whereas the straight-line and unit-of-production methods prorate the expense evenly over the life of the asset (assuming that the production is spread evenly over the life of the asset).

In choosing the method of computing depreciation, management should first examine its basic requirements and then select the method that yields the greatest advantage. A primary factor is the capital needs of the business. A firm that is short of funds should select the method providing the largest amount of funds during the early years of the asset's life. The following hypothetical example illustrates this point. Two new firms have purchased fixed assets costing $100,000. Assume that the life of these assets is 20 years, with no scrap value at the end of the period. Firm A uses the straight-line method; firm B employs the sum-of-the-years'-digits method. The following financial data show the impact that each method has on the cash flow of the firms.

	Firm A	Firm B
Net Sales	$100,000	$100,000
All Expenses except Depreciation	− 88,000	− 88,000
Profit Before Depreciation	$ 12,000	$ 12,000
Depreciation Charges	− 5,000	− 9,520
Profit Before Taxes	$ 7,000	$ 2,480
Taxes	− 1,540	− 546
Profit After Taxes	$ 5,460	$ 1,934
Depreciation	+ 5,000	+ 9,520
Cash Flow	$ 10,460	$ 11,454

The data reveal that firm B has $994 more for operational purposes than firm A. From this we may conclude that by using either the double-declining-balance or sum-of-the-years'-digits methods, a firm will be able to secure more funds from internal sources during the early years of the asset's life than will a company that employs the straight-line or unit-of-production method.

A second consideration that influences the choice is the fact that funds received today are worth more than those received at some later date. This is because a firm can re-employ the funds at profitable rates and thus produce additional funds. It is obvious that any technique that produces larger depreciation charges in the earlier years is superior from this standpoint to those that produce smaller amounts.

Depreciation is an expense and as such affects the tax bill of the firm. If a method permits a larger charge-off in the earlier years than in the later years, the firm will be called upon to pay less taxes during the years of the high depreciation charges. Conversely, the firm will have to pay more taxes during the later years of the asset's life. If the firm's relative profit position does not change, the higher taxes will offset the lower taxes, with the only advantage gained being the ability to reinvest the funds for a longer period of time. We may conclude that if all other things are equal, it is advantageous to use the depreciation method that allows larger write-offs during the early years of the asset's life. We should point out, however, that small firms may move into a higher tax bracket only to find that they are paying more taxes by using methods that permitted larger write-offs during the first years of the asset's life. The following tabulation illustrates this.

	Year 1	Year 2	Year 3	Year 4	Year 5
Revenue After All Costs Except Depreciation	$20,000	$30,000	$40,000	$50,000	$60,000
Sum-of-Years'-Digits Depreciation	5,000	4,000	3,000	2,000	1,000
Straight-Line Depreciation	3,000	3,000	3,000	3,000	3,000
Tax–Sum-of-Years'-Digits Method	3,300	5,980	11,260	16,540	21,820
Tax–Straight-Line Method	3,740	6,460	11,260	16,160	20,860

It is seem from these data that by using the straight-line method, the firm would realize a tax saving of $420 in actual dollars over the five-year period. Next, remembering that a dollar received today is more valuable that one received at a later date, it is necessary (1) to find the present value of the tax cost and (2) to decide which method is the most advantageous. The following data reveal this information, if the firm's cost of capital equals 10 percent. It may be noted that the straight-line method offers an advantage of $59 over the sum-of-the-years'-digits method.

When the time value of funds is considered, of course, the "real" dollar cost of the accelerated method decreases, since fewer dollars are paid out in the early years, whereas the opposite is true when the straight-line method is used.

The purpose of the discussion above is to point out to the student that there are certain conditions under which one method is more advantageous than an-

Year	Sum-of-the-Years'-Digits Method		Straight-Line Method	
	Tax	Present Value of Tax[a]	Tax	Present Value of Tax[a]
1	$3,300	$3,000	$3,740	$3,400
2	5,980	4,939	6,460	5,336
3	11,260	8,456	11,260	8,456
4	16,540	11,297	16,160	11,037
5	21,820	13,550	20,860	12,954
	$58,900	$41,242	$58,480	$41,183

[a] Discount rate equals 10 percent.

other. The finance officer's responsibility is to determine and to put to use the method that is the best for the business firm over the long run.

A word of caution should be sounded regarding the practices of building up idle capital (primarily cash) through improper depreciation policies and of retaining earnings in excess of need. Everyone would criticize a firm that sold equity or debt securities when its assets were unemployed; yet, many companies today raise funds from internal sources for which they do not have a legitimate need. Recognizing that such a practice may exist among business corporations, *Fortune* made a study of the cash position of the 1,000 largest corporations in 1969—a study that, to say the least, was quite revealing.[2] The data contained in Table 16-2 were either taken directly from the article or computed from the financial data compiled by *Fortune*. The principal finding of the survey was that a very large number of firms held excessive cash; for example, 20 of the 1,000 largest corporations in the United States held more than 24.4 percent of their total assets in cash.

Of interest also is that, although the firms listed in Table 16-2 held abnormal amounts of cash or "near" cash, they enjoyed an excellent return on invested capital. Of the 20 companies whose cash equaled 25 percent of their assets or better, only three earned less than 10 percent on invested capital. In the light of such an earnings record, it may be said that these firms have been operated successfully. But were they operated as efficiently as possible? The answer to this question is revealed by an examination of columns five and six. If each of these firms had reduced its cash or "near" cash accounts by 50 percent, either by paying additional dividends or by buying its own stock, it would have raised the rate of return on invested capital substantially. In fact, without exception, every firm could have increased its rate of return on invested capital by 16 percent or more, and one firm could have increased its return by nearly 60 percent.

The primary function of the finance officer is to raise funds when they are needed from the most advantageous source or sources, but never to obtain funds that will not be used in the most effective manner, regardless of the source.

[2]"Extremes of the Liquidity Spectrum," *Fortune*, June 1970, p. 174.

TABLE 16-2

STATUS OF THE CASH ACCOUNT OF
TWENTY COMPANIES IN 1969
(in millions)

	CASH OR NEAR CASH[a]				
Companies	Amount	Percent of Assets	Net Income, Percent of Invested Capital	Adjusted Percent of Invested Capital	Net Income,[b] Percentage Change
Tampax	$ 25.2	45.1	34.6	48.1	39.0
Dow Jones	42.9	44.2	31.7	47.0	48.3
Polaroid	209.2	43.2	14.9	19.8	33.0
Marmon Group	23.4	42.0	11.5	17.5	52.2
Federal Company	38.5	38.6	31.2	43.0	38.0
Skyline	14.3	38.0	40.9	62.6	53.0
Maytag	36.4	36.4	25.4	32.3	27.2
Beeline Fashions	6.3	35.9	22.7	31.8	44.5
Parke Davis	140.8	35.3	9.7	14.3	47.5
Screw and Bolt Corporation of America	12.6	34.9	8.8	11.9	35.2
Northwestern Steel & Wire	46.5	33.6	14.4	16.8	16.7
Zenith Radio	103.8	30.9	17.6	22.9	30.2
Rheingold	25.6	26.6	15.7	24.9	58.6
Olympia Brewing	13.4	26.5	13.8	16.4	18.8
Lane	14.3	26.5	11.8	14.1	19.5
General Battery	10.1	26.3	13.9	20.3	46.0
Masco	14.5	25.3	20.3	26.2	29.1
Cannon Mills	61.9	24.6	7.1	8.4	18.4
Pabst Brewing	50.0	24.5	14.2	16.8	18.3
Plough	23.6	24.4	20.1	23.7	17.9

[a] Bank deposits and all securities shown as current assets or government securities held as offsets against tax liabilities.
[b] Computed on invested capital remaining after the firm had theoretically paid out 50 percent of its cash in dividends.
Source: "Extremes of the Liquidity Spectrum," Fortune, June 1970, p. 174; "The Fortune Directory of 500 Largest Industrial Corporations," Fortune, May 1970, pp. 98-117; "The Fortune Directory of the Second 500 Largest Industrial Corporations," Fortune, May 1970, pp. 182-200.

Is Depreciation Adequate?

A word about the adequacy of depreciation charges may be worthwhile at this point. If the object of depreciation is to recover the original cost of the assets involved, many believe that the depreciation flows resulting from present methods are adequate. This is not true only when losses are such that depreciation charges are never earned. The problem confronting businesses today is that, although original cost may be recovered, depreciation still may not be adequate. Let us examine this point.

Management is not held responsible for an impairment of capital only when legitimate losses are incurred from operations. To illustrate, by law, directors are jointly and severally responsible for the payment of cash dividends when a corporation is insolvent or would become insolvent if dividends were declared. Yet the same law will not allow sufficient depreciation charges to be written off to replace existing fixed assets during periods of rising prices. It has been argued that under such conditions business firms are taxed on fictitious profits. Stated somewhat more strongly, the government is impairing the capital of the business firm.

The use of replacement cost rather than original cost has been advanced as one solution to this problem. In all fairness we should point out that the use of replacement cost has not yet been accepted as a solution. Another possible solution is to allow firms to charge off the difference between the original and replacement cost at the time the worn-out machine is replaced.

It is not the intent of the writer to explore the problems inherent in these two solutions, but only to point up one of the major problems confronting businessmen today and to recommend that serious thought be given to solving it.

17

Long-Term
Debt Financing

The average business firm utilizes three types of debt in the financing process: short-term, intermediate-term, and long-term. Since short-term and intermediate debt have already been discussed, we now direct our attention to the general subject of long-term debt. Long-term or funded debt refers to liabilities with a maturity longer than five years and is included under the long-term liabilities section of the balance sheet.

Long-term debt may be obtained through the issuance of formal instruments to the public as well as through informal instruments issued privately. The formal instruments are usually sold to the public by middlemen and may take the form of mortgage bonds, debentures, collateral trust bonds, equipment trust certificates, and income bonds. The informal instruments are usually long-term notes, placed directly in the hands of the investor by the issuer.

This chapter is concerned with the following facets of debt financing: (1) general characteristics of long-term debt instruments, (2) relative importance of this type of financing, (3) general nature of the indenture, and (4) the provisions contained in indentures.

IMPORTANT OF DEBT FINANCING

The principal reasons for using debt to finance working and fixed capital were set forth in Chapter 9, and it was emphasized that they applied to small businesses as well as to middle-sized and larger firms. However, from a quantitative standpoint, middle-sized and large firms are by far the most important users of bonds and other long-term debt. Table 17-1 reveals the volume of new securities issued during the years 1962-1969 and Table 17-2 shows the volume issued by various users. An examination of these tables reveals that the relative importance of bonds declined sharply during 1968 and 1969. In 1967 the dollar volume of bonds accounted for 89 percent of all new issues, but it fell to 79 percent in 1968 and to 69 percent in 1969. During the same period the sale of common stock rose sharply; the volume obtained through the sale of common stock rose 294 percent in this period. High interest rates probably caused some companies to employ common stocks rather than bonds as a method of raising long-term funds. In addition, management substituted short-term debt for long-term debt with the idea of refinancing when interest rates declined.

An analysis of Table 17-2 shows that firms in the manufacturing and public utility industries are by far the largest users of bonds. It is interesting to note that the decrease in the amount of bonds used by manufacturers accounted for the overall decline in bonds utilized by all industries. Stated differently, the demand for bonds remained reasonably constant in all industries except manufacturing.

Bonds were considerably more important than stock, accounting for 69 to 90 percent of the funds raised through the sale of new issues. This does not mean that business firms use more debt than equity in the financing process; it means rather that they rely more heavily on internal than external sources for equity funds.

The majority of bonds were sold to private investors during the years 1962-1965, but beginning in 1966 this trend was reversed. This is attributed directly to rising interest rates. That is to say, due to the increase in interest rates, investors other than financial institutions directed larger amounts of their funds into this market.

TABLE 17-1

TOTAL NEW ISSUES OF CORPORATE SECURITIES
(in millions)

| | | | GROSS PROCEEDS, ALL ISSUES | | | |
| | | BONDS | | | STOCK | |
Year	Total, Bonds and Stocks	Total Bonds	Publicly Offered	Privately Placed	Preferred	Common
1962	$10,705	$ 8,969	$ 4,440	$4,529	$422	$1,314
1963	12,211	10,856	4,713	6,143	343	1,011
1964	13,957	10,865	3,623	7,243	412	2,679
1965	15,992	13,720	5,570	8,150	725	1,547
1966	18,074	15,561	8,018	7,542	574	1,939
1967	24,798	21,954	14,990	6,964	885	1,959
1968	21,966	17,383	10,732	6,651	637	3,946
1969	26,744	18,347	12,734	5,613	682	7,714

NOTE: Figures rounded.

Source: Federal Reserve Bulletin, December 1970, p. A46.

TABLE 17-2

TOTAL NEW ISSUES, BY TYPE OF USER
(in millions)

YEAR	GROSS PROCEEDS, MAJOR GROUPS OF CORPORATE ISSUERS											
	Manufacturing		Commercial and Miscellaneous		Transportation		Public Utility		Communication		Real Estate and Financial	
	Bonds	Stocks	Bonds	Stocks	Bonds	Stocks	Bonds	Stocks	Bonds	Stocks	Bonds	Stocks
1962	$2,880	$ 404	$ 622	$ 274	$ 573	$ 14	$2,279	$ 562	$1,264	$ 43	$1,397	$ 457
1963	3,202	313	676	150	948	9	2,259	418	953	152	2,818	313
1964	2,819	228	902	220	944	38	2,139	620	669	1,520	3,391	466
1965	4,712	704	1,153	251	953	60	2,332	604	808	139	3,762	514
1966	5,861	1,208	1,166	257	1,856	116	3,117	549	1,814	189	1,747	193
1967	9,894	1,164	1,950	117	1,859	466	4,217	718	1,786	193	2,247	186
1968	5,668	1,311	1,759	116	1,665	1,579	4,407	873	1,724	43	2,159	662
1969	4,448	1,904	1,888	3,022	1,899	247	5,409	1,326	1,963	225	2,739	1,671

Source: *Federal Reserve Bulletin*, May 1970, p. A46.

GENERAL CHARACTERISTICS
OF LONG-TERM DEBT INSTRUMENTS

Long-term debt instruments take the form of bonds and long-term promissory notes. Although the two are similar, bonds are much more formal. A bond may be defined as a "written promise, under seal, to pay a specified sum of money at a fixed time in the future, usually more than ten years after the promise is made, with interest at a fixed rate, payable at specified interest dates."[1] The bond is covered by a trust indenture, which is a contract between the issuer and lender, usually made out to a trustee. A bond differs from a promissory note primarily in its formality; although long-term notes are not generally accompanied by indentures under the supervision of trustees, they are frequently represented by contracts containing essentially the same provisions. Since long-term promissory notes are usually connected with private placement, all further discussion pertaining to this type of instrument is deferred until Chapter 18.

Bonds are usually issued in amounts of $1,000; however, smaller denominations have recently become popular. Interest is based on the face amount of the bond; that is, the issuer promises to pay a fixed rate of interest on or before the dates specified in the bond contract. Interest payments, unlike dividends, are fixed charges and become a liability of the firm on the specified date of payment. Bond interest is considered an expense of doing business and is tax deductible. Because bond interest is a liability of the corporation, failure to pay it constitutes default and, in most cases, accelerates the maturity of the principal. Unless both are paid, the firm is subject to bankruptcy proceedings.

Bondholders do not as a general rule have any voting privileges and cannot be classified as owners of the business. Rather, they are classified as creditors and, as such, have prior claim to the firm's assets in the event of liquidation. The relative position of a particular creditor depends upon his relative position with other creditors.

Bonds may be secured by real property, personal property, or the general credit of the corporation. In cases of bonds secured by real property, the standard practice is to secure the issue with a mortgage. Specifically, this means that a lien against certain assets is given to the creditor, as in the case of mortgage bonds and equipment bonds. In the event of default of either the interest or principal, the creditor may seize the pledged assets and dispose of them at auction. If the assets are sold for an amount exceeding the debt, the creditor is paid and the remainder returned to the borrower. If the mortgaged property is sold for an amount less than the debt, the creditor receives the entire amount, and his status changes to that of a general creditor. In addition to real property, firms rely on stocks, bonds, and personal property as security. Col-

---

[1] Charles W. Gerstenberg, *Financial Organization and Management of Business*, 4th rev. ed. (Englewood Cliffs, N.J.: Prentice-Hall, Inc., 1959), p. 104.

lateral trust funds are examples of debt instruments secured by personal property.

Unsecured obligations are not literally lacking in security; they simply make no specific claim against either real or personal property. They are, however, secured by the general credit of the corporation. Debenture bonds are the most common type of unsecured bonds.

Regardless of the type of security supporting the bonds, they are usually issued in one of the following three forms: (1) bearer form, (2) fully registered as to principal and interest, or (3) registered as to principal only. Registration simply means that the name and address of the owner and the date of registering is recorded by the registrar. Bonds registered as to principal only are actually coupon bonds; that is, coupons are clipped and forwarded by the owner to the interest-paying agent.

The maturities of bonds vary; for example, a few bonds have been issued with maturities of 100 years, but these are rare, and the majority have maturities of from 10 to 30 years. In some cases the maturity of the bond is matched with the life of the assets it is used to finance; that is, if bonds are issued to pay for a machine whose life is 10 years, the bond's maturity will be approximately 10 years. When there is no particular asset associated with a bond issue, the size of the firm's cash flow generally guides management in establishing the bond maturity.

Companies may issue bonds that mature all at one time, or they may issue serial bonds, which means that a definite amount matures each year. To illustrate, bonds numbered 1 through 9 would mature in 1968, bonds numbered 10 through 19 would be due in 1969, bonds 20 through 29 would mature in 1970, and so forth.

THE TRUST INDENTURE AND
THE TRUSTEE

The trust indenture or deed of trust made out to the trustee is the contract between the bondholder and the issuing corporation. Although the various types of provisions contained in the contract are peculiar to the corporation involved, the most common ones may be divided into three groups. The first group includes provisions regarding (1) organizational and administrative matters, (2) description of the pledged property, (3) provisions assuring maintenance and insurance, and (4) provisions for action in the event of default.

The second group of contract terms is customarily requested by the borrower and is designed to provide flexibility for the firm. Examples of these features are (1) redemption and convertible clauses, (2) provisions for amending the indenture, and (3) provisions for adjusting the sinking fund requirements.

The third group includes terms designed to protect the lender. These terms are usually restrictive in nature; for example, provisions setting forth the conditions for (1) the declaration of dividends, (2) the creation of additional liens,

(3) the sale of additional securities by the firm or its subsidiaries, (4) lease financing, (5) mergers or consolidations, (6) the acquisition of additional assets, and (7) the reduction of bonded indebtedness through the use of sinking funds.

If any of these restrictions prohibits actions that are considered necessary for the well-being of the firm, management should immediately enter into negotiations with the lenders to amend or remove such provisions. If, after negotiation, lenders fail to amend or eliminate the provisions, management should seek ways to circumvent them legally. Although several of the above provisions cannot be legally avoided, there are some that are subject to evasion. For example, many lenders require the so-called acquired property clause to be included in the closed-end mortgage. This clause states in general that property acquired at some future time must serve as security for the existing mortgage. The problem is immediately obvious; that is, a firm would have difficulty in financing the acquisition of new property with a bond issue when the newly acquired property would be subject to the lien of a previously issued mortgage. If the bonds could be sold at all, they would receive a low rating and would carry a very high interest rate. Management can avoid the acquired property clause by any one of the following methods: refunding or redemption, purchase money mortgage, leasing, financing through subsidiaries, or consolidation.

Leasing property is an ideal way to circumvent provisions that prevent the issuance of additional debt. For example, a typical provision states that bonds shall not be issued if the net earnings applicable to the payment of interest for 24 months out of the 36 preceding are not equal to or greater than four times the amount of the interest charges. Since leases are not considered debt contracts and are not included in the balance sheet, they may be used as a substitute for debt without violating the terms of the indenture.

The provisions of an indenture are often so long and complicated that it is impractical for each bondholder to enforce its terms. To overcome this difficulty, a trustee is appointed by the corporation to act for the bondholders. Although the trustee is hired by the corporation, his primary responsibility is to the bondholders. If the trustee fails to fulfill this responsibility, the bondholders may have him removed and cause a new one to be appointed. In addition he may be held liable for damages by the bondholders. Although the specific duties of the trustee vary with provisions of the indenture, the following are the primary duties of the trustee: (1) authentication of bonds, (2) checking performance of covenants, and (3) enforcing the terms of the indenture.

The Trust Indenture Act of 1939 regulates trust indentures covering bonds, debentures, and notes sold in interstate commerce. The purpose of the act is twofold: (1) to provide for full disclosure of the provisions of the indenture at all times, and (2) to assure security holders that trustees will have high standards of conduct, thereby prohibiting individuals or firms who might have conflicts of interest with bondholders from serving in the capacity of trustees.

In addition to the trustee, there is usually a registrar whose primary function is to record the names of the registered bondholders. In some cases there is also an agent, who is responsible for interest payments on the bonds.

METHODS OF ELIMINATING
BONDED INDEBTEDNESS

As mentioned earlier, bonds have fixed maturity dates, and in order to prevent possible financial embarrassment, management should plan for their orderly liquidation. In addition to liquidating bonded indebtedness when it matures, management may find it advantageous to replace existing bonds with other debt instruments or with equity-type securities.

Bonds may be eliminated in several ways; these are: (1) purchasing the outstanding bonds with cash, (2) replacing existing securities with more desirable securities of the same general type, and (3) exchanging existing securities for securities of a completely different type.

Cash may be exchanged for outstanding securities upon maturity or before. Exchanging cash for debt securities upon maturity presents no problem and is generally handled by the trustee. Many firms provide the necessary cash for repurchasing purposes either by the creation of sinking funds or by borrowing the funds when redemption is to take place. In the case of a sinking fund, the funds may be used immediately by the trustee to retire the bonds, or they may be invested in other securities whose maturities coincide with those of the outstanding bonds. The exchange of cash for bonds before they mature necessitates: (1) the inclusion of an agreement (call provision) in the indenture, giving management the right to call the bonds at its discretion; (2) the purchase of bonds directly from the bondholder; or (3) the purchase of the bonds in the open market.

Management customarily includes a call provision in the indenture, anticipating that it will be advantageous to eliminate existing securities before they mature. This provision sets forth the date when the bonds may be called, as well as the price at which they will be repurchased. Generally, the date is set sufficiently far in the future to be attractive to investors. The price at which the bonds are to be called usually exceeds par for a specified time, thereafter declining to par. In addition to the call date and price, the amount of bonds to be called is clearly set forth in the indenture.

If bonds are to be redeemed under the call provision, it is the duty of the trustee to notify the bondholders that the call privilege is to be exercised. As the bonds are presented, the trustee makes payment and sends the bonds in for cancellation. When redemption is to take place without a call provision, the issuer negotiates directly with the bondholder. In such cases, the redemption price is determined by negotiation; however, if the issuer repurchases the bonds in the open market, the price is fixed by supply and demand.

The technique generally known as refunding may be used to eliminate debt securities by substituting a new security, usually another debt instrument, for the one that is outstanding. Refunding usually takes place prior to or near the maturity date of the outstanding security. The process can be effected by (1) the direct exchange of bonds with the bondholder, or (2) issuing new securities to the public and using the proceeds to liquidate the securities to be refunded. If a direct exchange is to be undertaken, the issuer will, after negotiation, exchange the old securities for new ones. If security holders do not wish to exchange securities, a new issue may be offered to the public, with proceeds of the sale used to liquidate the outstanding securities. This type of financing is generally referred to as secondary financing; that is, no new assets are acquired, nor is there any change in the amount of liabilities outstanding.

Persuading existing shareholders to accept new securities for existing obligations usually requires a premium. This premium may take the form of (1) cash bonuses, (2) higher rates of interest, (3) better security, or (4) some new and advantageous provisions.

The final method of eliminating existing debt obligations is to arrange for bondholders to exchange their securities for some other type of securities—for example, preferred or common stock. The privilege of converting one security for another is included in the bond indenture and may be exercised by the bondholder. We should mention that the issuer expects to receive some benefit from the conversion; otherwise such a provision would not have been included in the indenture. The primary advantages the issuer expects to receive are: (1) to improve the salability of the bonds, (2) to reduce the cost of raising funds, and (3) to lower the cost of capital by taking advantage of the best market at the time of the issue.

To assure conversion, management must set the conversion rate in a way that encourages the exchange. Usually the rate is stated in terms of an exchange of one bond for shares of stock at a specific price or one bond for a certain number of shares of stock. Occasionally the conversion price is improved (from the corporation's viewpoint) over time; for example, one bond is exchanged for 5 shares of stock until the end of December 1970; one bond exchanged for 4½ shares of stock until the end of December 1972; and so forth. The principal reason for such a schedule is to force conversion.

As a general rule, the time during which conversion is allowed is set forth in the bond indenture. Although it is difficult to generalize, most conversion privileges are limited; that is, after a certain date the conversion privilege is null and void. Furthermore, there is usually a period immediately following the issuing date when no conversion can take place. The length of time in both cases is based on the desires and objectives of the issuer. Several other provisions are ordinarily included in the indenture; these are: (1) an agreement that sufficient securities will be on hand at all times to effect the conversion without difficulty, (2) a provision adjusting interest and dividend charges at the time of conversion, and (3) provisions for the cancellation of the debt securities.

Management may prefer to eliminate bonds from its capital structure before maturity for several reasons; the most important are: (1) to replace bonds that have high interest rates with securities that are not as expensive, (2) to eliminate provisions that may act as a deterrent to new financing, (3) to eliminate contract terms that limit freedon of operations, and (4) to invest idle cash.

We should emphasize that since conditions constantly change, management should include provisions in all debt obligations that will allow it to purchase for cash or refund existing securities when such action is warranted.

WARRANTS

Many firms have found it extremely advantageous to include "sweeteners" in their indentures; that is, to increase the desirability of the bonds in order to attract a larger market. One such device is the warrant, which has become quite popular during the past several years.

Warrants are options to purchase a specific number of shares of a particular security, generally common stock, at a predetermined price. The price may or may not vary with time. To enhance the warrant's value it may be detachable, in which case it may be separated from the bond and sold.

The warrant has two values: theoretical and actual. The former is determined by subtracting the option price from the market price of the security and multiplying the result by the number of shares the warrant holder is authorized to buy. Assume the following: the Conec Company permits the owner of each warrant to purchase one share of common stock for $15. The stock and warrants are traded on the American Stock Exchange, priced at $30 and $20, respectively. In this case the theoretical value is $10 but the actual price is $20. In many cases the warrant will sell above its theoretical value; that is, the investor will pay a premium for the warrant (determined by subtracting the theoretical value from the market price of the warrant). Investors are willing to pay the premium because a greater percentage gain is possible from an investment in the warrant than from an investment in the stock with which the warrant is associated. To illustrate this concept, assume the following:

Date	Option Price	Market Price	Theoretical Value	Actual Price
January 1, 1970	$15	$30	$15	$15
October 1, 1970	15	45	30	30

Assume that an investor purchased one share of stock for $30 and sold it on August 1, 1970, for $45. Disregarding taxes and commissions, the investor realized a capital gain of $15, or 50 percent. Now assume that instead of the stock, the investor purchased a warrant for $15 and sold it on August 1, 1970, for $30. Instead of the 50 percent capital gain, the investor realized 100 percent gain. Since the investment potential, loss as well as gain, is more favorable for the warrant than for the stock, investors tend to bid up the price of the warrant. For example, suppose an individual were required to pay a premium of $5 or a total of $20 for the warrant. If the warrant had sold for $32.50 on August 1, 1970, the owner would have received a 62.5 percent return, which is still more than he would have received if he had purchased and sold the stock.

As a general rule, the premium paid for warrants declines as the price of the stock increases. The primary reason for this is that the advantage resulting from leverage decreases as the price of the warrant increases. In the above example, a much higher return was possible from the purchase of the warrant when it was priced at $15 than when it was $20. Also, the loss potential tends to increase when the price of the warrant increases.

EFFECTS OF CONVERTIBLE SECURITIES, OPTIONS, AND WARRANTS ON EARNINGS PER SHARE OF COMMON STOCK

At one time businesses were not required to adjust the earnings per share of common stock even if the capital structure contained convertible securities and bonds with warrants. This situation was changed by Opinion No. 15 of the American Institute of Certified Public Accountants. Briefly, the opinion states that companies with capital structures consisting principally of common stock are required to report only earnings per common share on the income statement. However, companies with capital structures containing convertible securities, options, or warrants that upon conversion or exercise will dilute earnings per share, are required to show primary earnings per share as well as fully diluted earnings per share.

Primary earnings per share is based on the number of common shares outstanding plus common stock equivalents, if dilutive. Options and warrants are common stock equivalents at all times, but should be included in the computation if dilutive. Convertible securities are common stock equivalents only if their cash yield at the time of issuance is below two-thirds of the current bank prime interest rate. In computing earnings per share, the proceeds that would have been received had options and warrants been exercised are assumed to be invested in treasury stock, thus reducing the number of shares of common stock outstanding. A more complex method is used if the exercised options and warrants cause the number of shares of common stock outstanding at the end of the period to increase more than 20 percent.

Fully diluted earnings per share is computed on the basis that all convertible securities, options, or warrants, if dilutive, have been converted or exercised.

The net effect of this method of reporting is to reduce the *actual* earnings per share that is reported on the profit-and-loss statement.

18

Long-Term
Debt Instruments

Long-term debt is created either by offering securities to the public through such organized exchanges as the New York Stock Exchange and the American Stock Exchange or by selling the securities directly to individual or institutional investors. The latter method was the most important during the years 1962-1965, but beginning in 1966 this trend was reversed. This reversal may be attributed to a rising interest rate; that is, as a result of very high interest rates, investors other than financial institutions and funds began to show an interest in bonds, thus causing companies to issue more debt securities publicly.

Of the various types of debt securities offered for sale, the most common include mortgage bonds, collateral trust bonds, equipment trust bonds, income bonds, real estate notes, and debenture bonds. Except for income bonds, the name of the instrument refers to the type of security supporting the issue. In the case of income bonds, the name refers to the condition under which interest is paid; that is, unless the issuer produces an income for the period, the interest on these securities will not be paid.

Sometimes the type of debt instrument used is not important; but often it is, and therefore we shall review each type carefully.

MORTGAGE BONDS

The mortgage bond, like any other bond, is nothing more than a formal promise to pay a definite amount of money at a specific time in the future, as well as a definite amount of interest at specified times throughout the life of the bond. It differs from a collateral and unsecured bond in that the issuing corporation executes a general mortgage on certain properties either presently owned or to be acquired.

Corporate mortgages covering the pledged property may be closed-end, limited open-end, and open-end. In the case of a closed-end mortgage only a certain amount of bonds may be issued. If other bonds are issued and secured by a mortgage on the same property, they must come under the lien of a subsequent mortgage—that is, they must be subordinated to the original issue. With a limited open-end mortgage, additional bonds are permitted but cannot exceed a definite amount. Such a mortgage allows a company to issue bonds covering part of its ultimate needs at one time and the remainder at a later date; but all the bonds will be secured equally under the same mortgage. An open-end mortgage is one that allows any amount of bonds to be issued under the same mortgage.

Obviously, the indentures will contain some form of restrictions concerning additional issues under the limited open-end and open-end mortgages. Although it is difficult to generalize about the exact nature of such restrictions, the majority are related to (1) earnings, (2) the mortgaged property, or (3) equity capital. Some typical restrictions are these: Earnings applicable to the payment of interest must exceed a certain number of times the amount of interest plus lease rentals; bonds cannot be issued if the par value of the issue exceeds a certain percentage—commonly about 75 percent—of the property to be acquired; and bonds cannot be issued if the total debt represented by long-term bonds exceeds a certain percentage of the stock outstanding.

Management frequently has the right to change the form, the terms of the contract, the rate of interest, or any other provision that it deems necessary, of each subsequent issue of bonds issued under limited open-end or open-end mortgages. That is, bonds issued under such mortgages may be issued in series. Needless to say, no new series is allowed to pre-empt the rights and privileges of previously issued bonds. The right to make changes allows management to take advantage of changes that occur as a result of a changing economy. For example, if the level of interest rates falls, management would be at a disadvantage if it had to charge a higher rate on a new issue of bonds.

Formerly the title to a mortgaged property was actually transferred to the mortgagee at the time the debt was made, and it remained in his custody until the debt was liquidated.[1] This made it extremely difficult for the mortgagor to repay the creditor, which, of course, restricted the use of mortgage bonds in the financing process. To eliminate this hardship, the equity courts ruled that the conveyance could be kept "dead" through the use of a "defeasance" clause; that is, as long as the obligations of the debtor are met, the mortgagor would retain

---

[1] The theory of the mortgage differs from state to state. In some states, the mortgage is considered a conveyance of title, whereas in others it is considered only a lien against the pledged property. Although there are important legal implications, these two theories are of little consequence to the financial officer.

title and use of the property. Should the debtor fail to meet the obligations promptly, title would be conveyed immediately, and the owner would lose the property without redress. Later this condition was changed so that, rather than transferring the property to the mortgagee when the terms of the indenture are not met, the creditor is required to put the pledged property up for sale. If the property is sold for more than the amount of the mortgage, the difference belongs to the mortgagee. (In most cases of insolvency and default under a corporate mortgage, the rights of bondholders and stockholders alike are worked out under some form of reorganization rather than by foreclosing the mortgage.)

Generally speaking, the title of a mortgage bond reflects its primary characteristics. For example, a first mortgage refunding bond is one that has first claim on certain properties in the event of default of interest or principal. Also, the funds raised from its sale are used to refund an outstanding obligation. Another example is the purchase money mortgage, which provides funds for an acquisition and is secured by a mortgage on the acquired property. Samples of different bonds titles are: divisional bonds, terminal bonds, first mortgage bonds, and consolidated and improvement bonds.

A business firm may have several secured bond issues outstanding at any one time. Each issue may have co-equal first mortgages on entirely different properties, or each may have successive claims on a single property. That is, one issue may be secured by a first mortgage, another by a second mortgage, and still another by a third mortgage on the same property. In the first instance, holders of bonds with first mortgages on different properties look to the value of the pledged assets for satisfaction in the event of default. In the case of bondholders who hold successive liens, payment is made in the order of priority. For example, suppose there are first, second, and third mortgages of $100,000, each outstanding against a building originally valued at $500,000. Assume further than the firm defaults and the building is liquidated for $250,000. The holders of the first and second mortgages receive $100,000 each, but the holder of the third mortgage bond receives only $50,000 and becomes a general creditor for the remaining $50,000.

In the event that a number of liens are outstanding against a particular piece of property, those with a prior claim are usually referred to as senior or underlying, and those with secondary claims are called junior or overlying.

COLLATERAL TRUST BONDS

The second major type of bond issued by corporations is the collateral trust bond. These bonds are secured by securities of the mortgagee—for example, by (1) bonds of the issuing corporation, (2) stocks and bonds of subsidiaries, and (3) stocks and bonds of firms other than subsidiaries. The use of bonds of the issuing corporation is not widespread, since most firms do not own their own securities in sufficient quantities to serve as security on bonds. However, the use of securities of subsidiaries has enjoyed a degree of popularity. This was true of holding companies during the latter part of the nineteenth and the first part of the twentieth centuries.

Collateral trust bonds are issued in the same manner as mortgage bonds except that the securities are actually held by the trustee. As long as the terms of the indenture are satisfied, the mortgagee receives the income (dividends and interest) from the securities and votes the pledged stock.

The strength of collateral trust bonds, like any other bonds, depends upon the strength (earnings) of the issuing corporation and the value of the security. If the earnings of the issuing corporation are weak, the strength of the issue rests entirely on the size and stability of the earnings of the companies represented by the pledged securities. We can readily see that collateral trust bonds supported by securities of blue chip firms are more acceptable than those supported by securities of firms of doubtful status. Moreover, collateral trust bonds secured by bonds are generally considered stronger than those secured by stocks. Needless to say, some stocks are stronger than certain bonds; but the bonds of any given company are stronger than its stock.

Collateral trust bonds have not enjoyed a particularly good reputation; therefore, a firm should consider floating other types of bonds before resorting to this type of security.

Debenture Bonds

Debenture bonds are secured by the general credit of the issuing company and are usually considered the strongest of all bonds. This obviously cannot be said of all debentures, but since debentures of reasonably strong firms are generally accepted by the investing public, it may be said that this type of bond enjoys an excellent reputation. We should remember, however, that a mortgaged bond of a relatively weak company is superior to a debenture of the same company, since the owners of the former instruments hold a prior claim on at least a certain amount of the firm's assets. Debentures of strong companies are comparable to mortgage securities of equally strong companies. In other words, firms that are capable of meeting their obligations are able to raise funds through the use of debentures on terms as favorable as those obtained by firms that employ mortgage securities.

The debentures enjoy a threefold advantage when compared to mortgage bonds. First, the interest cost of debentures is no higher than that charged for comparable mortgage securities; thus, the firm is not required to tie up assets in the form of mortgages. Second, the cost and expense connected with mortgaging fixed assets is eliminated, thus reducing the cost of flotation. Finally, considerably more flexibility is obtained through the use of debentures than from mortgage bonds. This is particularly true in the case of mergers and/or the sale of assets. The primary disadvantage is that the lender may require the borrower to agree to additional restrictive provisions.

Gerstenberg suggests that the following firms are capable of issuing debentures: (1) corporations that employ a relatively small amount of fixed assets,

(2) corporations with extremely high credit ratings, and (3) corporations that have mortgaged all their available assets and now must issue debentures in order to obtain sufficient funds for operational purposes.[2]

Debentures are often convertible; that is, the owner has the right to convert the debt security into common or preferred stock. By using convertible debentures, the issuer secures the advantages of lower cost (interest rates are usually smaller than for securities without this feature) and the opportunity of exchanging debt obligations for equity securities.

Many debentures contain a redemption clause allowing the issuer to call the bonds after a specified time, usually at a price in excess of par. A typical provision would permit the issuer to redeem the bonds at, say, 105, during the first year. If the bonds are not redeemed within the first year, they may be called at any time in the future by a call price of something less than 105; for example, during the second year they may be redeemed for 104, the third year for 103, the fourth year at 102, and so forth. In some cases the redemption clause also contains a provision that the debt cannot be refunded within a certain length of time at an interest rate below a certain figure, say 4.5 percent.

After World War II, consumer finance firms began issuing subordinated debentures to raise new funds. These securities differ from regular debentures in that their claims rank behind the claims of other unsecured debt in the event of insolvency. A few industrials have also used subordinated debentures in their capital structure.

In many cases subordinated debentures are used instead of preferred stock, since there are several advantages in this practice. First, like preferred stock, subordinated debentures provide the firm with additional borrowing power; second, the cost as compared to preferred stock is lower; and, third, the interest rate is tax deductible.

Equipment Trust Certificates

Equipment trust certificates (sometimes referred to as bonds or notes) are usually associated with the financing of moving equipment, particularly railroad cars and in some instances airplanes, trucks, and trailers. They offer another means of circumventing the after-acquired-property clause, because if the bonds are sold under the Philadelphia plan, the title of the property rests with the trustee, or if they are issued under the New York plan, the property is sold on a conditional sale basis.

To understand the use of this type of financing, let us examine these two practices. The New York plan, the more common method, employs the conditional sales technique. The property is sold to the user under a conditional sales contract; the buyer agrees to make a down payment of approximately 20 percent and periodic payments that will cover the remainder of the purchase price

---

[2]Charles W. Gerstenberg, *Financial Organization and Management of Business*, 4th rev. ed. (Englewood Cliffs, N.J.: Prentice-Hall, Inc., 1959), pp. 126-27.

plus interest and expenses. The manufacturer assigns its rights to an agent, who holds title to the property. If the financing is privately arranged through a financial institution, the company may act as its own agent. If the financing is not privately placed, the agent issues certificates to the public and uses the proceeds to pay off the manufacturer. The agent receives serial payments from the user and passes them on to the lender. Usually the bonds are in series, which permits orderly repayment.

The Philadelphia plan requires that the trustee, usually a trust company, and the seller enter into an agreement containing the following provisions: (1) the title of the property will be received and held by the trustee; (2) equipment bonds will be issued by the trustee and sold directly to the public, such bonds to become the obligation of the trustee (although the seller guarantees both the interest and principal); (3) the proceeds of the sale will be turned over to the seller; and (4) the bonds will be issued in series, and the maturities of the longest will approximate three-fourths to four-fifths of the economic life of the equipment used as security.

The trustee enters into an agreement with the user obligating the latter to pay periodic rentals. The agreement usually requires a down payment of approximately one-fifth to one-fourth of the cost of the equipment and periodic payments of a sufficient size to pay the interest on the outstanding securities plus an amount equal to the par value of the bonds that mature each year. Included in these payments is an amount equal to all costs associated with the trustee and with taxes. After each bond has been repaid (from the rental payments), the user pays a nominal amount, and the trustee transfers the title of the equipment directly to the user. Usually the schedule of repayments is designed so that the remaining book value of the equipment after the last bonds have been paid is equal to the amount of the down payment. An example of this type of bond is the Equipment Trust, Series T, 4 3/8 percent Equipment Trust Certificates issued by the Missouri Pacific Railroad. The certificates are to mature in 15 annual installments of $440,000 each on January 1 from 1965 to 1979. The certificates were issued with a 20 percent original cash equity.

Equipment trust bonds are usually considered to be excellent investments because (1) the value of the equipment always exceeds the amount of the bonds outstanding; (2) the equipment used in this type of financing is usually essential to the operation of the business, which forces the firm involved to work harder to avoid default; and (3) the equipment used to secure equipment trust bonds is usually in demand by similar companies. In the light of this, equipment trust bonds should be seriously considered not only by middle-sized and large firms that have after-acquired-purpose clauses in existing mortgages, but also by firms not strong enough to issue debentures but needing equipment that has wide acceptance among common businesses.

Income Bonds

These securities differ from other types of bonds in that interest is paid only when it is earned. Income bonds are similar in nature to preferred stock, but with the advantage that interest is tax deductible. The contractual provisions of income bonds, like those of other forms of bonds, vary. For example, some have no lien on specific property, whereas others may enjoy a junior claim. In a few cases, they actually have senior claims. The latter is indeed rare; moreover, there are fewer negative provisions than are found in indentures of mortgage bonds, debentures, or collateral trust bonds.

Income bonds have traditionally resulted from reorganizations; however, during more recent years, a few solvent firms have resorted to income bonds and strangely enough, the bonds have been accepted by the investing public. To increase their acceptance, management has included cumulative and convertible clauses. In some cases the cumulative feature does not become effective until a few years have lapsed. The purpose of the delay is to permit the firm to establish itself financially.

REAL ESTATE MORTGAGE NOTES

Long-term funds may be obtained directly from financial institutions such as commercial banks, savings banks, life insurance companies, mortgage companies, and other lenders, by mortgaging real estate that is owned by the business firm. The mortgage loan is represented by a long-term promissory note and mortgage. Notes of this type are not sold to the public; consequently, there is no indenture or trustee. The institutions providing this type of debt normally restrict the debt to a portion of the appraised value of the mortgaged property. Also, in most cases the mortgage is a closed-end mortgage—that is, limited in amount to the original issue.

MISCELLANEOUS BONDS

Many types of bonds may be discussed as a group, since they are neither well known nor widely used. Yet students of finance should be familiar with them. The first of this group is *guaranteed bonds*, which have been guaranteed as to interest, principal, or both, by some responsible third party. They may be mortgage bonds, debenture bonds, or collateral trust bonds, but because they are guaranteed, they assume a different classification. One peculiarity of this bond is that it is known by the name of the guarantor and is evaluated in the light of the guaranteeing firm.

Joint bonds are guaranteed bonds with two or more guarantors. *Assumed bonds* are securities for which a firm other than the issuer is responsible. The strength of this type of bond arises from the fact that the holders have a claim against the assets covered by the indenture under which the securities were issued, as well as a general claim against the assets of the firm assuming the bond. It does not follow that assumed bonds are stronger than ordinary bonds since their strength corresponds to the strength of the company that assumed the obligation. Generally speaking, assumed bonds originate from mergers and consolidations.

Receiver certificates are debt obligations issued by a firm that is in receivership. In order to make these instruments attractive, the courts generally place them ahead of existing securities insofar as the lien against the issuing company's property is concerned.

A *split-coupon bond* is one that carries a fixed rate of interest plus additional interest contingent on earnings. The interest that is contingent on earnings is restricted to a fixed amount, say 1 or 2 percent. *Participating bonds*, on the other hand, receive a fixed amount of interest plus an additional amount, provided earnings reach a certain level. The amount of additional interest is determined by the terms of the indenture, although as a general rule the amount is limited.

19

Equity
Capital

Equity or ownership capital of corporations is obtained either by the sale of common, classified, or preferred stock to individuals and institutions or by retention by a going concern of a part of its profits rather than payment in the form of cash dividends. The latter method provides more funds than the former (see Table 19-1, p. 187). The volume of funds obtained by selling stock fluctuates widely from year to year; for example, the sale of stock provided $8.4 billion in 1969, but only $1.4 billion in 1962. On the other hand, retained earnings ranged from $21.2 billion in 1967 to a low of $20.9 billion in 1969 (see Table 16-1, p. 155).

Equity sources will continue to provide the greatest percentage of corporate capital; this is why retained earnings are discussed in this chapter.

CHARACTERISTICS OF EQUITY CAPITAL

Many characteristics distinguish equity from debt capital. First, management is under no *contractual obligation* to pay a return for its use. The fact that no dividends are required does not mean that equity capital is free, since its cost is related to the earnings that shareholders expect. Although the corporation has no contractual obligation to pay a fixed amount to the owners, the owners are the residual claimants to all earnings after operating expenses, financial charges, and taxes have been deducted. Although shareholders come last, they have the advantage of receiving all that is left, which in most successful companies amounts to a higher return than is received by those who hold securities with a contractually limited return. (Although the return of preferred stock is usually limited, shareholders receive payment before the owners of common stock.)

A second characteristic is that the control of the corporate enterprise is vested in the owners of equity capital. In many cases this right is not exercised, but it is reserved for them exclusively. When control is exercised, it is accomplished by first electing the board of directors, and second, delegating to them the necessary authority to operate the firm. Although the right to operate is delegated, shareholders do not lose control; they can remove existing board members either directly or by not re-electing them.

A third characteristic is that there is no stated time at which capital is to be returned to the shareholders. If owners wish to retrieve their investment, they must either sell their stock or wait until the firm has been liquidated. It is this characteristic, coupled with the first one mentioned above, that causes corporate management to consider equity capital to be much less risky than debt.

TERMINOLOGY

Certain terms connected with equity securities are used in textbooks on the subject of finance as well as in all accounting and financial literature, and students should be familiar with them. The aggregate ownership interest of a business corporation is represented by the firm's *capital stock*. The total number of shares of stock, regardless of kind, that the firm's charter authorizes is referred to as the *authorized shares*. It should be pointed out that when a firm wishes to issue more shares than are authorized, it is necessary for shareholders to amend the charter. *Issued shares* are those that have been issued by the corporation. Stock that has been given or sold back to the company is known as *treasury stock*, and *outstanding shares* are those that have been issued and are presently held by individuals or institutions. Stock is issued as either *par* or *no-par stock*. Stock with a par value has been given a par or face value as is stated in the charter as well as on the face of the stock certificate. The stated value of a share of no-par stock is established in the charter or by resolution of the board of directors. Funds received in excess of the stated value are treated as capital surplus. In the absence of a stated value, the entire amount may be included in the capital account—that is, there will be no paid-in capital.

The *book value* of a share of stock of a business firm is computed by deducting liabilities from assets and dividing by the number of shares outstanding. For example, firm A has assets of $1 million, liabilities of $500,000, and 100,000 shares of stock outstanding. The book value in this case is $5 per share. To find the book value of common stock of a firm with preferred stock outstanding, first subtract the par or stated value of this stock from net worth, and then follow the same process as outlined above.

CERTIFICATE OF STOCK

All stock regardless of type is represented by *stock certificates*. The stock certificate is written proof of ownership. However, although the rights and privileges are not granted unless the individual's name has been recorded on the books of the corporation, the issuance of a certificate is not a prerequisite of ownership; an individual or institution becomes a legal owner immediately after the subscription and consideration have been accepted by the corporation. The information printed on the stock certificate is usually prescribed by the laws of the state in which the business is incorporated. As a general rule all the following information is included: name and state of the issuing corporation; certificate number; number of shares represented by the certificate; the par value, or a statement that the stock is no-par; the statement that the stock is fully paid and nonassessable; and the names of the officers authorized to sign the stock. The back of the certificate contains provisions for transfer of title, with spaces for dates, names of transferees, and signatures of the owners.

TECHNIQUES OF ISSUING
AND RECORDING SHARES OF STOCK

It was mentioned in Chapter 1 that issuing and transferring shares of stock is done with little or no difficulty. This function may be performed by the secretary of the corporation or by a transfer agent and a registrar. Large corporations usually employ the latter. The initial issuance of shares simply requires that the transfer agent, after verification by the registrar, issue a stock certificate to the buyer and record his name in the stock record book.

An owner who sells his stock completes the assignment on the back of the stock certificate and sends the certificate to the transfer agent. The transfer agent cancels the stock certificate, issues and countersigns a new certificate, and sends both to the registrar. The registrar checks to see that the number of shares issued is the same as those cancelled, and upon verification, he countersigns and returns both to the transfer agent. The transfer agent than attaches the cancelled certificates to the original stub and makes delivery of the new certificates. If the owner wishes to transfer only a part of the stock represented by his stock certificates, the same procedure is followed except that the transfer agent issues two certificates; one is sent to the transferee and the other—for the shares that were not sold—to the original owner.

TYPES OF STOCK

Common Stock

The one characteristic of all common stock is that its owners are the residual claimants of (1) all corporate earnings after operating expenses, financial charges, and taxes have been paid, and (2) all assets after prior claims have been satisfied. As a general rule, common stock enjoys most, if not all, of the so-called common-law rights; but it should be pointed out that when one or more of these rights is contracted away, the stock can no longer be classified in this category.

Financing with common stock is done by every corporate enterprise. Why is this true and what considerations influence its use? First, the equity capital represented by common stock serves as a cushion; that is, since owners of common stock are the last group to participate in the assets in the event of dissolution, any losses that may be incurred are absorbed by this group. Moreover, since dividends are not mandatory, the firm does not experience "legal" failure when it fails to earn a profit. Herein lies common stock's greatest advantage.

Other advantages also accrue to management when capital is raised through the sale of common stock. First, directors have the greatest possible latitude in making dividend policy. Not only is financial embarrassment avoided when there are no funds available for common stock dividends, but directors can raise a large part, if not all, of their capital needs by following a policy of plowing back earnings rather than paying dividends.

Second, common stock carries no fixed maturity and therefore does not require a refinancing process. Third, common stock, in many cases, is easier to sell than either preferred stock or debt. This is particularly true when the ratio of debt to equity has reached its maximum. Another factor supporting this contention is that the yield on common stock is higher than yields on preferred stock or debt securities (yield here refers to dividend yield plus capital appreciation). Also, common stock is desired by a large number of investors since it acts as a hedge against inflation.

Although there are several valid reasons for using common stock, there are also several disadvantages to the firm that employs common stock in the financing process.

1. In the majority of cases, management finds it necessary to price its stock so that it will yield a higher return than that paid to preferred stock or debt securities. Stated differently, common stock costs more than either preferred stock or debt securities.

2. The cost of selling common stock, like the cost of buying it, is generally higher than that of preferred stock or debt securities.

3. Interest expenses are deductible for tax purposes, thus causing equity capital to cost substantially more than debt capital.

4. Unless management is careful in establishing the price of a new issue of common stock, existing stockholders will lose a portion of their net worth. That is, when new stock is sold for a price less than the book value of the stock outstanding, the old shareholders are in effect transferring part of their net worth to the new shareholders.

5. An additional issue of common stock also dilutes the control of the existing shareholders. To avoid this situation, old shareholders are forced to exercise their pre-emptive rights in proportion to their present holdings, a situation that may present a problem in that the investors may not need or want additional shares of the stock.

6. Since common stock shares equally in income, management cannot increase the return on equity capital except by increasing the overall return on investment or trading more heavily on its equity. In the latter case, the additional risks incurred could create further problems.

The volume of common stock sold during any one year tends to fluctuate rather widely. For example, only $3,946 million was sold in 1968, but in 1969, $7,714 million was sold, an increase of 95 percent. Factors causing such a wide variation are numerous, and each changes in importance from period to period. Some of the elements that influence the sale of stock are (1) prices of securities (the general price level is represented by such averages as the Dow Jones averages for 65 stocks and 30 industrials), (2) price of debt instruments, (3) general state of the economy, and (4) volume of planned expenditures.

An examination of Table 19-1 reveals that the sale of common stocks increased substantially during 1968 and 1969. This rapid rise was somewhat unexpected, since the general price level of stock declined substantially during that period; the Dow Jones average for 30 industrials declined about 180 points, yet the sale of common stocks rose approximately 95 percent. It is reasonable to assume that the increase in bond interest had a tremendous influence on the decision to sell stock. Another reason that probably influenced management was the relative decline in undistributed profits during this period that we noted in Chapter 16.

TABLE 19-1

TOTAL NEW ISSUES
(in millions)

YEAR	BONDS			STOCKS	
	Total	*Publicly*	*Privately*	*Preferred*	*Common*
1962	$ 8,969	$ 4,440	$4,529	$422	$1,314
1963	10,856	4,713	6,143	343	1,011
1964	10,865	3,623	7,243	412	2,679
1965	13,720	5,570	8,150	725	1,547
1966	15,561	8,018	7,542	574	1,939
1967	21,954	14,990	6,964	885	1,959
1968	17,383	10,732	6,651	637	3,946
1969	18,347	12,734	5,613	682	7,714

Note: These stocks represent only those registered for sale through the Securities and Exchange Commission and do not include those sold without registration or registered only with the securities boards of the several states. Figures are rounded.

Source: Federal Reserve Bulletin, December 1970, p. A46.

It is reasonable to assume that the volume of stock sold will increase as long as bond interest remains high. This idea will be discussed further in the section titled *Preferred Stock*.

Classified Stock

During and after World War I, corporations experienced greatly increased growth in size as well as in earnings. Individuals owning fixed-income securities realized that in order to participate in this growth, they would have to buy equities, and they began demanding common stock. Recognizing a potentially large market, and convinced that this particular group was not interested in assuming the managerial function, management created a class of common stock that had all the rights and privileges of ordinary common stock except the right to vote. (Management usually calls the nonvoting stock Class A and the voting stock Class B.) This analysis proved correct, and classified common stock became quite successful. Very little classified stock was sold during the Depression, and up to the present time it has not regained the popularity that it experienced during the 1920s. This is mainly because the New York Stock Exchange and various federal agencies have discouraged its use by not permitting nonvoting stocks to be listed.

Preferred Stock

A preferred stock is one that receives some form of favorable treatment not enjoyed by common stock. Although the kind and degree of preference varies, the most common pertains to earnings and assets in the event of dissolution. As a general rule, all preferred stockholders are entitled to a share of the firm's profit, usually before any is distributed to the common shareholders. Moreover, they precede common stockholders in the distribution of assets in the event of dissolution. In addition, preferred stock of public utility companies enjoys certain advantages over common stock from the viewpoints of both the issuer and the investor. In the case of the former, public utilities receive a deduction for tax purposes for dividends paid on certain of their preferred stock—the deduction was equal to 28 percent in 1964 and 29.167 percent thereafter. The deduction is computed on the lesser of (1) preferred dividends paid during the tax year or (2) taxable income for the tax year (figured without the deduction for dividends paid on preferred stock). The owner of the preferred stock of taxable public utilities received a tax deduction of 61.2 percent for 1964 and 60.208 percent thereafter on dividends received, provided the utility companies involved were allowed a tax reduction on the dividend distributed.[1]

---

[1] A corporate owner that, together with the issuer, was a member of an affiliated group making the appropriate elections was eligible to receive a tax deduction of 72 percent in 1964 and 70.833 percent thereafter, rather than 61.2 and 60.208 percent; see sections 244 and 247 of the *Internal Revenue Code*.

To compensate for these advantages, preferred stockholders are required to forfeit certain common-law rights. It should be emphasized that the withholding of any right must be agreed upon not only by the common stockholder but by the preferred stockholder as well. The two rights most frequently contracted away are the right to vote and the right to subscribe to new stock issues in proportion to one's holdings. In many cases, the right to vote is not completely eliminated, but the privilege is greatly modified; that is, the shareholder cannot vote except under certain circumstances. The author knows of one preferred stock that does not permit shareholders to vote except when the issuing corporation fails to pay dividends or to provide for the sinking fund. Should either deficiency occur, the holders of the preferred stock have the right to elect one-fourth of all directors. In some cases, the holders of preferred stock actually possess a stronger voting privilege than common stockholders. Finally, Illinois and Mississippi require that preferred stockholders have the same voting privileges as common stockholders.

Directing our attention again to the preferential treatment with respect to dividends, the most common provisions found in preferred contracts pertain to the size and continuity of the dividend. As a general rule, dividends on preferred stock are fixed and are stated as a percentage of par value. For example, a $100 par, 7.5 percent cumulative preferred stock is one that pays $7.50 annually. If the dividend is not paid each year, the amount accumulates and must be paid before dividends can be paid to common stockholders. The cumulative feature is understood; that is, if management wishes to avoid this feature, it must be specifically excluded from the contract. Obviously, the cumulative feature may become a burden, since any arrearages must be settled before a dividend can be paid to the common shareholders. To reduce the burden, the cumulative feature may be modified or even eliminated after a reasonable time, say, five years. Management should always attempt to modify this particular provision if it believes the firm will encounter a prolonged period of financial embarrassment.

In addition to providing the cumulative feature, management often permits preferred stockholders to participate along with common stockholders in the distribution of earnings. That is, preferred stockholders are allowed to receive dividends in excess of the amount stated in the contract. Provision for participation varies from firm to firm; in fact, no one method of participation is more commonly utilized than another. In order to establish positively whether a stock is participating or nonparticipating, management should indicate its intention in the contract, since in some instances courts have ruled that the preferred stock is participating if not otherwise stated, whereas in other cases the exact opposite has been held.

The following features are often found in preferred stock contracts: (1) conversion privileges, (2) redeemable or callable provisions, and (3) sinking fund features. In order to improve the stability of the preferred contract, a conversion provision may be included permitting preferred stock to be exchanged for common stock at a predetermined time in the future. This provision is designed to favor the purchaser of preferred stock, but it also permits the firm to simplify the capital structure without repurchasing the preferred stock. The conversion rate is usually expressed in terms of so many shares of common stock for each share of preferred. In a great many cases, management restricts the time allowed the preferred shareholder for converting to common stock, either by including a redeemable clause in the contract or actually limiting the time during which the stock can be exchanged. These clauses are designed to aid management; however, several clauses are included to protect the conversion privilege. For example, this privilege may be reduced in value if any of the following occurs:

> A split-up of shares issuable upon conversion, or a change in such shares; a stock dividend; a sale of additional shares issuable upon conversion for less than a certain price; the issuance of subscription rights; the distribution of assets to the holders of senior securities; the issuance of other classes of stock having a preference upon redemption; liquidation, or dissolution; the issuance of another class of convertible securities offering the privilege of conversion into the same class of stock at a price lower than that offered to the first class of convertible stock.[2]

As a general rule, management will include provisions in the preferred contracts designed to nullify the dilutive effects of any of the above should they occur; in other words, the preferred status of the shareholder is generally assured over the life of the contract.

Preferred stocks are frequently callable or redeemable at the discretion of management. This type of provision obviously permits management to eliminate the rigidity caused by fixed dividends, cumulative features, and participation clauses. Through the elimination of preferred stock, the relative position of the common stockholders is improved, and in most cases, the price increases— meaning of course, that the firm's cost of capital is reduced.

Although the terms by which stock is to be redeemed or called vary greatly, a few are common to most preferred contracts: (1) the stock will not be redeemed until a certain period has elapsed, (2) the redemption price will exceed the par value of the stock, and (3) the premium will decline throughout the life of the contract, until finally the call or redemption price equals par.

Redemption is often accomplished gradually rather than all at one time. Some contracts for stock that is to be gradually redeemed contain provisions for a sinking fund. These provisions usually differ from contract to contract. For example, a specified sum may be set aside before common dividends are paid, an increasing amount may be set aside, or a certain percentage of profits after taxes may be earmarked for the sinking fund.

---

[2] Lillian Doris, ed., *Business Finance Handbook* (Englewood Cliffs, N.J.: Prentice-Hall, Inc., 1953), p. 611.

Policies Governing the Use of Preferred Stock

Preferred stock has been declining in relative importance as a source of funds. Several reasons account for this. First, the cost of preferred stock is higher than that of bonds, partly because dividends on preferred stock are not tax deductible, whereas bond interest is deductible as an expense. Also, the dividend rate on preferred stock is higher than bond interest. A simple illustration emphasizes this differential. Suppose company A has $1 million of 6.5 percent preferred stock and a like amount of 8 percent debenture bonds outstanding. The interest cost before tax is $80,000, whereas the annual preferred dividends amount to $65,000. Since bond interest is deductible for tax purposes, the company's saving on bond interest equals its tax rate; if the tax rate is 42 percent, the effective cost is $46,400 rather than $80,000. Moreover, the firm would have to earn at least $112,069, since the preferred stock dividend is paid after taxes.

The second major disadvantage is that in most cases, the contract provisions tend to restrict management's efforts. For example, the cumulative feature may cause arrearages to become so large that any type of future financing would be severely limited. This feature also curtails management's ability to retain earnings, thus restricting the growth of the company. Another disadvantage is the burden that results from the participation provision; that is, because common stock prices do not react favorably when there is a participating feature, the cost of funds increases.

A company enjoys several advantages by using preferred stock. First, preferred stock dividends are fixed and can, therefore be used to increase the rate of return on common stock (participating preferred cannot be used for this purpose); in other words, management can use preferred stock to trade on its equity. Preferred stock is superior to bonds for this purpose because the risk of insolvency is greatly reduced; it is not mandatory that dividends be paid, whereas interest charges must be paid or the firm faces bankruptcy.

A second advantage of preferred stock is that management may use this device to raise equity capital without losing control of the company. Third, if all things remain constant, the cost of preferred stock is lower than that of common stock, thus permitting the firm to participate in activities that might otherwise be unprofitable. Finally, the use of preferred stock allows a company to tap an otherwise closed source of funds; for example, certain institutional investors are unable to purchase common stock but are allowed to purchase preferred stock.

An interesting situation now taking place could have a major impact on the sale of preferred stock during the 1970s. Beginning in 1965, the cash flows of business firms have shown a decrease relative to interest costs. In other words, dollar costs of interest have risen rather sharply yet cash flow has remained relatively stable. Moreover, the majority of business firms, particularly corporations, have increased relative debt. As a consequence, interest coverage has deteriorated sharply. In addition, many firms will be called upon to refinance much of their long-term debt within the next few years. If interest rates continue at their present levels (the rate on Aaa bonds was approximately 8 percent in May 1970), businesses will be required to reduce their debt-equity ratio in order to maintain an acceptable interest-rate coverage. To accomplish this they will more than likely replace debt obligations with preferred stocks rather than common stocks, since the former will not affect return on equity as much as common stock. The student can see immediately that such action could have far-reaching effects. For example, (1) the popularity of preferred stocks would rise; (2) return on equity and earnings per share would decline, since there would have been a decrease in the amount of leverage employed; and (3) cost of capital would be affected.

Although these comments are strictly conjectural, it is believed that preferred stock will rise in popularity during the 1970s.

20

Primary

Security Markets

Because of their ability to tap the so-called capital market, middle-sized and large corporations have a definite advantage over small corporations and noncorporate enterprises when raising capital externally. Entry to this market is usually through a group of institutions whose primary function is to distribute new securities to individuals and institutions and to act as middlemen in the trading of old securities. The market for new securities is referred to as the primary market and the market for old securities is called the secondary market. It is called to the attention of the reader that new capital is not raised in the secondary market, since its primary function is to aid in the movement of existing securites among investors. The primary market, on the other hand, is the market through which large sums of new capital are raised each year, and since most firms sooner or later turn to this market for the purpose of raising new capital, it is necessary to examine its operations. Included also in this chapter is a discussion of the role that investment bankers play in this very important area.

THE PRIMARY MARKET:
IMPORTANCE AND CHARACTERISTICS

The primary market is the market through which all business firms, regardless of size, raise all the external funds used in the financing process. Funds obtained in this market may be raised formally or informally. In the formal process, the securities are registered with the SEC or with state securities commissions and are usually sold to the public through investment bankers. Funds are raised informally by selling securities directly to large investors, primarily financial institutions—see Chapter 21.

It is impossible to estimate closely the amount of new capital raised by all firms from external sources, since many small firms do not register their securities with either the SEC or state securities commissions. This information is available only for corporations that have registered their securities with one of these governmental bodies. For example, Table 20-1 depicts the amounts and the types of instruments used in the procurement of funds from the so-called external markets. An examination of this table reveals several interesting facts. First, the total amount of new capital has increased substantially since 1962. Second, corporations offered more securities publicly than privately in every year except 1963, 1964, and 1965. Third, stocks have fluctuated in importance as a source of funds. Finally, preferred stock does not play a very important role in the financing process.

TABLE 20-1

TOTAL NEW CORPORATE ISSUES
(in billions)

	BONDS			STOCKS	
Year	Total Corporate Bonds[a]	Publicly Offered	Privately Placed	Preferred	Common
1962	$ 9.0	$ 4.4	$4.5	$ .4	$1.3
1963	10.9	4.7	6.1	.3	1.0
1964	10.9	3.6	7.2	.4	2.7
1965	13.7	5.6	8.2	.7	1.5
1966	15.6	8.0	7.5	.6	1.9
1967	22.0	15.0	7.0	.9	1.6
1968	17.4	10.7	6.7	.6	3.9
1969	18.3	12.7	5.6	.7	7.7

[a]Subtotals do not equal totals because of rounding.
Source: Federal Reserve Bulletin, December 1970, p.A46.

Since registration with the SEC—or with a state security commission if an offering is made intrastate—is required of almost all companies offering corporate securities to the public, business firms have traditionally enlisted the aid of investment bankers in the distribution process. Let us examine the institution of investment banking, particularly in the area of equities, and its role in the important process of raising funds through public offerings.

TYPES OF INVESTMENT BANKERS

Investment bankers may be defined as financial institutions whose primary function is to aid business enterprises and governmental units in the private or public distribution of their securities. The student should not confuse this type of banker with the commercial banker, since the investment banker assists business and governmental units in acquiring funds for relatively long periods of time, whereas commercial banks aid in acquiring funds for relatively short periods of time.

When investment bankers first began to operate, it was possible to classify them on the basis of the kinds of securities they handled as well as the number of functions they performed. For example, many were called bond houses; moreover, some were classified as specialists, as in the case of houses that dealt only in municipal or federal bonds. This method of classifying investment bankers has lost its significance, since for the most part they have diversified their activities.[1]

It should also be pointed out that investment banks were originally classified as wholesalers, retailers, and dealers. The primary function of wholesalers is to distribute securities to other houses either for their own account or for the purpose of distributing the shares to the public; in other words the purchasers are retailers of securities. The dealer sells from the list of larger houses and receives a dealer's discount. Present-day investment bankers cannot be so classified since they tend to engage in all phases; therefore, no useful purpose is served now by classifying investment bankers according to such narrow areas of activities.

FUNCTIONS OF INVESTMENT BANKERS

Investment bankers perform several functions for firms attempting to raise funds from external sources. Their most important service is the distribution of securities; in fact, if it were not for this function, investment bankers would be hard to put to justify their operations in the primary market. Due to the importance of the distribution function, most of this chapter is directed to a discussion of methods used by investment bankers in the capital-raising process.

Although functions tend to vary among firms, the following are performed by most investment bankers. First, they offer investment advice to the firm, for which service they are highly qualified, since they deal constantly with new securities or securities soon to appear in the secondary market. In many instances, their advice is given to the clients of the investment banking firm; however, some investment banking firms actually manage the portfolios of business firms, charging a fee for this service. In times past, investment bankers have been criticized for conflict of interest, since they are sellers of securities as well as independent advisers. This is resolved rather easily by most investment bankers in that they do not recommend or purchase for their clients any security in

---

[1]T. A. Wise, "The Bustling House of Lehman," *Fortune*, December 1957, pp. 157-60, 185-92. This article describes the variety of functions that the modern investment banker performs.

which they have an interest. It should be remembered that an investment banker will, in most cases, avoid any act that would detract from his reputation, since he cannot compete successfully in the securities market without an unimpeachable reputation.

A second function performed by the investment banker is acting as a broker or dealer in the secondary market. Most investment firms act as brokers in organized exchanges as well as the over-the-counter market. In many instances, this particular function provides the investment firm with its major source of income. In addition to serving as brokers for stocks and bonds, some act as commodity brokers, and in a few instances they participate in the sale of commercial paper.

A third function, closely allied with the first one mentioned, is that of providing financial advice relative to (1) expansion through mergers, consolidations, and the outright purchase of fixed assets of other firms; (2) interim financing; (3) short-term financing; (4) reorganization, recapitalization, and liquidation; and (5) any other financial activity. Many firms that have developed a contact with investment bankers would not consider a financial act without asking their advice.

Finally, investment bankers are often called upon to distribute large blocks of existing securities in the secondary market. For example, stock of many firms is closely held and therefore does not find a ready market. To create a market, the investment banker distributes the shares being held by a relatively few stockholders to a large number of shareholders. This often entails almost the same type of activities needed to sell securities in the primary market. Examples include the sale of the common stock of the Ford family in 1948 and the stock of Transiton Corporation in 1958.

ROLE OF THE INVESTMENT BANKER
IN THE DISTRIBUTION PROCESS

The investment banker's most important function, the distribution of securities in the primary market for the purpose of securing capital to be used by business firms for operational purposes, is accomplished by three methods: underwriting or outright purchases, stand-by underwriting, and best efforts selling. Underwriting is by far the most important method and accounts for the greatest number of securities handled by investment bankers. It is nothing more than the outright purchase (alone or in conjunction with other investment bankers) of stocks and bonds that the issuer proposes to offer to the public. The investment banker thus assumes the risk normally associated with price fluctuations during the time the issue is being marketed. The profit realized is the difference between the price paid for the security and the price for which it is sold (called the spread), less any expense incurred in the process.

The right to underwrite the issue may be obtained either by negotiation or by competitive bidding. The latter method results when (1) the states require public sealed bids for municipal issues; (2) the SEC requires competitive bids, with certain exceptions, on the securities of public utility holding companies and their subsidiaries; (3) the Federal Power Commission requires competitive bidding on new issues; (4) the Interstate Commerce Commission requires sealed bids, with certain exceptions, on all public sales of railroad securities over $1 million; and (5) many state public service commissions require competitive bidding on public utility issues. Arguments have been advanced for and against competitive bidding, and certainly there is considerable validity to the contentions of both sides. It is recommended that students familiarize themselves with these arguments, since competitive bidding accounts for a large part of total underwriting.

Negotiated underwriting results from direct negotiations between the underwriter and issuer. As a general rule, the buying or underwriting department performs the function of acquiring the securities; in addition, this department is charged with developing new business, recommending effective financial plans, and assisting the issuer both in selecting the provisions to be included in the contract and in the actual writing of the prospectus or indenture.

Since securing the right to distribute securities through negotiation is quite different from competitive bidding, it is necessary to set forth briefly the various steps involved in the negotiation process. The process usually includes (1) the investigation of the merits of the proposed issue by the buying department; (2) the negotiation of an informal agreement with the issuing firm; (3) the formation of an underwriting group, if warranted (and when necessary, the selection of a manager of this group); (4) registration with the SEC or a state securities board if required; (5) the creation of a formal agreement between the participating members of the underwriting group and manager; (6) the creation of a selling group, if the issue is so large that more than one seller is required; (7) negotiation with the issuer with respect to price and spread; (8) signing of the purchase contract with the issuer, subject to clearance by the SEC or the appropriate state agency; and (9) the sale of securities to the public, subject to delivery after the closing.

A brief description of these steps will be helpful to the student. First, the buying department of the originating house analyzes the general nature of the firm's business; that is, it determines the firm's relative position in the total market, assesses the potential of the firm's future demand, and ascertains the ability of the management. Second, an investigation is made of the firm's past and its future potential. This normally includes past financial data and a forecast. Third, the firm's facilities are carefully examined by the investment banker and, if necessary, an outside engineering firm or other professional group may be called upon to assist in evaluating the firm's assets and requirements. The buying department then bases on these data its recommendation on the desirability of the proposed financing and the amount and type of new securities to be issued.

If the proposal is acceptable to both the company and the investment banker, an informal agreement is drawn up, setting out the amount and type of securities to be offered and when the offering is to be made. If the offering is relatively small, the originating house may manage the account alone; however, if the account is so large that assistance is needed, the issuing company helps the manager to form an underwriting group. The selection of the dealers may be agreed upon, but they cannot be officially signed until the registration statement becomes effective.

The registration statement is drawn up by the following individuals and groups: the manager of the underwriting group, the financial officers and any other interested officers of the issuing firm, lawyers of both the issuing firm and underwriting firm, accountants of both, and any additional specialists whose services are necessary. After completion, the registration statement is filed with the SEC, or with the state securities commissioner if the issue is to be sold intrastate.

Two agreements are necessary at this point in the negotiation, one between the participating members of the underwriting group and the manager of the originating house, and the other between the issuing corporation and the underwriter. The latter agreement is commonly referred to as the purchase contract and includes the price of the securities to be issued to the public and the price the underwriter is to pay. Once the purchase contract has been signed, the underwriter is obligated to buy the entire issue from the company. (Included in each purchase contract, however, is an "out" clause, setting forth the conditions under which the underwriter is not required to fulfill the agreement.)

The final step is the actual sale of the securities. After all the above steps have been completed, the sales department of each member of the underwriting group assumes the responsibility of selling a proportionate share of securities to the investing public. If the securities have not been sold during the period agreed upon by the underwriters, either of two courses is open. The period may be extended in the hope that the securities will be sold. Or if failure is acknowledged, the agreements may be dissolved, with each firm taking its proportionate share of unsold securities either to hold until the stock can be moved at the offering price or to sell at any price that can be obtained.

A second method of raising new capital involves the process generally referred to as "stand-by" underwriting. This method entails an agreement by the investment banker (or group) to sell securities that, for one reason or another, are offered for sale by the issuer. For example, suppose a firm makes available 50,000 shares of common stock to its stockholders through its pre-emptive agreement. To assure itself that the entire issue will be sold, the issuer signs a stand-by agreement with an investment banker to take up the securities that are not sold by the business firm through the pre-emptive right process. In some cases, the underwriter charges a small fee for this service; for example, $0.25 per share for all shares of the issue plus an additional $1.00 per share on all shares the investment banker is called upon to sell. Occasionally, investment bankers charge a fee for the actual amount they are required to sell.

A third method employed by investment bankers to raise new capital for corporations is called "best efforts" selling. Under this technique investment bankers serve as agents for the issuing company but, unlike underwriters, they do not own the shares; they exercise their best efforts to sell the security and are compensated in direct relation to the number of units sold. Again unlike underwriters, investment bankers assume no risk, since they do not take a position in the issue. Generally "best efforts" distribution is employed in highly speculative issues and in cases of securities that are new and untried.

COST OF RAISING CAPITAL

The term *cost of flotation* as used by the Securities and Exchange Commission refers to the total cash cost of selling securities. This cost is made up of two items: underwriters' compensation and expenses. Underwriters' compensation is the gross amount that underwriters obtain for their efforts; it is the difference between the price they pay the issuing company and the price they receive from the ultimate purchasers. Expenses are the total cash outlay made by the firm in connection with the issue. They include expenses incurred in connection with the registration statement, accountants' fees, attorneys' fees, outside consultants' fees, etc. They do not include the costs related to the staff of the issuer.

It is difficult to indicate specific cost figures, since costs are influenced by (1) the type of issue, (2) the size of the issue, and (3) the size of the firm. The data in Table 20-2 indicate the cost of flotation of debt as securities in the period 1951-1955, as well as preferred and common stocks for the periods

TABLE 20-2

COSTS OF MARKETING PUBLIC ISSUES,
1951–1955 AND 1963–1965, EXPRESSED
AS A PERCENTAGE OF TOTAL ISSUE

SIZE OF INCOME (in millions)	COMMON STOCK (percent)		PREFERRED STOCK (percent)		DEBT ISSUES (percent)	
	1951– 1955	*1963– 1965*	*1951– 1955*	*1963– 1965*	*1951– 1955*	*1963– 1965*
Under 0.5	27.2	18.5	—	16.0	—	N.A.
0.5–1.0	21.8	14.6	12.6	11.1	11.5	N.A.
1.0–2.0	13.6	11.6	8.1	11.4	8.2	N.A.
2.0–5.0	10.0	9.1	4.9	6.1	3.8	N.A.
5.0–10.0	6.2	7.6	3.7	1.6	1.8	N.A.
10.0–20.0	4.7	6.9	2.9	1.8	1.5	N.A.
20.0–50.0	5.4	5.6	3.2	3.1	1.3	N.A.
50.0 and Over	—	2.6	2.5	1.7	1.2	N.A.

Source: Cost of Flotation of Registered Equity Issues, 1963-1965 (Washington, D.C.: Securities and Exchange Commission), March 1970, p. 10; and *Cost of Flotation of Corporate Securities, 1951-1955* (Washington, D.C.: Securities and Exchange Commission), June 1957, p. 37.

1951-1955 and 1963-1965. These figures show the effects of size and type of securities on cost. A small common stock issue is considerably more expensive than a large one. Further, common stock issues are more expensive than bond issues. Finally, preferred stocks, because of their characteristics, fall in between.

21

Private Placement

and Government

Financing

In recent years, two primary changes in financing have received increased attention. First, business firms of all sizes are issuing securities privately rather than publicly. Second, the Congress of the United States has created two types of institutions for the purpose of aiding in the financing of small businesses. Prior to the decade of the 1960s, the majority of all funds raised from external sources was secured through the sale of securities to the public by middlemen; but by 1963 the sale of securities privately had grown in importance to a point where firms offered more securities privately than publicly. From all indications it appears that this method of raising funds will decline some in importance, but will continue to be a major source of external capital.

It is not unusual for the United States government to participate directly or indirectly in the financing process. What is unique, however, is that the federal government has created institutions whose primary purpose is to finance only one size of business firm. A discussion of these two developments is included in this chapter.

THE SALE OF SECURITIES PRIVATELY

The increasing importance of financial institutions has brought about a new concept in raising funds from external sources. During the 1920s and 1930s, the principal method of raising funds from external sources was through the sale of securities to the public via a middleman. This method began to decline in importance during the latter part of the 1930s, and businesses turned to raising funds by selling securities directly to institutional investors, such as insurance companies and funds of all kinds. Corporations sold more securities privately than publicly for the first time in 1962, when such sales amounted to $5.9 billion, or 55.1 percent of the total securities offered both publicly and privately (see Table 21-1). Private placement has declined in importance primarily because interest rates have risen to their highest levels in several decades, causing individuals to increase their demand for bonds.

TABLE 21-1

NEW CORPORATE SECURITIES: TOTAL
OFFERED, TOTAL PRIVATELY PLACED, AND
TOTAL DEBT INSTRUMENTS PRIVATELY
PLACED, 1962-1968
(in millions)

YEAR	TOTAL, ALL OFFERINGS	TOTAL PRIVATE PLACEMENTS	TOTAL BONDS PRIVATELY PLACED	
			Amount	*Percent*
1962	10.7	5.9	5.7	96.6
1963	12.2	7.3	7.0	95.9
1964	14.0	8.6	8.3	96.5
1965	16.0	9.8	9.6	98.0
1966	18.1	10.5	10.3	98.1
1967	24.8	9.4	9.2	97.9
1968	22.0	9.2	8.6	93.5
1969	26.7	NA	NA	NA

Source: Federal Reserve Bulletin, October 1970, p. A46; and New York Stock Exchange *Fact Book*, 1969, p. 63.

Examining the nature of securities sold through the private placement process, we may note that the amount of equity capital raised through the sale of stocks privately is negligible when compared to the amount of debt capital secured. To illustrate, between 1962 and 1968, debt instruments sold privately never accounted for less than 93.5 percent of all securities sold and rose as high as 98.1 percent of the total. Although the same trend is seen in publicly offered securities, the ratio of equity to debt is much higher.

Three industry groups—manufacturing, financial and real estate, and electric, gas, and water—are the major users of private placement as a method of distributing securities. In 1961, funds raised by these groups accounted for 75 percent of the total raised in this manner. Incidentally, this ratio remained fairly constant during the five-year period from 1957 through 1961 (see Table 21-2). Although amounts given in the table have undoubtedly varied during the past several years, it is logical to believe that these industries are still the major users of the private placement technique.

TABLE 21-2

PRIVATE PLACEMENT OF CORPORATE SECURITIES
BY TYPE OF ISSUER, 1957-1961
(in millions)

Year	Manufacturing	Extractive	Electric, Gas, and Water	Railroad
1957	$1,657	$147	$ 666	$ 0
1958	1,397	105	617	0.5
1959	979	59	677	22
1960	958	113	518	18
1961	1,837	181	824	50

	Other Transportation	Common Section	Financial and Real Estate	Commercial and Other
1957	$ 419	$137	$ 415	$184
1958	505	176	502	187
1959	659	101	983	275
1960	386	107	1,093	304
1961	396	173	1,110	427

Source: Securities and Exchange Commission, *28th Annual Report* (Washington, D. C.: Government Printing Office, 1963), p. 178.

ADVANTAGES AND DISADVANTAGES
OF PRIVATE PLACEMENT

Several factors account for the importance of private placement. Although the following elements are generally conceded to have contributed most to the growth and development of this method of financing, it is believed that no one reason is more important than another, because of the variations in the nature and characteristics of the companies employing this method of financing.

First, the financing process is achieved much more rapidly through the private sale of securities than through public offerings. Although the Securities and Exchange Commission attempts to expedite the registration process, the average time lapse between the original filing and the effective date of registration is so long that a definite risk is incurred. Unfortunately this period is becoming longer; for example, the average amount of time between the original filing of 3,316 registration statements and their effective dates or registration was 65 days in 1969, 44 days for 2,131 registrations in 1968, and 36 days for 1,460 registration statements in 1967.[1]

The increasing length of time required to process registration is one of the problems confronting the SEC today. To reduce this time period, the SEC has initiated several policies which, they believe, will expedite the registration pro-

---

[1] Securities and Exchange Commission, *35th Annual Report* (Washington, D. C.: Government Printing Office, 1969), p. 32.

cess. One such policy is not to

> ... accelerate the effective date of the registration statement unless the preliminary prospectus contained in the registration statement is distributed to underwriters and dealers who it is reasonably anticipated will be invited to participate in the distribution of the securities to be offered or sold. The purpose of this requirement is to afford all persons affecting the distribution a means of being informed with respect to the offering so that they can advise their customers of the investment merits of the security.[2]

Another action taken to expedite the registration process is the requirement of a summary sheet as an exhibit to each statement or amendment. The sheets are designed to facilitate the automatic processing of data through the use of the Commission's computer.[3]

A second advantage of private placement is that the cost of raising funds by this method is usually lower than the cost associated with public offerings. In the main, these savings result from (1) lower costs of flotation, (2) the elimination of registration and listing requirements, (3) lower accounting and legal fees, and (4) reduction in the costs normally associated with the trustee.[4] Although savings are generally realized regardless of the size of the issue, the greatest savings are possible in the smaller issues. The data contained in Table 21-3 show that savings are quite large in issues of less than $2 million.

Third, small or lesser known businesses usually receive a higher price for securities sold through private sale than for those sold publicly. This is because a single large purchaser often studies the firm more closely and evaluates more accurately the investment merits of a small, relatively unknown firm than is apt to be the case when a large number of smaller investors purchase publicly offered securities. Also, since private placement purchasers are not primarily interested in market ability, they will pay a higher price than the average investor for privately offered securities. The average bondholder cannot afford to pay as high a price for such securities because he may be called upon to sell quickly in order to adjust his portfolio to changing conditions. Private placement buyers, on the other hand, seldom need to sell securities to adjust their portfolios. As a result, smaller companies actively offer their securities in the private placement market.

Fourth, contract terms are easier to adjust in securities that have been sold privately because of the smaller number of owners. This is advantageous for a relatively new firm as well as for firms that tend to change character. In addition to this type of flexibility, privately issued securities are easier to change in the event of financial reversal. Also, contract terms may be designed more nearly to meet the requirements of the issuer than is possible in the case of securities that

---

[2]*Ibid.*, p. 27-28.

[3]*Ibid.*, p. 28.

[4]In all public offerings of debt, there is a trustee whose primary purpose is to protect the interest of the bondholders. In the case of private placement, no trustee is required; thus the expenses normally associated with this function are eliminated.

TABLE 21-3

COST OF FLOTATION OF SECURITIES
BY SIZE OF ISSUE
(costs as percent of proceeds)

SIZE OF ISSUE	DEBT ISSUES		COMMON STOCK	
	Public	Private[a]	Public	Private[b]
Under 0.3		3.4	N.A.	16.0
0.3–0.5		2.7	18.5	18.0
0.5–1.0	11.5	2.1	14.6	13.5
1.0–2.0	8.2	1.6	11.6	8.2
2.0–5.0	3.8	1.1	9.1	7.2
5.0–10.0	1.8	0.8	7.6	15.2
10.0–20.0	1.5	0.6	6.9	N.A.
20.0–50.0	1.3	0.4	5.6	2.7
50.0 and over	1.2	N.A.	2.6	N.A.

[a]Obtained by adding together compensation paid to agent and expenses for two different samples of offerings in 1951-1955.
[b]Obtained by adding together compensation paid to agent and expenses for two different samples of offerings in 1963-1965.
Source: Cost of Flotation of Registered Equity Issues (Washington, D.C.: Securities and Exchange Commission), March 1970, pp. 24 and 54; and *Cost of Flotation of Corporate Securities, 1951-1955* (Washington, D.C.: Securities and Exchange Commission), June 1957, pp. 37, 64, and 66.

are sold to the public. In the latter case, the investors are much less sophisticated than the very large purchasers and usually do not accept complicated provisions.

Finally, sale of securities through private placement allows the issuer to retain a high degree of secrecy and at the same time to develop a sound outlet for its securities.

Despite the impressive list of advantages of private placement and its place of prominence as a method of financing, there are several disadvantages connected with its use. A serious drawback is that it tends to restrict a firm's potential market, since securities are not made available to all investors. Another disadvantage is that a firm is unable to purchase its securities in the open market and thus is unable to take advantage of an increase in the general level of interest rates. (The price of the bond declines when interest rates increase.) In some instances purchasers of securities offered privately demand restrictions more severe than those attaching to securities offered publicly. This last disadvantage is debatable, since a comparison is extremely difficult to make. Finally, some issuers are unable to receive as high a price for their securities when sold privately as publicly, thus causing the cost of capital to be higher.

ROLE OF THE INVESTMENT BANKER
IN PRIVATE PLACEMENT

Business firms may negotiate the private placement of securities; however, many business firms continue to rely on investment bankers to perform this important function. The relation between the investment house and the issuer in private placement is not the same as that usually found in publicly offered issues. To illustrate, the investment banker does not underwrite the issue that is to be placed privately; rather, his primary function is to find a buyer among the many institutional investors who, incidentally, may be customers for securities that are being underwritten and offered publicly. For this service, the investment banker receives a fee. In addition to finding potential customers, investment bankers also provide advice and recommendations concerning (1) the provisions of the indenture, (2) the type of securities to be issued, (3) the amount of securities to be offered, (4) the timing of the offering, (5) the preparation of the financial information that is to accompany the issue when the sales presentation is made, and (6) any future matters that may arise with regard to the issue.

The cost of the services of the investment banker for private placement issues is usually below that charged by the investment banker for the publicly offered issue. In private placement, the investment banker acts as an agent for the issuer and receives a fee for his services. The size of the fee is in direct relation to the size of the issue and the number of functions he performs. A study of privately placed issues conducted by the Securities and Exchange Commission reveals that fees paid to agents for services performed in connection with debt issues ranged from 0.22 to 1.86 percent of the value of the issue, but that the fees charged in connection with the sale of equity were higher; for example, they ranged from 4.5 to 6.2 percent. Incidentally, the study also revealed that agents' fees were paid on 57 percent of issues. This does not mean that investment bankers were used in each of the cases; rather, it means that firms relied on outside help in 57 percent of the cases. This help may have been obtained from investment bankers, financial consultants, or middlemen.

Although many issuers of securities do not require the services of an investment banker, we should bear in mind that saving the fee for this service may be the most expensive "saving" that a firm can make. Remember, the investment banker is a specialist who can and does offer valuable services. Unless the firm is able to perform these services effectively, it pays in the long run to employ the services of a qualified investment banker.

GOVERNMENT AS A SOURCE OF FUNDS

In general, government is not a major supplier of capital to large businesses during normal periods. This has not been the case with small businesses; in fact, the financial problems of small businesses have received increasing attention from national, state, and local governments. This interest comes from the belief that if we are to have true competition in our economy, small businesses must continue to operate and must therefore receive assistance from governmental agencies. This concept is debatable, but the various aspects of the argument will not be presented here. Nevertheless, students of finance should be familiar with the nature and characteristics of the financing techniques and the agencies of the government that provide funds to small businesses.

Prior to 1953, several agencies provided funds to both large and small businesses. In 1932, the Reconstruction Finance Corporation was created by the federal government which owned outright all the stock of the RFC; the primary purpose of this agency was to provide loans to distressed banks, insurance companies, railroads, agricultural financing institutions, and relief and construction projects. In 1934, lending activities were extended to solvent companies that could secure financing from other sources. The loans were long term in nature (three to eight years) and were used to refund existing debt as well as to expand fixed and current assets. During World War II the function of the RFC was extended, and it participated in financing the war effort either directly or through such subsidiaries as the Defense Plant Corporation. Between 1932 and 1953 the RFC made 640,000 loans and loaned or invested approximately $48,750 million.

A 1934 amendment to the banking acts authorized each Federal Reserve bank to make working capital loans to businesses that were unable to secure financial assistance through normal channels. The loans were to be repaid in installments over a period of not more than five years, and usually within three years or less. This program was discontinued in 1950 after $851 million in loans had been processed.

In 1944, Congress passed the Servicemen's Readjustment Act for the primary purpose of aiding servicemen to enter into or expand existing businesses. Most of the 231,207 loans made between 1944 and 1958 were made by banks; only one-third were guaranteed by the government.

In 1953, the RFC was discontinued and its functions were assumed by the newly created Small Business Administration. The SBA makes available two types of loans to small businesses.[5] First, it makes business loans for plant construction and the acquisition of land, materials, and supplies for war, defense, or essential civilian production. The maturities of these loans may extend up to ten years, and the maximum amount to any one borrower cannot exceed $250,000. The SBA may make the loan directly if the borrower cannot borrow the funds from regular sources; as a general rule, however the SBA prefers to participate with local banks in making the loan. Second, the SBA is authorized to make disaster loans to business concerns or home owners who suffer losses from catastrophes such as floods and hurricanes.

The volume of loans made by the SBA either directly or through participation is not very large when compared to private lending agencies such as banks. In addition to aiding in the financing process, SBA assists small businesses by (1) advising them in financial affairs, (2) assisting in the procurement of govern-

---

[5] Manufacturing firms are small if they employ less than 250 persons or sell less than 5 percent of the total sales of an industry with few competitors. Wholesale firms are considered small if their yearly sales are $5 million or less. In most instances a retail firm is small if its sales do not exceed $1 million.

ment contracts, and (3) providing them with literature concerning various functions of the business.

The Small Business Administration makes debt funds available to small businesses (either directly or through participation with private financial institutions), but it does not engage in any form of equity financing. To stimulate the flow of equity capital and long-term loan funds to small businesses, the Small Business Investment Act was passed by Congress in 1958. This act authorized the Small Business Administration to perform the following functions:

1. To charter and license small business investment companies (SBICs)
2. To lend funds to such companies
3. To regulate and examine such companies
4. To lend money to state and local development corporations

The SBICs are privately owned and operated, and the only role played by the government is that of promoting the program by lending funds to persons wishing to start an SBIC, and regulating the company after it comes operative.

Briefly, although the SBICs may be chartered by the state or federal government, they must be licensed by the SBA. In order to qualify for a license, the SBIC is required to have a paid-in capital and surplus of $300,000. Capital may be obtained through the sale of stock or by borrowing, either from private sources or in limited quantities from the government. The SBA is authorized to match the capital invested by the promoters dollar for dollar up to $400,000. Also, SBICs may borrow funds from the SBA at a cost of 5 percent.

SBICs provide both equity and debt capital. They may purchase preferred or common stock, and they may invest in convertible debentures. Although the type of capital they provide is not restricted, they cannot have an aggregate investment in any one company in excess of 20 percent of the combined capital and surplus of the SBIC, or $500,000, whichever is less. Loans must be of good quality or supported by adequate security. Long-term loans cannot have a maturity of less than five years or more than twenty years. Moreover, the law includes provisions pertaining to repayment, extension, or renewal.

In order to facilitate the growth of SBICs, the federal government allows them certain tax advantages. For example, losses resulting from the sale of investment in equity securities can be written off against ordinary income. The companies may also deduct from ordinary income for tax purposes 100 percent of all dividends received. Further, an SBIC may elect to be taxed as a regulated investment company, which means that the federal corporate income tax is eliminated on income distributed to shareholders as ordinary dividends. In addition to the advantages accruing to the SBIC, investors have certain tax advantages; for example, should an investor sell at a loss, the total loss may be deducted from income rather than treated as a capital loss. On the other hand, profits from the sale of stock may be treated as capital gains.

It is difficult to say whether SBICs have been successful, since some have shown phenomenal growth and others have become bankrupt and have liquidated. Moreover, some question exists of whether the SBA has accomplished its primary goal, which is to provide adequate equity capital to all small businesses.

22

Secondary
Security Markets

The student of finance may wonder why an entire chapter of a business finance book is devoted to a study of the secondary market, since business firms do not receive funds from the sale of securities in this market. The secondary market is nevertheless essential to good financial planning, because without it the primary market would be almost nonexistent. For example, if such a market did not exist, investors would hesitate to purchase securities of business firms because they would be "locked in" and unable to change the level or character of their portfolios. Furthermore, the secondary market is necessary if a business firm is to determine accurately its cost of capital. This information is vital, since most decisions concerning expenditures are directly related to this cost. Another service of the secondary market is that it provides information that allows the finance officer to enter the market at the right time. The stock market is extremely sensitive to changes in the economy and reflects events currently happening or about to occur that might prevent the firm from entering the market. Observing these movements, the finance officer can seek other sources of capital that would appear to be more advantageous to the firm. The secondary market provides additional services but those given are sufficient to show that this subject is one of major importance and should be included in any study of financial management.

NATURE AND IMPORTANCE
OF SECONDARY MARKETS

The secondary market is a place where the buyer and seller of securities meet, with the idea that a transaction will result. The transaction normally passes through a middleman, commonly referred to as a broker, who charges a fee if a sale is made. In some cases a dealer as well as a broker, will operate in the market. The primary difference between the two is that the broker is an agent of the buyer or seller and never takes title to the security; that is, he is truly a middleman and is rewarded for his efforts by being paid a commission. The dealer, on the other hand, acts as a principal and in most cases actually takes title to the securities. The dealer buys the securities for his account and then sells them, and his compensation is determined by the spread between the purchase price and the sale price.

The securities sold in the secondary market consist of listed as well as unlisted securities. The market for listed securities is the "floor" of one or more of the stock exchanges, whereas the market for unlisted securities is the over-the-counter market (A few unlisted securities, however, are traded in the exchanges).

ORGANIZED EXCHANGES

As of June 30, 1969, 13 stock exchanges were registered under the Securities Exchange Act. In addition, four other exchanges existed but were not required to register. A list of the exchanges follows:

American Stock Exchange	Philadelphia-Baltimore-
Boston Stock Exchange	Washington Stock Exchange
Chicago Board of Trade	Pittsburgh Stock Exchange
Cincinnati Stock Exchange	Salt Lake City Stock Exchange
Detroit Stock Exchange	Spokane Stock Exchange
Midwest Stock Exchange	Colorado Springs Stock Exchange*
National Stock Exchange	Honolulu Stock Exchange*
New York Stock Exchange	Richmond Stock Exchange*
Pacific Coast Stock Exchange	Wheeling Stock Exchange*

*Exempted from registration by the SEC pursuant to Section 5 of the Securities Exchange Act.

The two largest exchanges are the New York Stock Exchange and the American Stock Exchange. The New York Stock Exchange is by far the largest; for example, on December 31, 1968, the market value of all stock listed in the New York Stock Exchange amounted to $692 billion and the market value of all bonds listed equaled $120 billion, making a total of $812 billion. (Of the total stock market value, 98 percent was in common stock.) The value of all securities listed on the American Stock Exchange amounted to only $61.2 billion on

December 31, 1968. The market value of all securities listed exclusively on all other exchanges is even smaller: $6.0 billion, or less than 1.0 percent of the total (see Table 22-1).

TABLE 22-1

MARKET VALUES OF SECURITIES LISTED
ON EXCHANGES AS OF
DECEMBER 31, 1968
(in millions)

	NUMBER OF ISSUES	MARKET VALUE
Stocks		
New York Stock Exchange	1,767	$692,337
American Stock Exchange	1,084	61,214
Exclusively on other exchanges	379	5,954
Total	3,230	$759,505
Bonds		
New York Stock Exchange	1,455	$120,407
American Stock Exchange	167	2,729
Exclusively on other exchanges	21	17
Total	1,643	$123,153
Total Stocks and Bonds	4,873	$882,658

Source: Securities and Exchange Commission, *35th Annual Report* (Washington, D.C.: Government Printing Office, 1969), p. 73.

It is interesting to note that although the market value of all stock listed on the New York Stock Exchange was about eleven times larger than that of the stock listed on the American Stock Exchange, the number of stock issues listed on the New York Stock Exchange exceeded those listed on the American by only 312 issues. The obvious reason for this is that the average price of the stocks listed on the New York Stock Exchange is much higher than that of stocks listed on the American Stock Exchange; companies whose stocks have a relatively small market price seem to prefer the American Stock Exchange, whereas the opposite is true of companies with higher-priced stock.

An organized exchange consists of a group of individuals and organizations who have purchased seats (memberships) for the primary purpose of trading in listed securities. The price of seats on the exchange is determined by supply and demand.[1] The highest price ever paid for a membership on the New York Stock Exchange—$625,000—occurred in February, 1929; the lowest price, amounting to only $4,000, occurred in 1876. The highest price paid in 1968 was $515,000 and the lowest was $385,000. Since 1963, the NYSE has had 1,366 memberships (seats) held by 646 organizations, of which 203 were corporations. Inci-

---

[1] The cost of a seat on the New York Stock Exchange includes the price of the seat plus an initiation fee of $4,000 and annual dues.

dentally, the number of corporations has increased relatively during this time; only 50 corporations held memberships in 1957.

Trading in securities takes place on the floor of the stock exchange. In 1968, 1,767 listed stocks and 1,455 bond issues were traded at 19 posts on the New York Stock Exchange. To indicate the tremendous activity that occurs on the floor, there were 3,299 million shares of stock traded in round and odd lots with a market value of $145 billion in 1968, as well as bonds with a market value of $3.8 billion.[2]

In order for a stock to be listed on an exchange, certain requirements must be met by the business firm. A few of the more commonly known requirements that the NYSE makes are:

1. Demonstrated earning power under competitive conditions of $2.5 million before federal income taxes for the most recent year and $2 million pre-tax for each of the preceding two years.
2. Net tangible assets of $14 million.
3. A total of $14 million in market value of publicly held common stock.
4. A total of 800,000 common shares publicly held out of 1,000,000 shares outstanding.
5. All common stock has the right to vote.

Companies that list on the American Stock Exchange are not expected to be as large; consequently, the listing requirements are somewhat lower than those of the New York Stock Exchange. For example, the minimum listing standards of the American Stock Exchange are: (1) net tangible assets of at least $1 million; (2) net earnings after all charges and taxes of $150,000 for the latest fiscal year, and an average of $100,000 for the past three fiscal years; (3) 200,000 publicly held shares with a market value of at least $1 million; (4) an aggregate market value of $2 million for the total outstanding shares; and (5) 750 shareholders including 500 holders of lots of 100 shares or more.

Why should a firm list its stock on one of the organized exchanges, particularly when there is such an effective over-the-counter market? One way to answer this question is to review briefly the more obvious advantages:

1. Listing tends to broaden the market for the securities, since many investors restrict their purchases to listed securities.
2. Exchanges provide a more orderly market for securities, thus increasing a security's marketability.
3. Listed securities receive more publicity, since several hundred newspapers report their market prices daily.
4. Listing tends to increase a security's prestige.
5. Improved marketability tends to increase a security's value from the standpoint of collateral.

Although the advantages above are claimed, many operations choose not to

---

[2] All these data were taken from the 1969 *Fact Book* of the NYSE.

list their securities. Generally the reasons for not listing are:

1. Many companies do not want to make public the information required by the exchanges.
2. Management may want to have a nonvoting stock in the capital structure.
3. The cost of filing may be considered high for certain companies, although it appears that it is reasonable when compared to the advantages associated with listing.
4. Finally, the spread of securities that are not widely distributed may not increase, since over-the-counter dealers would no longer actively retail the securities.

OVER-THE-COUNTER MARKETS

As we pointed out in the previous section, many business firms do not want to list their shares on an exchange, preferring that their stock be traded in the unlisted or over-the-counter market. Organized exchanges are auction markets and each transaction goes through a broker, but in the over-the-counter market, dealers buy and sell securities at negotiated prices. For example, the prices appearing in the financial pages of such newspapers as *The Wall Street Journal* are "bid" and "ask" prices for stocks in the retail market and are furnished by the National Association of Securities Dealers (NASD). The bid price is the price a dealer will pay for a reasonable number of shares of stock, whereas the asked price is the price at which he is willing to sell. The dealer receives as compensation the spread (gross profit margin), which is the difference between the bid and asked prices.

Dealers may act as either wholesalers or retailers. As wholesalers they make available to other dealers "prices" that are not generally known to the public. When acting as retailers, they pay the bid price and sell at the asked price. Brokers also operate in the over-the-counter market; that is, they buy unlisted securities for their customers in one of two ways. First, they buy from the dealer as an agent of the customer, charging the dealer's asked price plus a commission. Second, they buy from dealers and resell to their customers at a price that includes a small profit. When a broker is performing the selling function for a customer, he charges a brokerage commission. That is, the customer will receive the dealer's bid price less the brokerage commission. In some cases the broker actually buys the stock from the customer at a price below the dealer's bid price and immediately resells to the dealer at the bid price.

With less well-known securities, a dealer may buy for his own account and list these stocks on quotation sheets. If the dealer does not want to tie up large sums of funds, he takes options on them or acts as an agent.

The major securities traded in the over-the-counter market are government bonds, state and municipal bonds, corporation bonds, bank stocks, insurance company stocks, and stocks of companies that for one reason or another, fail to qualify for exchanges. We should note here that many listed stocks and bonds are traded over the counter rather than on an exchange. This situation comes about when holders of large blocks of listed bonds or stocks want to sell an entire block. The owner knows that such a sale would cause a break in the price, and rather than taking a chance on this happening, the owner offers the block of securities in the over-the-counter market.

Several observations of interest to the student of finance may be made about the over-the-counter market. First, it is believed that the price of actively traded securities of comparable quality fluctuates about as much in one market as in another. Second, securities traded on listed exchanges usually have a higher collateral value than comparable securities traded on the unlisted market. Finally, it is impossible to prove the statement that prices on the unlisted market are lower than those on the listed market.

REGULATION OF THE
SECURITIES MARKETS

In 1932 the Senate Committee on Banking and Currency initiated a thorough study of the securities business with the idea of correcting unfair and unethical practices that were commonplace during the latter part of the 1920s. The findings of this committee resulted in the enactment of the Securities Act of 1933 and the Security Exchange Act of 1934, as well as the creation of the Securities and Exchange Commission. The Securities Act of 1933 was designed to make absolutely sure that companies issuing securities disclose fully all facts surrounding the securities to be issued. The act prohibited not only the issuance of misleading information, but also the intentional withholding of material information.

The primary purpose of the Securities Exchange Act of 1934 is to assure a fair and orderly securities market and to prevent the excessive use of credit in the purchase of securities. To accomplish these goals, the act (1) requires registration of all exchanges of substantial size with the SEC; (2) governs the listing and delisting of securities, short selling, floor trading, and the practices of the exchanges; (3) requires periodic reports of firms whose securities are listed; (4) establishes regulations governing proxy requests by firms whose stocks are listed; (5) requires registration of all brokers and dealers except those dealing exclusively in public bonds; (6) prohibits market manipulation, misrepresentation, deception, and fraudulent practices with regard to securities transacted on the exchanges; and (7) restricts credit granted by brokers and dealers on any securities other than those listed or "exempted." Although few people favor the act in its entirety, it is generally conceded that it has accomplished its goals rather well.

To assure the investing public that firms have fully disclosed all facts surrounding the securities they are about to issue, the Securities Act of 1933 requires that any new security issues offered for sale in interstate commerce be registered with the SEC unless specifically exempted. The content of the registration statement varies among different types of issuers, but the following information is generally required: description of the business, nature of services or products, description of assets owned by the firm, list of officers and directors, complete financial statements for the past three years, and any other material facts that would affect the value of the securities to be issued.

If an investor suffers damages because of a false statement or an omission of a material fact, one or all of the following may be held liable: the issuer, the firm's directors and/or officers, the investment banker who aided in the preparation of the statement, and the accounting and/or engineering personnel who provided the data included in the registration statement.

After the registration statement has been submitted, it is carefully examined by the staff of the SEC. If the SEC is satisfied, the statement becomes effective 20 days after it is filed; however, if the SEC is not satisfied, it can request additional information, request that corrections be made and the statement reissued, or issue an order preventing the statement from becoming effective.

Not only must a registration statement be filed with the SEC, but a prospectus must be delivered to each buyer of a registered security by the seller, either before or at the time of the delivery. This document contains basically the same information found in the registration statement.

The Securities Act applies to all issues except those specifically exempted which include mainly government issues, municipal bonds, and the securities of railroads. Issues amounting to $300,000 or less need not be registered, but the SEC must be notified of their issuance. Finally, securities issued and sold exclusively intrastate are exempt from registration by the SEC; however, they are not necessarily exempt from registration by state securities boards. Generally, the procedure required when registering under a state's security law is the same as that followed by the SEC. The student should not think that the requirements for registration are easier under state statutes than under federal law, because the opposite is true in some cases. For example, not only does the Texas Security Act require full disclosures, but certification may not be permitted if

> ... he [commissioner] finds that the registrant has not proven the proposed plan of business of the issuer to be fair, just and equitable and also any consideration paid, or to be paid, for such securities by promoters is fair, just and equitable when such consideration for such securities is less than the proposed offering price to the public and that the securities which it proposes to issue and the methods to be used by it in issuing and disposing of the same will be such as will not work a fraud upon the purchaser thereof.[3]

The Securities Act of 1933 and the Securities Exchange Act of 1934 were created to control activities in the organized markets. In 1938, Congress adopted the Maloney Act, which amended the Securities Exchange Act of 1934 by

---

[3] Section 7C, *The Securities Act*, State of Texas.

adding Section 15A, covering the regulation of the over-the-counter market. The act provides for such regulation by national securities associations registered with the SEC. The NASD was registered under Section 15A in 1939 and is presently the self-regulatory arm of the over-the-counter (OTC) market. Regulation of the OTC is achieved through rules designed to promote just and equitable principles of trade and is enforced by district committees consisting of men operating in the securities business. The NASD is to the OTC what the NYSE and other organized exchanges are to the organized markets.

The following is a list of the main purposes of NASD as set forth in the association's certificate of incorporation:

To promote the investment banking and securities business

To standardize its principles and practices

To promote high standards of commercial honor and to promote among members observance of federal and state securities laws

To provide a medium through which the membership may consult with governmental and other agencies

To cooperate with governmental authority in the solution of problems affecting this business and investors

To adopt and enforce rules of fair practice in the securities business

To promote just and equitable principles of trade for the protection of investors

To promote self-discipline among members

To investigate and adjust grievances between members and between the public and members.

The NASD bylaws consist of fifteen articles, all of which are designed to achieve the purposes listed. To illustrate, the following are examples of activities covered in the bylaws: conditions of membership, registration of registered representatives, supervision of registered representatives, rules of fair practice, procedures for handling complaints, and the uniform practice code.

In general we may say that the Securities Act of 1933, the Securities Exchange Act of 1934, and the NASD have served a definite purpose in that they have contributed to the protection of the investor. However, the financial community has also contributed to the protection of the investor. The following is a list of the more important associations whose primary function is to further the economic well-being of the securities business:

The Association of Stock Exchange Firms

The Bond Club of New York

The Investment Bankers Association of America

The Life Insurance Association of America

The National Association of Investors' Brokers

The National Association of Investment Companies

The National Association of Securities Dealers, Inc.

The National Federation of Financial Analysts' Societies
The New York Financial Writers' Association, Inc.
Pension Funds Association

23

Expansion

of the Business Firm

Most businesses, regardless of size or legal form, are interested in expanding their sphere of operations. This desire is the result of many reasons, most of which may be classified into three broad categories: (1) personal ambitions of promoters, owners, and management; (2) desire to improve the profit potential of the existing operation; and (3) desire to increase efficiency. The finance officer is seldom called upon to decide whether expansion will take place; his function is to assist management in deciding which method should be used to expand, determining the best possible price to pay for the assets or stock to be acquired, and selecting the methods of raising the funds to be used in the expansion process. Therefore the purpose of this chapter is to examine the techniques of expansion as well as the methods used in pricing the assets to be acquired. A discussion of the sources of funds that may be utilized is covered elsewhere in this book.

METHODS OF EXPANSION

The expansion process implies an increase in any or all of the productive, distributive, and financial activities of a business firm, requiring either an increase in total assets or the replacement of less efficient assets with more efficient ones. Operational facilities may be expanded by internal or external means, or by a combination of these. When the first method is used, management acquires the additional assets with funds that have been secured either from retained earnings or from the sale of securities to the public. If expansion is achieved by external methods, it simply means that management has increased its assets by combining several businesses under a holding company or has acquired them through merger, consolidation, lease, or some combination of these.

Regardless of the method or methods used in the expansion process, the growth may be classified as vertical, horizontal, circular, or conglomerate. *Vertical expansion* involves the acquisition of the several stages of business activity; for example, a firm that produces a particular product will acquire the outlet through which it is distributed. Richman Brothers, manufacturers and distributors of men's clothing, is an example of a vertically integrated company; that is, they manufacture and distribute their own products. *Horizontal expansion* is accomplished when a firm acquires another firm that is engaged in similar operations, for example, when one grocery store acquires another grocery store. *Circular expansion*, on the other hand, brings together firms that produce different products with the idea that economies may be effected by having a common channel of distribution; General Foods Corporation is a perfect example of a firm that has grown in this manner. Finally, *conglomerate expansion* involves firms engaged in different lines of business activity. All these methods are currently employed, but conglomerate expansions have received the most publicity lately.

EXTERNAL VERSUS INTERNAL EXPANSION

Growth by combination or external expansion may be more desirable than expansion from within. Valuable time is often conserved, for example, since a going concern already exists, and immediate advantage can be taken of the opportunities presented by external expansion. The primary disadvantage of external as compared to internal expansion lies in the complexities that result from attempting to ascertain an appropriate price for the assets to be acquired. It is generally presumed that values vary more widely when the assets are fully operative; that is, the true value of the assets is more difficult to compute. Moreover, rarely if ever would all the assets of the acquired business fit into the operational pattern of the acquiring firm; thus losses are inevitably incurred.

Internal expansion, on the other hand, has certain advantages when compared to growth by external means. The principal advantage is that management is able to locate the new assets in the location most desirable from a cost standpoint. Moreover, the value of the assets acquired is more easily ascertained, since each asset is usually new and not a part of a going concern. Another major advantage is the absence of the need for obtaining approval. To illustrate, if a merger is the technique used to acquire additional facilities, the permission of the shareholders of both firms is required. However, if a like amount of assets is purchased with retained earnings or funds obtained from the sale of securities, no permission is required from the interested shareholders. It is true that under certain conditions stockholder permission is required if funds are raised by selling new securities, but such permission is not nearly as difficult to obtain as that required when an exchange of stock is involved.

THE VALUATION PROCESS

A major problem of growth is the determination of how much to pay for the assets to be acquired. As we have seen, the problem is less complicated if expansion results from internal growth, since management is called upon to evaluate separate assets. If expansion results from the partial or complete absorption of other business units, the problem is more complicated, because management is required to evaluate a mixture of assets that produces or will produce a stream of income. In this case it is the income stream that is being purchased and not the assets, and thus the size and regularity of the stream actually determine the value of the assets. If the assets fail to produce income, their value will decline to a level equal to their alternative uses. Management may employ a variety of techniques to determine a sound purchase price. Some of the more important ones are: (1) cost minus depreciation, (2) market value of stock, (3) appraisal price, and (4) capitalized value.

Although the following discussion includes a description of the various techniques used by management to arrive at a sound price, we should emphasize that no asset has a value in a business sense unless it produces a stream of income; therefore, the most logical of the methods presented is the one that relates cost to income. Even though it is agreed that the price dictated by this method is theoretically sound, it is the most difficult to put into practice because of the many errors that may result when determining the income flow. For this reason management also employs several other methods of valuation.

Cost Less Depreciation

The cost of an asset may be viewed from the standpoints of (1) what the asset cost at the time of its purchase or (2) what it would cost to replace it. One method of ascertaining the value of a firm is to determine the original cost of all its assets and then to reduce this cost by the valuation reserves—depreciation, depletion, and bad debts. (If the firm has any outstanding liabilities, it is necessary to adjust the book value by subtracting the amount of the outstanding liabilities.) These "cost" figures ignore changes in the price level and may have little or no relation to current price. The use of replacement cost tends to eliminate this particular disadvantage. However, its use also creates at least one other major disadvantage—that is, inability of management to arrive at the correct replacement price for identical equipment.

A second weakness of this method is that the valuation reserves may be incorrect. For example, one firm may follow the practice of a fast write-off, whereas another may use the straight-line method of computing depreciation. The assets of a firm using accelerated depreciation will have a lower value than those of the firm that employs the straight-line method. Finally, book value ignores the ability of the assets to produce future income. In fact, this method may place the same value on two assets, yet one may produce income for ten years whereas the other will produce income for only five years.

Market Value of Stock

Occasionally a fair price may be computed by multiplying the market price of each share of stock and the number of shares outstanding. If preferred stock is outstanding as well as common stock, its market value should be added to that of the common. This method has the advantage of considering future income, since the market value of stock is usually predicated on the stream of future income. Although the technique is advantageous from this standpoint, it does have some shortcomings. Which market price will be used—the average price or the most recent price? The market price tends to be influenced by factors other than potential earnings; therefore, in order for the value to be realistic, the market price should be adjusted to eliminate market fluctuations resulting from factors other than earnings, and this is difficult to accomplish. Finally, all stock does not have a market price—for example, stock in closely held companies. In such cases the market price must be computed. If earnings are used as a base for the market price, management may not know which earnings figure it should use. That is, should it use past earnings, present earnings, future earnings, or an average of all three?

Capitalized Value

In arriving at the price (present value) of a firm through the use of the capitalized-value technique, one must (1) ascertain the size of the income stream that may be expected, (2) determine a fair capitalization rate, and (3) compute the fair value of the firm. The accurate determination of the income stream requires a careful study of the future in order that past earnings may be adjusted. This is no easy task, since our economy is fraught with changes. A small error in judgment may bring about a large dollar change in the predicted price. To illustrate, suppose the income stream has been forecast as $100,000 and the capitalization rate is equal to 10 percent. In this case the present value is equal to $1 million ($100,000 divided by 10 percent). Now suppose the income forecast is off by 10 percent; that is, income is predicted to be an average of $110,000. Using this assumption, the price would amount to $1.1 million rather than $1 million. Suppose further that stock is sold for $100 per share and that the $1.1 million is paid for the firm. The firm is placed in operation, and at the end of the first year the firm produces an income of $100,000 rather than the expected $110,000. In this case, the market price of the stock will more than likely decrease to $90.91 if the price-earnings ratio remains at 10 to 1. In some cases the price-earnings ratio will decline when expected earnings are not realized; if so, the price of the stock will be even lower.

The difficulty involved in the selection of a correct capitalization rate also creates a problem for management. This rate is the rate of return that may reasonably be expected; as a general rule it varies directly with the degree of risk inherent in the business. One method used to determine the capitalization rate is to ascertain rates of return of like firms operating under similar conditions. The importance of selecting a proper capitalization rate cannot be overemphasized. To illustrate, management would pay $250,000 more for a business firm with an income stream of $100,000 if it used an 8 percent rather than a 10 percent capitalization rate.

The capitalized value should be adjusted (1) if some of the assets can be sold without reducing the size of the average stream of income, or (2) if additional funds are required in order to assure the predicted level of income.

In summary, we may say that values determined by the capitalization of income and the market value of a firm's stock are superior to the value arrived at by adjusting either original or replacement cost. In some cases neither of these methods is acceptable to the parties concerned. When this is true, the value is usually arrived at by negotiation or by having an expert establish an acceptable price by appraising the tangible and intangible assets.

TECHNIQUES OF EXTERNAL EXPANSION

Growth by external expansion may be accomplished through (1) mergers and consolidations; (2) holding companies; (3) gentlemen's agreements, communities of interest, and interlocking directorates; and (4) leases.

Little information exists concerning the relative importance of each method from the standpoint of the total economy; there are, however, studies that deal with smaller segments of our economy. For example, J. Fred Weston's survey of the growth patterns of 74 firms between 1900 and 1948 revealed that formal combinations accounted for one-fourth of the growth, whereas funds obtained from internal sources financed the growth of approximately one-half of the firms.[1]

Although combinations result from many and varied reasons, the principal ones are economic in nature. Writers in this important area usually list the following: (1) reducing the tax bill, (2) increasing the size of the market, (3) obtaining the economies that result from large-scale operation, (4) decreasing instability resulting from a nondiversified type of operation, and (5) increasing the firm's ability to keep up technologically.[2]

---

[1] J. Fred Weston, *The Role of Mergers in the Growth of Large Firms* (Berkeley: University of California Press, 1953), pp. 24-30.

[2] For a full discussion of these and other reasons, read J. Fred Weston and Eugene F. Brigham, *Managerial Finance*, 3rd ed. (New York: Holt, Rinehart & Winston, Inc., 1969), Chapter 21, and James C. Van Horne, *Financial Management and Policy* (Englewood Cliffs, N.J.: Prentice-Hall, Inc., 1968), Chapter 22.

Mergers and Consolidations

If one firm acquires the assets of another and the latter loses its identity, the combination is said to be a merger. On the other hand, when two or more companies transfer their assets to a newly created firm, the operation is said to be a consolidation. The differences between these two methods of combination are legally significant, but the end results are fundamentally the same when viewed from the economic or financial standpoint.

Legally, mergers and consolidations are effected only when specific statutory procedures are followed. Generally speaking, the following steps are followed in a legal merger or consolidation. First, the officers of the companies concerned meet and work out a plan. Second, the plan is submitted for approval to the directors of the companies involved. Third, if the plan is accepted by the board, the board passes a resolution and submits it to the shareholders of the respective companies for their acceptance or rejection. Fourth, if accepted, the plan is filed with the secretary of state. The secretary, upon acceptance, issues a certificate of merger or consolidation.

In statutory mergers and consolidations, the creditors are protected in that their rights and privileges are usually transferred to the surviving firm—some states require an exact transfer of rights; in others, certain claims may be modified. Minority rights are protected by law; that is, if a voluntary agreement cannot be reached, shareholders may file a claim in the proper court to settle the disagreement. For example, if the shareholders' dissension concerns price, the court will set the price upon which both parties must agree.

Although mergers and consolidations can be legally effected only when statutory procedures are followed, from a financial standpoint the same results can be accomplished when a firm (1) purchases for cash or stock all or a portion of the assets of another company, or (2) purchases the controlling interest of one or more firms.

Fusion by a Sale of Assets

The acquisition of assets by direct purchase is the simplest technique of combination, in that approval is necessary only from shareholders of the selling company or companies. Most states have statutes governing the sale of assets either for cash or stock. In general the following procedure prevails: (1) the board of directors adopts a resolution recommending the sale and directs that the resolution be presented for vote at a regular or special meeting of the shareholders; (2) approval, usually requiring the affirmative vote of four-fifths of the voting shares outstanding is obtained; and (3) the assets are conveyed as in any other sale. At this point in the process, and after all liabilities have been satisfied, the board of directors of the selling company usually declares a liquidating dividend and the firm is dissolved. If stock of the purchasing company has been issued in payment for the assets, the selling firm may either (1) spin off the stock to the existing shareholders and distribute any cash left after liabilities are satisfied or (2) retain the stock in the company's treasury and act as a holding or investment company.

The price to be paid for the assets is usually determined by (1) the capitalization of income, (2) appraisal, (3) cost (original or replacement) minus valuation reserves, and (4) the market value of stock or negotiation. See the discussion of the valuation process above for a description of these methods.

Fusion by the Holding-Company Device

Under certain circumstances, a firm may not be interested in the purchase of another firm's assets but may desire control of its operations. This objective may be achieved by purchasing sufficient stock to control the affairs of the company. The maximum required for control purposes is 50-plus percent; however, in most cases, control may be acquired through the ownership of much less than 50 percent of the voting shares. The major advantage of this technique is that it allows the acquiring company an opportunity to evaluate the fusion before taking steps to acquire the assets, either through statutory merger or by outright purchase. A second major advantage is the ability of the holding company to control large sums of assets with a minimum investment. To illustrate, it is possible to control the assets of several corporations merely by holding the controlling interest in only one firm. This type of operation is common among public utility companies, which are limited with respect to the number of levels that they may control by the Public Utility Company Act of 1935.

OTHER TECHNIQUES

The use of the lease as a means of controlling assets has been discussed in Chapter 15. The informal arrangements—gentlemen's agreements, communities of interest, and interlocking directorates—usually are for purposes that may be described as monopolistic, such as the control of prices and sales territories, rather than the achievements normally associated with the reasons for growth listed at the beginning of this chapter. Moreover, these techniques do not normally provide lasting control of assets. Finally, these acts are often in violation of antitrust laws. For these reasons no further discussion of these methods is presented here.

24

Financial Difficulties and the Replanning Process

As we mentioned earlier, one of the most important functions of financial management is the periodic evaluation of performance in the light of existing policies. If the evaluation reveals that the end results of the firm's activities meet predetermined standards, it may be presumed that existing objectives, policies, and procedures are being achieved and that they require no revision. If the analysis proves otherwise, management must (1) ascertain which policies are ineffective, and (2) initiate changes that are necessary if the firm's goals are to be achieved—that is, *replan* the firm's financial activities.

When should the evaluation and replanning process take place? As a general rule, evaluation should be continuous, since the economic environment in which the policies operate is constantly changing; likewise, it is essential that each policy be evaluated and reshaped whenever necessary to meet the changing conditions. Whereas evaluation is a continuous function, replanning is undertaken only when it has been proved that changes are needed. We should emphasize that inefficiencies result not only from ineffective policies but from inefficient operating personnel as well. Our concern in this chapter is to ascertain the effectiveness of existing policies and to determine ways and means of correcting them rather than to discuss ways and means of improving performance of management personnel. However, a word of caution is necessary at this point: the financial manager should be absolutely sure it is the policy that is at fault before changes are made. If the personnel are at fault, a change in policy will not cure the problem.

BASIS FOR THE REPLANNING PROCESS

Replanning should not be undertaken unless there is positive knowledge that existing policies are ineffective or will become ineffective within the foreseeable future. To establish proof of this requires management to examine performance in the light of pre-established norms or standards. The function of comparing operations is simple enough, but the creation of standards for measuring performance is extremely difficult, since it requires that management first establish the level of activity that the firm should achieve. For example, should the firm earn 5 percent or 50 percent on its assets? With no additional information, it is impossible to say whether 5, 10, 15, or some other figure is correct. However, it is possible to arrive at an acceptable figure by examining each influencing element.

Management can approach this problem in two ways. First, it can translate the firm's goals into what are considered acceptable standards of performance and then compare actual operations with the predetermined goals. If deviations occur, the reason for the inefficiency must be determined; when this is known, corrective action can be taken. A second approach is to establish minimum and maximum standards, and if operations do not fall within these boundaries, causes can be determined and corrective action taken.

Regardless of the method used, standards must be established for each operational area as well as for the total operation. To illustrate, suppose management of a firm has decided that it should receive a return of 10 percent on investment after taxes. Assume further that the goal has not been reached. To determine the problem area or areas requires that an analysis be made of each component part of the operation that affects total return. To make such an analysis requires the setting of standards for each operational area. Only when these have been established and a comparison has been made is it possible to determine the causes of the deviations.

STAGES OF FINANCIAL
EMBARRASSMENT

Fortunately there are many signals that indicate to management when a firm's policies are ineffective and in need of replanning, long before complete financial embarrassment is a fact. That is to say, there are various stages of failure, and by careful examination financial management can detect the failure symptoms and ascertain and correct their causes before it is too late. A word of warning: the causes must be determined and corrected if management wishes to avoid a recurrence. If only the symptoms are corrected and not their cause, most likely the difficulty will reappear, probably more severely the second time. To illustrate, suppose a firm is constantly short of cash. If management borrows additional funds without ascertaining the real cause for the cash shortage, the firm will probably experience a serious cash shortage within a very short time. On the other hand, if the cause is ascertained and corrected, management can raise the necessary cash and be reasonably certain that in the future the cash flow will not be interrupted in such a manner as to create a similar problem.

Financial embarrassment may be divided into three phases: economic, financial, and legal. Economic failure exists when the rate of return realized on assets falls below the firm's cost of capital, thus causing the firm to drift toward the second and third stages of failure. Failure should be detected at this stage for several reasons, and three of the more important are: (1) replanning is much more effective if it is initiated at this time; (2) the actions required to eliminate the causes for economic failure are not nearly as drastic as those required to "cure" the causes usually present in the financial and legal stages of failure; and (3) when failure is detected early, the confidence of the investing public is less likely to be impaired. This last is very important, because when confidence is shaken, the price investors charge for their funds increases, and this, in turn, tends to force the firm into the position of not being able to accept otherwise profitable projects.

Economic failure, unlike financial and legal failure, does not mean that a firm is insolvent in the usual sense. That is, creditors have not incurred a loss. In fact, if management is able to reshape its policies, the firm will most likely be able to meet all maturing obligations as they come due. If, however, the "causes" are not removed, the firm will be called upon to refund existing obligations, ultimately defaulting because sufficient funds will not be available to satisfy the obligations. If management initiates action at this stage to eliminate the problem areas, the creditors are generally willing to renew their obligations and even to make available additional funds for operational purposes.

If the causes for economic failure are not ascertained and corrected, the firm can be expected to move into the second stage of failure, which may be referred to as financial failure. A firm in this phase is insolvent in that it is unable to meet its maturing obligations, but it is not insolvent in the bankruptcy sense; that is, liabilities do not exceed assets. We should point out that although drastic action is usually necessary to restore the firm to a sound position, it is not necessary to liquidate the business endeavor. A number of remedies in a wide range are available to management to aid in the correction of financial insolvency. Included among these remedies are readjustments, extensions, out-of-court composition settlements, and reorganization under Chapters X and XI of the Bankruptcy Act.

The ultimate stage of financial embarrassment may be referred to as legal failure. The firm is said to be legally bankrupt when its liabilities exceed its assets. To correct this situation, usually management must reorganize under the Bankruptcy Act or enter into voluntary or involuntary liquidation. The latter is accomplished through the courts and under the jurisdiction of the Bankruptcy Act.[1]

---

[1] For a thorough discussion of the techniques used to remedy financial and legal failure, see Charles W. Gerstenberg, *Financial Organization and Management of Business*, 4th rev. ed. (Englewood Cliffs, N.J.: Prentice-Hall, Inc., 1959), Chapters 26 and 27.

ACTION TAKEN IN THE
REPLANNING PROCESS

Effective management cannot wait until the firm has experienced legal failure to take action, since in most cases the only remedies then available are reorganization or liquidation. In either case creditors generally lose, and ill-will results. To avoid insolvency and at the same time to realize the highest possible return on investment, management must engage in continuous analysis for the earliest possible detection of causes for financial embarrassment. Corrective action taken when failure is imminent not only can be effective, but in most instances is less drastic than that called for if the symptoms remain undetected until either the financial or the legal failure stage. The following example shows the importance of this approach.

The XYZ Company, a middle-sized corporation operating in the midwestern and eastern parts of the United States, is engaged in the manufacture and sale of communication and navigation equipment for aircraft, as well as electronic equipment and component parts. These products are sold directly to manufacturers, with no contact with the public. Mr. Wilson, vice-president for finance, is very cost-conscious and maintains cost records on all phases of the firm's operation. Past history shows that the cost of capital is equal to 10 percent, and the board of directors has adopted the policy that return on investment should be equal to at least 5 percent more than the cost of capital. That is, investment should not be made in projects unless they return at least 15 percent, except when the investment is made for strategic reasons; in these cases, the directors reason that the low return would be offset by projects with returns exceeding 15 percent.

Wilson realizes that the rate will fluctuate above and below this standard; therefore, his staff maintains a record in graph form of the movement of the overall rate in order to determine any downward trends at the earliest possible time. Figure 24-1 depicts the movement of the firm's rate of return during the past twelve months.

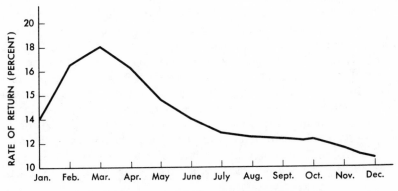

FIGURE 24-1 XYZ Company Rate of Return

In conjunction with his staff, Wilson observed that since February the rate of return had declined steadily. Furthermore, the forecast for the next three months indicates that the rate of return will not rise above 12 percent. The analysis also revealed the following: sales had declined 10 percent during the past nine months; cash had increased 15 percent over the level previously established by policy; receivables and inventories accounts had declined by approximately 12 percent during the past 12 months; turnover of capital had declined from 2.5 times to 2.1 times; and earnings as a percentage of sales had also declined.

Wilson reasoned that immediate steps were necessary if the firm was to regain its previous position and achieve the goals that the board had established. Also, he recognized that to initiate effective changes, an analysis should be made to isolate the cause or causes for the present condition. Wilson made the analysis and found the following conditions. The firm's prices were in line with those of its competitors, but earnings as a percentage of sales had declined below the average for the industry. In studying costs, he determined that although variable costs were in line with those of other firms in the industry, fixed costs were excessive. In addition, the study revealed that the demand for three of the firm's major products had declined steadily over the past year. As a result, the firm was producing at less than full capacity, thus causing the per unit cost to increase. In determining the reasons for declining inventories, Wilson discovered that the purchasing officer tied inventory levels directly to sales, and since sales had declined, he had reduced the level of inventories. As a result, the flow of funds had been interrupted, allowing cash to build up to a level exceeding that which had been established by policy.

Wilson concluded that the decline in the rate of return was the result of overexpansion of fixed assets and buildup of idle working capital. He knew that temporary changes could be initiated that would cause the firm's rate of return on investment to rise, but it would be necessary to institute permanent changes if the required return were to be maintained. The following temporary and permanent policy changes were recommended to eliminate these two basic problems.

First, the board should allocate funds for a crash research program with the primary objective of finding substitutes for the three products for which demand had declined. Once this program was under way, the firm should initiate a permanent research program for the development of new products that could be introduced as quickly as the demand for existing products tended to soften.

Second, if it became apparent to management that the new products could be developed within a short time, management could invest its idle cash in short-term government securities and convert them into cash whenever the need to build up inventories reappeared. Investments of this nature have the effect of improving the firm's rate of return and, at the same time, providing flexibility. On the other hand, if management concluded that the new products could not be introduced within a reasonable time, it could use the excess cash to liquidate short- and intermediate-term loans, thus reducing the level of investment. Such action would have two effects: (1) the operating ratio would improve and (2) investments would decline, thus causing the rate of return to improve.

Finally, if possible, management would want to reduce the size of its plant until products were found that would cause production to increase. This might be accomplished by not replacing existing equipment until demand increased or by selling idle equipment. If this policy were followed, investment turnover would increase, thus causing the rate of return to improve.

Wilson might have found other causes that would have had the same effects as those listed above. For example, the decline in inventories might have been caused by the failure of the purchasing officer to follow consistently sound purchasing policies, and the decline in sales might have resulted from inadequate inventories. On the other hand, prices might have been entirely out of line with those of comparable producers. Also, incorrect credit terms might have forced buyers to look elsewhere for their supplies. Furthermore, the analysis might have indicated that the sales effort was concentrated on unprofitable lines, thus causing total demand as well as profits to decline, or that cash was increasing because the firm retained excessive funds in relation to need.

The discussion above shows how important it is for management to approach the problem of replanning logically; that is, before replanning is undertaken, management should follow the same steps taken when plans were first developed. Briefly, the decision-making process as it applies to replanning includes five steps: (1) seek out the real causes for the failure of present policies, (2) analyze the critical factors that influence the areas concerned, (3) develop alternative plans, (4) select and initiate the best plan available, and (5) check the solution after it has been installed in order to determine its effectiveness.

CROSS-INDEX TO FINANCE TEXTBOOKS

ESSENTIALS OF FINANCIAL MANAGEMENT	BIERMAN	JOHNSON	WESTON & BRIGHAM	VAN HORNE	NORGAARD & VAUGHN	BRIGHAM et. al.
	Chapters				*Cases*	
Chapter:						
1 Role of Financial Management in the Business Firm		1	1	1		
2 The Legal Forms of Business Organization		2				
3 Formation and Control of the Business Corporation		2			3, 41	24
4 Internal Financial Analysis		4	3, 4	25, 26	1, 4, 5, 9	2
5 Cost of Capital	4, 5	11	11	4	19, 46	13, 14
6 Planning Fixed-Assets Expenditures		8	7, 8	3, 5	15, 16, 18	6, 7, 8, 9
7 Working-Capital Management				15		
8 Working-Capital Management (continued)	1, 3	5, 6, 7, 9	5, 13, 14	16, 17, 18	6, 7, 8, 10 11, 12, 14, 44	5, 17, 18
9 Equity versus Debt Financing	6, 11	10	9	27	27	10, 35
10 Capital Structure Determination	7			7, 8	33	
11 Income Taxes and Financial Planning			2		39	36
12 Dividend Policies	8, 10	22	12	9, 10	40	15, 16
13 Short-Term Capital		12		17, 19	26	19
14 Short-Term Credit, as Supplied by Financial Institutions		13, 14	15	19, 20	20, 21, 22	19

	Bierman	Johnson	Weston & Brigham	Van Horne	Norgaard & Vaughn	Brigham et al.
15 Intermediate Financing		15, 19	16	21, 22	17, 20, 23, 24, 25	20, 21
16 Internal Sources of Funds					20	26
17 Long-Term Debt Financing		17	17, 19	11	32, 46	
18 Long-Term Debt Instruments	12, 13, 14, 15, 16, 17	18, 20	20	12, 14	28, 46	27, 28, 29, 30
19 Equity Capital		20, 21	18	13	29, 30	25, 27, 28
20 Primary Security Markets		17				
21 Private Placement and Government Financing		15			46	
22 Secondary Security Markets						22, 23
23 Expansion of the Business Firm		23, 24	10, 21	23	31, 34, 35, 36, 37, 38	11, 12, 31, 32
24 Financial Difficulties and the Replanning Process			22	24	42, 43	33, 34

Bierman, Harold, Jr., *Financial Policy Decisions.* New York: The Macmillan Company, 1970.

Johnson, Robert W., *Financial Management*, 4th ed. Boston: Allyn & Bacon, Inc., 1971.

Weston, J. Fred, and Eugene F. Brigham, *Managerial Finance*, 3rd ed. New York: Holt, Rinehart & Winston, 1969.

Van Horne, James C., *Financial Management and Policy*, 2nd ed. Englewood Cliffs, N.J.: Prentice-Hall, Inc., 1971.

Norgaard, Richard L., and Donald E. Vaughn, *Cases in Financial Decision Making.* Englewood Cliffs, N.J.: Prentice-Hall, Inc., 1967.

Brigham, Eugene F., Timothy J. Nantell, Robert T. Aubrey, and Stephen L. Hawk, *Cases in Managerial Finance.* New York: Holt, Rinehart & Winston, Inc., 1970.

PRESENT VALUE OF $1

Years Hence	1%	2%	4%	6%	8%	10%	12%	14%	15%	16%	18%	20%	22%	24%	25%	26%	28%	30%	35%	40%	45%	50%
1	0.990	0.980	0.962	0.943	0.926	0.909	0.893	0.877	0.870	0.862	0.847	0.833	0.820	0.806	0.800	0.794	0.781	0.769	0.741	0.714	0.690	0.667
2	0.980	0.961	0.925	0.890	0.857	0.826	0.797	0.769	0.756	0.743	0.718	0.694	0.672	0.650	0.640	0.630	0.610	0.592	0.549	0.510	0.476	0.444
3	0.971	0.942	0.889	0.840	0.794	0.751	0.712	0.675	0.658	0.641	0.609	0.579	0.551	0.524	0.512	0.500	0.477	0.455	0.406	0.364	0.328	0.296
4	0.961	0.924	0.855	0.792	0.735	0.683	0.630	0.592	0.572	0.552	0.516	0.482	0.451	0.423	0.410	0.397	0.373	0.350	0.301	0.260	0.226	0.198
5	0.951	0.906	0.822	0.747	0.681	0.621	0.567	0.519	0.497	0.476	0.437	0.402	0.370	0.341	0.328	0.315	0.291	0.269	0.223	0.186	0.156	0.132
6	0.942	0.888	0.790	0.705	0.630	0.564	0.507	0.456	0.432	0.410	0.370	0.335	0.303	0.275	0.262	0.250	0.227	0.207	0.165	0.133	0.108	0.088
7	0.933	0.871	0.760	0.665	0.583	0.513	0.452	0.400	0.376	0.354	0.314	0.279	0.249	0.222	0.210	0.198	0.178	0.159	0.122	0.095	0.074	0.059
8	0.923	0.853	0.731	0.627	0.540	0.467	0.404	0.351	0.327	0.305	0.266	0.233	0.204	0.179	0.168	0.157	0.139	0.123	0.091	0.068	0.051	0.039
9	0.914	0.837	0.703	0.592	0.500	0.424	0.361	0.308	0.284	0.263	0.225	0.194	0.167	0.144	0.134	0.125	0.108	0.094	0.067	0.048	0.035	0.026
10	0.905	0.820	0.676	0.558	0.463	0.386	0.322	0.270	0.247	0.227	0.191	0.162	0.137	0.116	0.107	0.099	0.085	0.073	0.050	0.035	0.024	0.017
11	0.896	0.804	0.650	0.527	0.429	0.350	0.287	0.237	0.215	0.195	0.162	0.135	0.112	0.094	0.086	0.079	0.066	0.056	0.037	0.025	0.017	0.012
12	0.887	0.788	0.625	0.497	0.397	0.319	0.257	0.208	0.187	0.168	0.137	0.112	0.092	0.076	0.069	0.062	0.052	0.043	0.027	0.018	0.012	0.008
13	0.879	0.773	0.601	0.469	0.368	0.290	0.229	0.182	0.163	0.145	0.116	0.093	0.075	0.061	0.055	0.050	0.040	0.033	0.020	0.013	0.008	0.005
14	0.870	0.758	0.577	0.442	0.340	0.263	0.205	0.160	0.141	0.125	0.099	0.078	0.062	0.049	0.044	0.039	0.032	0.025	0.015	0.009	0.006	0.003
15	0.861	0.743	0.555	0.417	0.315	0.239	0.183	0.140	0.123	0.108	0.084	0.065	0.051	0.040	0.035	0.031	0.025	0.020	0.011	0.006	0.004	0.002
16	0.853	0.728	0.534	0.394	0.292	0.218	0.163	0.123	0.107	0.093	0.071	0.054	0.042	0.032	0.028	0.025	0.019	0.015	0.008	0.005	0.003	0.002
17	0.844	0.714	0.513	0.371	0.270	0.198	0.146	0.108	0.093	0.080	0.060	0.045	0.034	0.026	0.023	0.020	0.015	0.012	0.006	0.003	0.002	0.001
18	0.836	0.700	0.494	0.350	0.250	0.180	0.130	0.095	0.081	0.069	0.051	0.038	0.028	0.021	0.018	0.016	0.012	0.009	0.005	0.002	0.001	0.001
19	0.828	0.686	0.475	0.331	0.232	0.164	0.116	0.083	0.070	0.060	0.043	0.031	0.023	0.017	0.014	0.012	0.009	0.007	0.003	0.002	0.001	
20	0.820	0.673	0.456	0.312	0.215	0.149	0.104	0.073	0.061	0.051	0.037	0.026	0.019	0.014	0.012	0.010	0.007	0.005	0.002	0.001	0.001	
21	0.811	0.660	0.439	0.294	0.199	0.135	0.093	0.064	0.053	0.044	0.031	0.022	0.015	0.011	0.009	0.008	0.006	0.004	0.002	0.001		
22	0.803	0.647	0.422	0.278	0.184	0.123	0.083	0.056	0.046	0.038	0.026	0.018	0.013	0.009	0.007	0.006	0.004	0.003	0.001	0.001		
23	0.795	0.634	0.406	0.262	0.170	0.112	0.074	0.049	0.040	0.033	0.022	0.015	0.010	0.007	0.006	0.005	0.003	0.002	0.001			
24	0.788	0.622	0.390	0.247	0.158	0.102	0.066	0.043	0.035	0.028	0.019	0.013	0.008	0.006	0.005	0.004	0.003	0.002	0.001			
25	0.780	0.610	0.375	0.233	0.146	0.092	0.059	0.038	0.030	0.024	0.016	0.010	0.007	0.005	0.004	0.003	0.002	0.001	0.001			
26	0.772	0.598	0.361	0.220	0.135	0.084	0.053	0.033	0.026	0.021	0.014	0.009	0.006	0.004	0.003	0.002	0.002	0.001	0.001			
27	0.764	0.586	0.347	0.207	0.125	0.076	0.047	0.029	0.023	0.018	0.011	0.007	0.005	0.003	0.002	0.002	0.001	0.001	0.001			
28	0.757	0.574	0.333	0.196	0.116	0.069	0.042	0.026	0.020	0.016	0.010	0.006	0.004	0.002	0.002	0.002	0.001	0.001	0.001			
29	0.749	0.563	0.321	0.185	0.107	0.063	0.037	0.022	0.017	0.014	0.008	0.005	0.003	0.002	0.002	0.001	0.001	0.001	0.001			
30	0.742	0.552	0.308	0.174	0.099	0.057	0.033	0.020	0.015	0.012	0.007	0.004	0.003	0.002	0.001	0.001	0.001	0.001	0.001			
40	0.672	0.453	0.208	0.097	0.046	0.022	0.011	0.005	0.004	0.003	0.001	0.001										
50	0.608	0.372	0.141	0.054	0.021	0.009	0.003	0.001	0.001	0.001												

PRESENT VALUE OF $1 RECEIVED ANNUALLY FOR N YEARS

Years (N)	1%	2%	4%	6%	8%	10%	12%	14%	15%	16%	18%	20%	22%	24%	25%	26%	28%	30%	35%	40%	45%	50%
1	0.990	0.980	0.962	0.943	0.926	0.909	0.893	0.877	0.870	0.862	0.847	0.833	0.820	0.806	0.800	0.794	0.781	0.769	0.741	0.714	0.690	0.667
2	1.970	1.942	1.886	1.833	1.783	1.736	1.690	1.647	1.626	1.605	1.566	1.528	1.492	1.457	1.440	1.424	1.392	1.361	1.289	1.224	1.165	1.111
3	2.941	2.884	2.775	2.673	2.577	2.487	2.402	2.322	2.283	2.246	2.174	2.106	2.042	1.981	1.952	1.923	1.868	1.816	1.696	1.589	1.493	1.407
4	3.902	3.808	3.630	3.465	3.312	3.170	3.037	2.914	2.855	2.798	2.690	2.589	2.494	2.404	2.362	2.320	2.241	2.166	1.997	1.849	1.720	1.605
5	4.853	4.713	4.452	4.212	3.993	3.791	3.605	3.433	3.352	3.274	3.127	2.991	2.864	2.745	2.689	2.635	2.532	2.436	2.220	2.035	1.876	1.737
6	5.795	5.601	5.242	4.917	4.623	4.355	4.111	3.889	3.784	3.685	3.498	3.326	3.167	3.020	2.951	2.885	2.759	2.643	2.385	2.168	1.983	1.824
7	6.728	6.472	6.002	5.582	5.206	4.868	4.564	4.288	4.160	4.039	3.812	3.605	3.416	3.242	3.161	3.083	2.937	2.802	2.508	2.263	2.057	1.883
8	7.652	7.325	6.733	6.210	5.747	5.335	4.968	4.639	4.487	4.344	4.078	3.837	3.619	3.421	3.329	3.241	3.076	2.925	2.598	2.331	2.108	1.922
9	8.566	8.162	7.435	6.802	6.247	5.759	5.328	4.946	4.772	4.607	4.303	4.031	3.786	3.566	3.463	3.366	3.184	3.019	2.665	2.379	2.144	1.948
10	9.471	8.983	8.111	7.360	6.710	6.145	5.650	5.216	5.019	4.833	4.494	4.192	3.923	3.682	3.571	3.465	3.269	3.092	2.715	2.414	2.168	1.965
11	10.368	9.787	8.760	7.887	7.139	6.495	5.988	5.453	5.234	5.029	4.656	4.327	4.035	3.776	3.656	3.544	3.335	3.147	2.752	2.438	2.185	1.977
12	11.255	10.575	9.385	8.384	7.536	6.814	6.194	5.660	5.421	5.197	4.793	4.439	4.127	3.851	3.725	3.606	3.387	3.190	2.779	2.456	2.196	1.985
13	12.134	11.343	9.986	8.853	7.904	7.103	6.424	5.842	5.583	5.342	4.910	4.533	4.203	3.912	3.780	3.656	3.427	3.223	2.799	2.468	2.204	1.990
14	13.004	12.106	10.563	9.295	8.244	7.367	6.628	6.002	5.724	5.468	5.008	4.611	4.265	3.962	3.824	3.695	3.459	3.249	2.814	2.477	2.210	1.993
15	13.865	12.849	11.118	9.712	8.559	7.606	6.811	6.142	5.847	5.575	5.092	4.675	4.315	4.001	3.859	3.726	3.483	3.268	2.825	2.484	2.214	1.995
16	14.718	13.578	11.652	10.106	8.851	7.824	6.974	6.265	5.954	5.669	5.162	4.730	4.357	4.033	3.887	3.751	3.503	3.283	2.834	2.489	2.216	1.997
17	15.562	14.292	12.166	10.477	9.122	8.022	7.120	6.373	6.047	5.749	5.222	4.775	4.391	4.059	3.910	3.771	3.518	3.295	2.840	2.492	2.218	1.998
18	16.398	14.992	12.659	10.828	9.372	8.201	7.250	6.467	6.128	5.818	5.273	4.812	4.419	4.080	3.928	3.786	3.529	3.304	2.844	2.494	2.219	1.999
19	17.226	15.678	13.134	11.158	9.604	8.365	7.366	6.550	6.198	5.877	5.316	4.844	4.442	4.097	3.942	3.799	3.539	3.311	2.848	2.496	2.220	1.999
20	18.046	16.351	13.590	11.470	9.818	8.514	7.469	6.623	6.259	5.929	5.353	4.870	4.460	4.110	3.954	3.808	3.546	3.316	2.850	2.497	2.221	1.999
21	18.857	17.011	14.029	11.764	10.017	8.649	7.562	6.687	6.312	5.973	5.384	4.891	4.476	4.121	3.963	3.816	3.551	3.320	2.852	2.498	2.221	2.000
22	19.660	17.658	14.451	12.042	10.201	8.772	7.645	6.743	6.359	6.011	5.410	4.909	4.488	4.130	3.970	3.822	3.556	3.323	2.853	2.498	2.222	2.000
23	20.456	18.292	14.857	12.303	10.371	8.883	7.718	6.792	6.399	6.044	5.432	4.925	4.499	4.137	3.976	3.827	3.559	3.325	2.854	2.499	2.222	2.000
24	21.243	18.914	15.247	12.550	10.529	8.985	7.784	6.835	6.434	6.073	5.451	4.937	4.507	4.143	3.981	3.831	3.562	3.327	2.855	2.499	2.222	2.000
25	22.023	19.523	15.622	12.783	10.675	9.077	7.843	6.873	6.464	6.097	5.467	4.948	4.514	4.147	3.985	3.834	3.564	3.329	2.856	2.499	2.222	2.000
26	22.795	20.121	15.983	13.003	10.810	9.161	7.896	6.906	6.491	6.118	5.480	4.956	4.520	4.151	3.988	3.837	3.566	3.330	2.856	2.500	2.222	2.000
27	23.560	20.707	16.330	13.211	10.935	9.237	7.943	6.935	6.514	6.136	5.492	4.964	4.524	4.154	3.990	3.839	3.567	3.331	2.856	2.500	2.222	2.000
28	24.316	21.281	16.663	13.406	11.051	9.307	7.984	6.961	6.534	6.152	5.502	4.970	4.528	4.157	3.992	3.840	3.568	3.331	2.857	2.500	2.222	2.000
29	25.066	21.844	16.984	13.591	11.158	9.370	8.022	6.983	6.551	6.166	5.510	4.975	4.531	4.159	3.994	3.841	3.569	3.332	2.857	2.500	2.222	2.000
30	25.808	22.396	17.292	13.765	11.258	9.427	8.055	7.003	6.566	6.177	5.517	4.979	4.534	4.160	3.995	3.842	3.569	3.332	2.857	2.500	2.222	2.000
40	32.835	27.355	19.793	15.046	11.925	9.779	8.244	7.105	6.642	6.234	5.548	4.997	4.544	4.166	3.999	3.846	3.571	3.333	2.857	2.500	2.222	2.000
50	39.196	31.424	21.482	15.762	12.234	9.915	8.304	7.133	6.661	6.246	5.554	4.999	4.545	4.167	4.000	3.846	3.571	3.333	2.857	2.500	2.222	2.000

Index